Cinema Off Screen

The publisher and the University of California Press Foundation gratefully acknowledge the generous support of the Robert and Meryl Selig Endowment Fund in Film Studies, established in memory of Robert W. Selig.

Cinema Off Screen

Moviegoing in Socialist China

Chenshu Zhou

UNIVERSITY OF CALIFORNIA PRESS

University of California Press
Oakland, California

Library of Congress Cataloging-in-Publication Data

Names: Zhou, Chenshu, 1985– author.
Title: Cinema off screen : moviegoing in socialist China / Chenshu Zhou.
Description: Oakland, California : University of California Press, [2021]
    | Includes bibliographical references and index.
Identifiers: LCCN 2020056151 (print) | LCCN 2020056152 (ebook) |
    ISBN 9780520343382 (cloth) | ISBN 9780520343399 (paperback) |
    ISBN 9780520974777 (epub)
Subjects: LCSH: Motion pictures—China—History—20th century—
    Case studies. | Socialism and motion pictures—China—
    20th century—Case studies. | Motion picture audiences—China—
    20th century—Case studies.
Classification: LCC PN1993.5.C4 Z5726 2021 (print) |
    LCC PN1993.5.C4 (ebook) | DDC 791.430951—dc23
LC record available at https://lccn.loc.gov/2020056151
LC ebook record available at https://lccn.loc.gov/2020056152

30 29 28 27 26 25 24 23 22 21
10 9 8 7 6 5 4 3 2 1

Contents

Illustrations

Acknowledgments

It is still hard to believe that I have written a book that in no small part relies on interviews. My parents used to exert a great deal of effort trying to make me talk to strangers. "Jingjing, you go buy the popsicle yourself." I was five. "Jingjing, you go ask for directions." I was in high school but still protested. Yet when an interest in spectatorship led me to the point where I desperately wanted to hear what the audiences themselves thought about their moviegoing experiences, I knew I had to do the inevitable.

I want to thank everyone that has offered their help in the interviewing process, especially the few people who were instrumental in broadening my pool of interviewees. It was my parents who brought in the first group of interviewees by mobilizing their networks of old colleagues, neighbors, and friends. Lu Yunnan, a meticulous sociology student much more experienced than me in the art of interviewing, conducted ten interviews in Xinjiang for this project, bringing in perspectives from audiences that were otherwise out of my reach. Later, when I tried to interview more factory workers, Chen Kaihang, who saw my call for help on Weibo, accompanied me to the factory community where she grew up and introduced me to many retired workers. Others who have offered to connect me with their parents and grandparents, who have allowed me into their homes, and who have spoken with me, sometimes for up to two or three hours, are too numerous to name here (a list of my interviewees can be found in the appendix). This book was inspired by the experiences of several generations of Chinese people born before me. It was driven by an urge to understand and articulate these experiences, to reclaim them from the realm of everyday trivia. Without the knowledge, enthusiasm, and patience of my interviewees, this book could not have been written. I owe them my deepest gratitude.

This book was also made possible by archival sources found at the following libraries and archives: National Library of China, Beijing Municipal Archives, Shanghai Municipal Archives, and UC Berkeley Library. A heartfelt thanks goes to the Cui Yongyuan Oral History Research Center, now affiliated with the Communication University of China. Though not open to the public at the time, the Center kindly allowed me to browse through their amazing collection of interviews and internal documents. The used-book website Kongfuzi also deserves a special mention. Through its many sellers, I not only was able to procure unique archival materials; it is also on this website where I first came across the poster that eventually became the cover of this book.

At Stanford University, where this book was first conceived as a PhD dissertation, I was fortunate to have received guidance and support from amazing scholars who have forever shaped the way I approach scholarship. Ban Wang is the best advisor one can ask for. Whenever I had doubts about my ideas or felt disillusioned about academia, I took comfort in the fact that I could turn to him for both pep talks and concrete suggestions. The intellectual rigor and breadth of Haiyan Lee has been a constant inspiration. Her comments, at once relentless and constructive, often left me in deep thought, challenging me to strengthen my arguments and be a better scholar. I also gained many insights from my conversations with Jean Ma, who has been an irreplaceable source of encouragement, criticism, and references. I thank her for helping me see the contributions of my project when I felt clueless myself. My dissertation research at Stanford was assisted by the Graduate Research Opportunities Fund and a Mellon Dissertation Fellowship.

After receiving my PhD in 2016, I was a beneficiary of the precious time granted to me during my two postdoctoral fellowships at Stanford University and New York University Shanghai. The University of Pennsylvania, my current institutional home, graciously allowed me to postpone the beginning of my employment so that I could concentrate on revising this book in the summer and fall of 2020. I thank my colleagues in the History of Art Department and the Cinema and Media Studies Program for their understanding and patience. I am excited that this book is coming out into the world as I enter a new community and a new stage in my career.

Over the years, my thinking and writing have been shaped by interactions with many scholars and mentors. Paul Pickowicz, Wang Zheng, and Carma Hinton, as conference discussants, gave valuable early feedback on papers that became important building blocks for this book. Two scholars that have particularly inspired me are Yomi Braester and Francesco Casetti. I remember one conversation I had with Yomi near the end of an Association for Asian Studies conference. Sitting on a brownish couch of a generic hotel lobby, he wondered out loud about whether there was more beyond the binary framework of dominance and resistance. This conversation has eventually led me to redirect my book from questions of ideology and subject formation to an exploration of the multiple dimensions of film exhibition. I am also grateful for his continuing mentorship. Another "light bulb" moment occurred during Francesco Casetti's presentation at a Society of Cinema and Media Studies Annual Conference in which he emphasized with passion that cinema was not a visual medium but an environmental medium. The different strands of my thinking suddenly came into clarity and I was able to solidify a decision to foreground seemingly trivial and anecdotal aspects of moviegoing that are not typically considered as part of audience "reception." Although I was too shy to talk to Casetti at the moment, I am glad that he later read parts of the book and offered both encouragement and useful suggestions. Another scholar and friend I am especially indebted to is Immanuel Kim, who not only read multiple drafts of my book proposal but was always ready to call back within minutes whenever I had questions about the book publishing process.

My gratitude also goes to the many teachers and friends that have impacted me intellectually and personally, including Qin Gao, Ran Ma, Jie Hu, Xinran Guo, Michelle Bloom, John Kim, Perry Link, Hongjian Wang, Claire Yu, Fontaine Lien, Xi Tian, Regina Yung Lee, Nan Ma, Yun Liu, Pavle Levi, Keren He, Yao Wu, Wei Peng, Renren Yang, Hangping Xu, Elise Huerta, Yu-chuan Chen, Tiffany Lee, Eldon Pei, Emma Yu Zhang, Xiao Rao, Longlu Qin, Yanshuo Zhang, Luciana Dobre, Kevin Singleton, Paul Ganir, Melissa Hosek, Parna Sengupta, Ellen Woods, Blakey Vermeule, Adam Johnson, Bronwen Tate, Zenia Kish, Elise Stickles, Ping Zhu, Ling Zhang, Panpan Yang, Hongwei Thorn Chen, Weihong Bao, Yiman Wang, Yanping Guo, He Bian, Asli Berktay, Jing Wang, Kuo-an Ma, Fang He, Rebecca Karl, and Jie Li.

Having written most of the book during two postdoc fellowships, multiple attempts at the job market, and my son's first and fifth birthdays, I was always rushing to meet the next deadline. This made the support and feedback I have received from University California Press extra important. I thank Raina Polivka for generously taking a chance with a first-time author like me. The two reviewers for my book proposal provided helpful comments that allowed me to clarify the direction of the book at an early stage. Later, my manuscript further benefitted from the feedback of Jenny Chio, Emily Wilcox, and Jason McGrath, who challenged me to improve my arguments and strive for better execution of ideas. I am deeply grateful for their detailed comments and thoughtful suggestions. I also thank Madison Wetzell for her editorial support and timely responses to my questions.

The book would not have been possible without the love and support of my family. I cannot overstate my gratitude to my parents, who have provided me with infinite willingness to help as I figure out how to be a scholar and a mom at the same time. During the COVID-19 pandemic when I could not return to China as planned, my parents helped me obtain image scans and mailed me important materials across the Pacific. Whether the world is in a pandemic or not, parents always find ways to make it work. I hope this book makes them proud. During the uncertain postdoc years when I did not know where I would end up, it was my husband Jason McCammond that kept me calm. With his amazing abilities to take care of everything around the house, I was able to focus on my work; and thanks to his humor and positivity, I never stopped laughing. To my son Wukong, I thank you for your resilience as we moved you from school to school, one continent to another. I know my constant need to work must have frustrated and puzzled you. I hope one day you will understand and be proud of Mommy.

Finally, I save a special place in my heart for my academic sisters Yige Dong, Belinda Qian He, and Mei Li Inouye. You have shown me the incredible power of female friendship as you listened to me, encouraged me, ranted with me, laughed with me, and took on the world with me. This book is dedicated to all the amazing women, female scholars, and academic moms that continue to forge new paths and support each other every day.

Parts of chapter 1 and chapter 3 have appeared in an article published in *Journal of Chinese Cinemas* 10, no. 3 (2016): 228–46. An earlier, Chinese version of chapter 2 was published in *Dangdai dianying* (Contemporary cinema) 10 (2019): 54–59.

MAP 1. Administrative divisions of China. Central Intelligence Agency, 2011.

Introduction

"Projecting Cinema"

In 1996, American writer and critic Susan Sontag (1933–2004) famously announced the "decay of cinema." While she expressed disappointment at the quality of new commercial films, the "decay" was mainly found in the ways in which films were consumed:

> You wanted to be kidnapped by the movie—and to be kidnapped was to be overwhelmed by the physical presence of the image. The experience of "going to the movies" was part of it. To see a great film only on television isn't to have really seen that film. It's not only a question of the dimensions of the image: the disparity between a larger-than-you image in the theater and the little image on the box at home. The conditions of paying attention in a domestic space are radically disrespectful of film. Now that a film no longer has a standard size, home screens can be as big as living room or bedroom walls. But you are still in a living room or a bedroom. To be kidnapped, you have to be in a movie theater, seated in the dark among anonymous strangers.[1]

In other words, the movie theater is supposed to provide size, darkness, immersion—an authentic experience of cinema, whereas home viewing is but a downgrade. If this lament rings a familiar bell for film critics and scholars in the contemporary West, the following account may give readers pause:

> Screen up, projector set, focus adjusted, the first light beam appeared, aiming at the screening. Everybody started casting hand shadows and throwing their hats in the air. This was called "projecting cinema" (*fang dianying*). It wasn't

the case that only when you showed a film that it was considered "projecting cinema." The rest was also a part of it. You watched the newsreels and then the main feature until the end credits finished rolling. After the light went back on, you stayed behind to watch people put away the equipment and fold the screen. Then you went home after everybody left. This whole process was "projecting cinema." It was like a festival.[2]

Cui Yongyuan (b. 1963),[3] a famous television producer and host who rose to fame in China in the late 1990s, made these remarks on *Childhood Flashback* (*Tongxin huifang*), a television show that was aired on China Central Television from about 2004 to 2015. The show was dedicated to rebroadcasting classic Chinese films made since 1949, the year of the founding of the People's Republic of China (PRC). It also included interviews with guests that center on childhood experiences of moviegoing. Born in 1963, Cui based his understanding of cinema largely on his experience attending open-air screenings (*lutian dianying*) in the early 1970s, a period more well known for Mao Zedong's Cultural Revolution (1966–1976). As we can see, cinema for Cui was less defined as a location (as the movie theater was for Sontag) than as a ritualistic process that began with the installation of the screening apparatus and ended with its disappearance, during which watching films was only one among other activities. Whether one could be "kidnapped" by the film, or whether one got to watch a good film or not, did not seem to be a concern.

As different as these two accounts of moviegoing appear to be, what is striking is how they are similar: Sontag and Cui, important cultural figures in the United States and China, were responding to the same global challenge posed to cinema by broadcast and digital media. During the mid-90s when Sontag published her article, television, videotapes, VCDs, and the newly developed DVD were already offering Western audiences an unprecedented amount of programming that they could enjoy in the comfort of their homes, film being one type of content among others. Consequently, as Sontag notes, "the love of cinema has waned."[4] It is not that people stopped watching films. What she means is that a particular kind of cinephilic engagement with cinema in the theatrical setting was disappearing. Cui, on the other hand, was well aware in the interview that the kind of cinema that he described belonged to a bygone era. Like Sontag, he was facing a situation of increasing home media consumption. In the mid-2000s when Cui's interview took place, Chinese consumers not only had access to many local and cable television channels, but also could easily buy VCDs and

DVDs, both legal and pirated copies. Internet download software like BitTorrent was also popular.

Meanwhile, in addition to new delivery technologies, what made Cui's model of moviegoing obsolete was major shifts in the ways in which cinema as an institution was conceptualized and organized by the Chinese state. From 1949 to the early 1990s, film exhibition remained largely state sponsored as part of the socialist planned economy and a major site for the production of socialist culture and socialist subjects. In the socialist system of film exhibition, exhibition outlets and mobile film projection teams attached to local cultural bureaus, workers' unions, workplaces known as work units (*danwei*), and the military showed films in movie theaters, factories, universities, parks, villages, and military bases—guided by an official recognition of the Chinese Communist Party (CCP) that film was both an effective propaganda tool and a mass entertainment medium. Despite post–Cultural Revolution ideological shifts and attempts at reform during the 1980s, the mechanisms of film distribution and exhibition were not completely upended by market logic until after 1992, the year during which Deng Xiaoping's influential tour of southern China took place and the Fourteenth Party Congress announced the development of "socialist market economy" as the official goal of China's economic reforms. In 1994, Hollywood movies began to appear regularly on Chinese screens on a revenue-sharing basis. In the early 2000s, a more efficient, demand-driven "theater circuit system" (*yuanxianzhi*) was put in place as the state opened up the film market for private investment. The commercial movie theater, particularly the multiplex, has since become the standard location for "going to the movies" in urban China.[5] Open-air screenings still happened in rural areas through state initiatives, but their importance as the center of communal cultural life had dwindled. Unlike Sontag, who witnessed the decline of the movie theater, the mode of film exhibition described by Cui was partly displaced by the *rise* of commercial movie theaters in postsocialist China.

Both Sontag and Cui were also unapologetically nostalgic. Their nostalgia was so straightforward because they did not see changes in practices of cinema as progressive updates of a medium whose identity remained stable. For André Gaudreault and Philippe Marion, cinema has died eight times—every time new technologies seemingly shook up the foundations of cinema, calling into question its identity—and yet cinema has persisted.[6] Sontag and Cui did not partake in such a view. For them, cinema is defined through a particular mode of exhibition and consumption, whereas divergence from the model constitutes a deterioration, a betrayal of what cinema really is. One may interpret their rhetorical act as one that articulates an ontology of cinema (i.e., what cinema is) based on a cultural memory of cinema (i.e., what it has been). Cultural memory, in the sense defined by Jan Assmann, is distinguished from communicative memory. While the latter happens in the realm of everyday oral communication, cultural memory depends on cultural formation (texts, images, rites, monuments) and institutional communication, which allow it to transcend the temporality of the everyday. In this way, cultural memory supplies a storage of knowledge from which a group can derive its unity and identity.[7] What Sontag and Cui accomplished, one by penning a widely circulated article and the other by speaking on national television, was turning their individual experience into cultural memory, on which an identity of cinema emerged and then offered itself to the respective audiences in the United States and China for collective identification. Yet a leap from cultural memory to ontology is only easy for someone securely rooted in an ostensibly homogeneous community. How do we, as critical observers of both Sontag and Cui, reconcile their different versions of cinema?

For the Western(ized) critic, it may be tempting to apply the label "alternative" to the experience of open-air cinema described by Cui, though from Cui's perspective, his experience was probably not alternative at all. Speaking with the same convicted tone as Sontag, Cui does not present the mode of open-air cinema familiar to his childhood self as a deviation from the standard of theatrical viewing still taken as a normative starting point by many film theorists. To him, what he experienced was not Chinese cinema, Chinese socialist cinema, or an instance of world cinema, but cinema itself. We should then be compelled to ask two questions. First, as Brian Larkin asks in relation to colonial cinema in Nigeria, "does cinema have a stable ontology that simply reproduces itself in different contexts over time and across space or, if we wish to examine the role of cinema outside of the experience of Berlin in the 1920s or New York in the 1920s, does that force us to rethink our conception of cinema?"[8] Second, what does it mean for our understanding of cinema if we stop treating the "alternative" as a mere "alternative"?

These questions are central to this book, which investigates the history, experience, and memory of film exhibition and moviegoing in China from 1949 to the early 1990s—that is, the socialist period—with 1992 as a symbolic end point. On an empirical level, this book contextualizes contemporary Chinese memories of cinema such as Cui Yongyuan's.

How were films shown and watched in relation to the political usage of cinema as propaganda? What were the institutions, technologies, and strategies of exhibition? What kinds of experience and memory of moviegoing were generated as China left its socialist legacy behind and entered an era of postsocialism? Drawing on both archival sources and audience testimonies, I approach film exhibition in socialist China through the notion of "cinema off screen," which is distinguished from an approach that centers on the film, or "cinema on screen." Recent scholarship on film exhibition, moviegoing, and audiences has gathered momentum under the rubric of "new cinema history." Moving away from formal analysis of the film text as well as notions of the spectator as a textual construct, "new cinema history" has brought together scholars from across the disciplines of film studies, sociology, anthropology, economics, geography, and cultural studies in a collective effort to reconceptualize cinema as an institution deeply embedded in local space, everyday life, and social relations. China has yet to become a site for extensive research in this particular subfield, which is evidenced by the absence of China in several recent anthologies that offer mostly case studies of film exhibition and moviegoing in Western countries.[9]

While extending the concerns and methods of "new cinema history" to China, this book departs from earlier studies by identifying specific "off screen" interfaces in film exhibition, points or boundaries of interaction other than the film text, such as the exhibition environment and the body—both the projectionist's and the viewer's—as well as the screening apparatus. It will show that film exhibition is best seen as a system in which the film shown on screen is only one among many interfaces. The interface effects of all that is non-filmic or "off screen" cannot be ignored. In socialist China, the state consciously implemented film exhibition as an institution that communicated to audiences through multiple interfaces, which in turn shaped cinematic experience in unexpected ways. The concept of cinematic experience includes but is by no means limited to an experience of films. Experience, as Francesco Casetti understands, is "a cognitive act, but one that is always rooted in, and affects, a body (it is 'embodied'), a culture (it is 'embedded'), and a situation (it is 'grounded')."[10] It is such embodied, situated experiences of Chinese audiences under socialism that this book brings to light.

Meanwhile, the recognition of "cinema off screen" goes beyond China. Just as Cui Yongyuan aspires to a discourse of cinema from what would normally be deemed as a marginalized position in the global order, this book makes a case for the broader implications of Chinese socialist film exhibition. Beyond the empirical, it destabilizes what is universal and what is seen as alternative. Joining scholars who have identified limitations of paradigms derived from Western cinematic practices, I point out how seemingly universal assumptions about film exhibition and moviegoing are historically situated and what appears unique and "deviant" may in fact be shared conditions. The coexistence of multiple interfaces in film exhibition should not be seen as a Chinese or a Chinese socialist phenomenon, but as an inherent potential of cinema that can manifest in stronger or weaker forms under different material and cultural conditions. In other words, this book develops a theory of film exhibition based on an empirical study of China.

WHAT CAN CHINA TELL US ABOUT CINEMA?

Speaking of the status of film theory in relation to Chinese cinema, Paul Pickowicz, one of the pioneers of Chinese cinema studies in the United States, has posed the following questions: "Why are all the 'universal' theories of European or American origin? How would Europeanists or Americanists react if 'universal' theories based on empirical studies of China were applied to the European case? I suspect that they would not like it at all."[11] Is Pickowicz right? Has he rightly predicted the fate of this book? There are few references I can rely on to come up with an answer. In cinema and media studies, China remains largely excluded from the discursive space known as theory. It is this separation that this book aims to challenge and reconfigure.

Theory has been the driving force behind film studies since its emergence as an academic discipline in Anglo-American universities in the 1960s and 1970s. As Richard Rushton and Gary Bettison suggest, film theory may simply be seen as a tool that helps us understand the medium better: "By framing general questions about cinematic phenomena, theorists try to disclose the way films work, how they convey meaning, what functions they provide, and the means by which they affect us. Exploring theoretical questions about the medium helps us to grasp the phenomenon of cinema, its broad systems, structures, uses, and effects—and these prototypical features can, in turn, enable us to better understand the workings of individual films."[12] There is no doubt that asking general, theoretical questions about cinema is beneficial. What is problematic, however, is when these questions are only asked from a Western point of view, informed by European and American traditions of filmmaking and moviegoing. These historically specific experiences are then generalized as "prototypical features," as what define cinema itself.

Two recent examples may be mentioned to illustrate these tendencies. One is film phenomenology, which Christian Ferencz-Flatz and Julian Hanich define as an attempt to describe "invariant structures of the film viewer's lived experience when watching moving images in a cinema or elsewhere."[13] However, relying heavily on thick, first-person descriptions, phenomenological studies produced by Western film scholars have only illuminated experiences of Western subjects watching (mostly) Western films in settings familiar to mainstream Western audiences.[14] Some scholars like Laura Wilson have sufficiently acknowledged the role of subjectivity in their analyses.[15] Yet this does not change the fact that the Euro-American focus has biased film phenomenology to frame certain questions as more significant while ignoring others (see chapter 5). Without more comparative analysis, one is also left without recourse to distinguish "invariant structures of the film viewer's lived experience"—which supposedly remain stable across time and space— from what is historically particular to the specific social, cultural, affective, and cognitive structures in which viewings occur.

Discussions about the identity of cinema prompted by digital technologies constitute another area where Western experiences of cinema tend to dominate. Is cinema still alive in the digital age? Are the boundaries between cinema and other media being erased? Does the transition from analog to digital matter more or less than the relocation of films from big screens to iPads and smartphones? To answer these questions, theorists are compelled to develop narratives of what cinema once was and where it was—such narratives rarely go beyond the dominant models of cinema in Europe and America. For example, in his book *When Movies Were Theater: Architecture, Exhibition, and the Evolution of American Film* (2016), William Paul asks: "If movies are no longer inescapably an art of the theater, have we lost an understanding of the art form that seemed self-evident to past audiences?"[16] But were movies ever "inescapably an art of the theater"? We can find numerous counterexamples not only in non-Western contexts but also in the West, where "alternative" modes of viewing—non-theatrical, rural, itinerant, museum, home exhibitions—have long existed in the shadow of the movie theater. Outside of the privileged space of theory, film studies witnessed the "historical turn" in the 1980s–90s and the rise of world cinema as an academic discourse in the 2000s. The fact that Paul still makes such a universalist assumption after many studies have demonstrated the diversity of film exhibition suggests that what is at stake is more than a matter of knowledge; it is a question of power. The movie theater was and still is the privileged exhibition site of the dominant commercial film industry. If an understanding of cinema was "self-evident" to "past audiences," it was only so to audiences that were produced by, and deeply imbricated with, this industry.[17]

On the other hand, the growth of English-language scholarship on Chinese and Sinophone cinemas since the 1980s took place as historians and literary scholars discovered cinema as a rich site where society, culture, and politics intersect. The filmic text, in this case, is seen as another conduit for the expression of national cultures or the dominant issues and structures of feelings of given historical periods.[18] Such a framing produces and sustains the gap between the empirical and the theoretical. "Theory," as Yingjin Zhang observes, is habitually used by China scholars to refer to Western theories.[19] The question of how to situate theory in relation to Chinese and Sinophone cinemas thus becomes one about whether one can ethically apply Western theory to non-Western cases. For some scholars, this is not a problem between the universal and the particular, but a matter of cross-cultural reading politics in an uneven global order in which the West continues to occupy a position of epistemological superiority.

Lingering orientalism is what some fear would take over an analysis of Chinese cinema that derives its interpretive authority from "theory." Yingjin Zhang worries that dangers in cross-cultural analysis would arise "every time a Western(ized) critic subjects the 'raw material' of a film from another culture to an interpretive 'processing' exclusively in Western analytic terms."[20] Pickowicz proposes that to study cultural production in China, one must develop China-centered theories—theories grounded in empirical research that takes into account the distinct history of China.[21] Emilie Yueh-yu Yeh goes so far as to call for the field to de-Westernize. In her view, the automatic acceptance of Western theory bespeaks an unconscious colonial desire. Hence, there is the need for "intellectual decolonization," which involves "a re-search of ourselves, seeking a lost object that was deferred, suspended or undermined in the process of colonial assimilation."[22] One way to achieve this goal is to introduce what she calls "reverse assimilation" into Chinese film historiography, meaning translating and using indigenous concepts in English scholarship rather than resorting to Western concepts. Yeh's example is the early twentieth-century concept of *wenyi*, which describes a unique genre of Chinese films that is similar but cannot be entirely captured by the Western concept of melodrama.[23]

While it is necessary to question the validity of theory, Western or non-Western, attempting to de-Westernize a field that itself depends on Western academic infrastructure to exist seems self-defeating at best. Attending any conference on Chinese cinema, literature, and culture nowadays, there is no denying that (Western) theory is unavoidable. Rather than circumventing theory, we need a better, more productive relationship with theory.

It is important to examine what we are missing when we describe the problem in terms of Western theory vs. Chinese materials. In this binary formation, theory is not only seen as foreign, but a given, a fait accompli. Advocating for a use of theory that is self-reflexive and dialogic, Yingjin Zhang writes that "the issue is not that Western theory cannot be applied, but that it should not be applied or imposed unilaterally so as to dominate or domesticate an alien cultural text."[24] What is assumed here is that before a theory is translated and relocated, it is already finished; what is at stake afterward is mainly how the theory is deployed rather than how it can be revised and updated. However, if we look at the fate of any French theory, the Frankfurt School, or German media theory in Anglophone scholarship, it is clear that theory is far from "dead" when it is translated, which rather gives it a second life, a chance to be rediscovered and renewed. For Casetti, an assumption becomes a theory if "besides expressing knowledge, it also succeeds in proposing itself as a community's heritage."[25] As a shared property of a community, theory should be open to collective authorship. A theoretical discourse, as Victor Fan suggests, can thus be an epistemological space emerging out of networks of debates rather than something that is systematically laid out in an article or a book.[26] For various reasons scholars of Chinese cinema and culture have felt excluded from the community that is "theory." As the focus is on the application of theory, what is precluded is the right to either participate in the ongoing revision of theory or question its production in the first place. What is also not considered is whether a study of China can have general significance beyond China. The scope of Chinese film studies is thus usually limited to the particular geographical area and historical period of a study. It is tempting to assume, as Pickowicz does, that Europeanists and Americanists would not be interested in any "China-centered" theory.

This book is more optimistic about the reception of "China-centered" theory beyond China. The optimism stems from the conviction that what is designated as "alternative" has equal right to participate in the definition of cinema; what Cui Yongyuan believes is cinema should also be recognized as cinema. Mobile projection and open-air cinema, for example, are two overlapping modes of exhibition that the book foregrounds. One may see these as configurations particular to China, or more specifically, China under socialism. Without falling back to a rigid Cold War worldview, one can still maintain, as Larkin does, that there is a fundamental difference between capitalist modes of cinema which treat cinema as a commodity form and spectatorship driven by politics—colonial or socialist.[27] Indeed, there were features that resulted from the unique combination of socialist ideology and conditions of underdevelopment that may be hard to generalize beyond China. The ways in which film projectionists were portrayed as model workers, as their manual labor was celebrated in the news media or the mode of atmospheric spectatorship Chinese viewers call "*kan renao*," may be uniquely "Chinese." But both mobile projection and open-air cinema are also global paradigms with characteristics shared across national boundaries. If testimonies of Chinese audiences urge us to see how material experiences of interfaces including the space, the atmosphere, and the technical apparatus of film exhibition constituted the bulk of their cinematic experience, then, the book urges its readers to consider, does not a similar, multichannel, multisensory engagement with cinema also exist elsewhere? A thorough look at film exhibition interfaces in socialist China will call attention to parallel elements in other contexts that may otherwise be marginalized or ignored. If there are indeed "invariant structures" of cinematic experience, then the seeming alterity of the Chinese socialist film culture should precisely be the reason why it needs to be introduced into the discursive space of theory. It is only by traversing the heterogeneous that we can distinguish what is particular to a social space and what is ontologically stable about cinema, or whether cinema even has a fixed ontology (my answer, in the end, is "no").

FILM EXHIBITION AS A SYSTEM OF INTERFACES

Central to my theorization of film exhibition is the concept of interface, which can be broadly defined as the communication boundary between two parts or systems. Having first emerged as a popular word in computer science in the 1960s, *interface* has become an important concept in media studies. Existing approaches have emphasized the interface as a filter of information or culture. The human-computer interface has been characterized as a "cultural interface" that filters the ways in which users interact with cultural data, including other media objects.[28] Mobile interfaces from the book to the mobile phone are recognized as sources of agency that can "enable people to filter, control, and manage their relationships with the spaces and people around them."[29] Interface is also associated with the recent trend in media studies to shift the object of disciplinary inquiry from specific media objects or communication technologies (such as radio, film, and television) to processes of mediation. Observing interfacing relations in diverse situations, media theorists have conceptualized interfaces as effects,[30] as dynamics of contact and transformation,[31] and as the bridging of segmented spheres of knowledge.[32]

My evocation of the interface concept branches from these broad discussions and considers film exhibition as a situation rich with interfacing dynamics. In film studies, Seung-hoon Jeong has located the screen as one link along a series of interfaces that "range from the filmic object through the medium (camera-film-screen) to the body (eye-mind)," all of which constitute what classic film theory refers to as the cinematic apparatus.[33] In this model, cinematic experience is easily reduced to a matter of visual perception and cognition, a linear process of information "passing through" the screen, the eye, and the mind. But what happens *during* an encounter with the screen is far more than what goes on *between* the screen and the embodied viewing subject. Interface can be a productive concept for reframing film exhibition precisely because it allows us to expand attention from the film or the screen as a portal into the filmed world to other surfaces, boundaries, and points of interactions associated with film exhibition through which communication or mediation also takes place.

In socialist China, especially during the early years of the PRC known as the Seventeen Years period (1949–1966), film exhibitors and projectionists actively sought to explore, inscribe, and control various interfaces on and off screen to convey state-mandated messages. From the exhibition space to the lecturing of the projectionist, from the screening apparatus to the various media objects (photography, slides, etc.) exhibited alongside films, additional interfaces were emphasized and made meaningful no less significantly than the showing of films, which frequently constituted only one aspect of film exhibition despite being the rubric that tied everything together. This approach to film exhibition can be seen as presupposing what John Fiske refers to as the "process" school of communication or what Weihong Bao describes as the linear model of the medium.[34] In this model, the sender tries to ensure that their message is efficiently and accurately transmitted to the receiver. From the perspective of exhibitors and projectionists, who were trained to be representatives of the state, a central question was thus how different interfaces could be deployed or curated to maximize the effect of mass communication. As Barbara Mittler observes, one strategy that Chinese propagandists adopted during the Cultural Revolution was redundancy, repeating the same messages across multiple platforms.[35] If we adopt an expanded view of film exhibition and pay attention to non-filmic interfaces, we can see that this principle was built into the premise of the socialist film exhibition system as well. Film reels were finished products whose integrity needed to be protected. Projectionists could not change or enhance the films. What they could do, and were instructed to do, was to exercise their agency on other interfaces so that the showing of films could be more effectively integrated into the CCP propaganda machine, whose changing and sometimes conflicting messages must be made intelligible through creative labor on the ground.

From the perspective of audiences, their experiences of cinema were not only filtered by multiple interfaces but were frequently of a different register from what is normally considered as reception. Although "new cinema history" and empirical studies of film audiences have foregrounded sociohistorical context as a defining factor of spectatorship, the concept of reception, as Lakshmi Srinivas notes, still habitually refers to how audiences engage with cultural texts.[36] In China studies, there has been a wave of recent scholarship focusing on cultural forms of Chinese socialism including visual culture, music, model operas (*yangbanxi*), literature, film, drama, dance, architecture, and museum exhibitions. Under the stigmatized label of "propaganda," these cultural forms used to be dismissed and ignored by China scholars. But following the boom in scholarship focusing on the Mao era (1949–1976), the current scholarly consensus is that Chinese socialist culture was born out of complex negotiations of shifting political and artistic needs and was never monolithic.[37] The reception of propaganda has also remained a shared interest. Mittler, for instance, draws the conclusion that Cultural Revolution propaganda art, which aspired to be a form of popular culture, was actually enjoyed by many, although not all audiences identified with its political messages. Based on her interviews with audience members, Mittler suggests that Chinese audiences vacillated between a "deluded" and "passive" reception of Cultural Revolution propaganda and a "parasitic" and "subversive" one.[38] Chang-tai Hung makes a similar point that audiences were able to engage with political images, texts, and monuments in creative and unpredictable ways.[39] In these studies, reception is treated primarily as a relationship between audience members and cultural texts or their intended messages. Of course, Chinese audiences attended screenings with the purpose of watching and enjoying films. But if film exhibition is a system of interfaces, then reception becomes a more general state of interfacing in the presence of films. While it involved engagement with the semiotic and symbolic content which exhibitors strived to control, audiences not only perceived signifying structures but interacted with surfaces (screen, seats, etc.,), atmospheres, bodies (the projectionist's, other viewers', and their own), objects, landscapes, and weather in a manner that involved their entire bodies: eyes to see, hands to touch, torso, legs, and feet to feel cold, tired, uncomfortable, and yet excited. These were first and foremost *material* experiences.

Even though political ideology played a part in shaping these experiences, what is striking is how moviegoing is so often remembered as something apolitical. In memoirs and in my own interviews with audience members, people talk about the place of moviegoing in their lives (sometimes important, sometimes marginal), the rituals involved, the senses activated, and the anecdotes they remember vividly after years. If one looks for evidence of political indoctrination or quiet resistance in audience accounts, one can certainly find it. But a large portion of cinema-related memory has little to do with audiences' reaction to ideological positioning or even their enjoyment of the films. In a traditional approach to reception, such memory might appear too trivial and anecdotal to warrant serious consideration. However, once the assumption that consumption of the film is always at the center of an experience of cinema is challenged, it is clear that for many, the seemingly small, non-film-related incidents can be exactly what make up the substance of cinematic experience.

Furthermore, such experience did not derive meaning only from the exhibition interfaces but also from the ways in which moviegoing was embedded in the general flow of life. Exhibition is the interface between cinema and life. While life shapes attitudes toward cinema, through exhibition, cinema has the power to alter everyday rhythms, cultivate communities, and punctuate memory. To understand this effect of cinema, we can evoke a tradition in media studies that John Durham Peters recently summarizes as one that "takes media as modes of being."[40]

He places into this tradition theorists such as Lewis Mumford, Martin Heidegger, Marshall McLuhan, Bruno Latour, and Friedrich Kittler. What these theorists share in common, Peters suggests, is that they are not concerned with media as information channels or interested in the analysis of texts, audiences, and institutions that occupies mainstream media studies. Instead, their conception of "media" (though some did not use this term) is both broader and more fundamental: "they see media as the strategies and tactics of culture and society, as the devices and crafts by which humans and things, animals and data, hold together in time and space."[41] Building on this tradition, Peters expands the concept of media to understand our existence within a larger ecological system in the digital age. Using the term *elemental media*, he draws attention to "the taken-for-granted base"—both natural and cultural— that forms enabling environments and anchors our being.

Cinema is not part of Peters's original conceptualization, but a similar approach can be appropriated for thinking about the impact of cinema on everyday life, for beyond the transmission of meaning, cinema also participates in the reorganization of experience by inserting into life schedules, rituals, conversations, escapes, heterotopic moments, and feelings that run the gamut. In this sense, cinema can be grouped together with calendars, clocks, indexes, maps, lists, and money as what Peters calls logistical media. "The job of logistical media is to organize and orient, to arrange people and property, often into grids. They both coordinate and subordinate, arranging relationships among people and things," writes Peters.[42] From this point of view, we need to understand the experiences of moviegoers in socialist China by asking not how they interpreted films, but what kinds of experiences were generated through the particular ways in which environment, bodies, and technological apparatus were arranged by the socialist modes of film exhibition, and what significance is attached to these experiences in retrospect.

It also follows that socialist culture needs to be distinguished from political culture, which has been defined as "shared values, collective visions, common attitudes, and public expectations created by high politics."[43] Focusing on political culture as the center of inquiry, a researcher naturally asks how the CCP employed symbols, rituals, rhetoric, narratives, and visual images to instill shared values among Chinese citizens, and to what degree the production of socialist subjectivity was successful.[44] But this does not encompass all aspects of socialist culture, which was also a media culture, a technological culture, a popular culture, and a communal culture. Approaching socialist culture in these terms means that the explanation of a cultural form or practice does not always need to resort to ideology. A medium or technology in a socialist context still carries its own "message" that cannot be reduced to a political usage of the medium. The mobile, open-air mode of exhibition, for instance, introduced a porous atmosphere that defined spectatorship as a form of embodied presence distinct from the dominant mode of attentive viewing in theatrical settings. Although open-air screenings, being mostly free and easily accessible, may be seen as a manifestation of the Maoist ideal of "serving workers, peasants, and soldiers" (*wei gongnongbing fuwu*), to focus only on the political significance would foreclose attention to the multifaceted and embodied ways audiences engaged with exhibition practices, which cannot all be explained by ideology.

BETWEEN ARCHIVES AND MEMORY

The two perspectives the book explores—that of the institutions and individuals behind the formation of the exhibition interfaces and that of the audiences—required a methodology that combined archival and memory research, which yielded two sets of overlapping and yet frequently divergent sources. The book is divided into a historical analysis based on archival materials of how the various exhibition interfaces came into being (chapters 1 to 3) and an examination of audiences' retrospective accounts (chapters 4 to 6) that reveal how they interfaced with cinema and remember moviegoing on their own terms, in ways that often exceeded state control.

Three types of archival materials informed the book's historical narrative. Widely circulated publications, including official CCP newspapers *People's Daily* (*Renmin ribao*, established in 1948) and *Guangming Daily* (*Guangming ribao*, established in 1949), as well as the popular film magazine *Mass Cinema* (*Dazhong dianying*, established in 1950) functioned as high-profile platforms that showcased developments in the socialist film exhibition system as achievements in nation building and modernization. In particular, they celebrated the rural film projectionist as a model socialist worker through reports of their arduous travel in the countryside, their dedicated labor, and personal sacrifices (chapter 2). These newspapers and journals may be seen as a print interface that instructed readers on the ideological significance of film exhibition. Government documents such as work reports and meeting summaries, which I was able to find at Shanghai Municipal Archive and Beijing Municipal Archive, provided glimpses into the inner workings of cultural bureaus and their administration of exhibition outlets. One consistent challenge these documents reveal was the difficulty of maintaining a balance between political education and the sustained operation of exhibition outlets, which depended on audience interest to generate revenue on top of limited state subsidy. For learning about projectionists' daily exhibition practices, the best sources are publications intended for exhibition workers, including training manuals, internal pamphlets, and trade journals. Most notably, I draw from a journal known as *Film Projection Resources* (*Dianying fangying ziliao*) from 1953 to 1956, as *Film Projection* (*Dianying fangying*) from 1957 to 1966, and as *Film Popularization* (*Dianying puji*) during most of the 1980s.[45] Abundant with articles submitted by projectionists and theater workers, this journal functioned as a public forum for practitioners within the exhibition system to exchange experience and debate best practices in areas such as how to increase attendance, how to conduct the so-called "pre-screening propaganda" (*yingqian xuanchuan*), and how to help audiences understand films through lecturing (*jieshuo*). One may question the extent to which the strategies and techniques recommended in the journal were routinely implemented on the ground; occasionally there were in fact criticisms pointing out that not all projection teams were fulfilling their duties properly. But it is safe to assume that the journal represented what many thought they *should* do to effectively serve the goals of socialist film exhibition. Viewed together, these archival sources allow me to excavate both the socialist rhetoric surrounding cinema and film projectionists and the operations of the exhibition system at different administrative levels.

In this book, however, I do not rely on the archive as my main source to describe audience experiences. Film magazines like *Mass Cinema*, in fact, published many accounts by audience members. For example, there was a recurring section in early issues of the magazine from 1950 called "Learning-from-films Awards" (*dianying xuexi jinjiang*), which featured short essays submitted by readers talking about how they had learned valuable moral lessons from films they watched. These essays were handpicked by editors, who would award a first place and a second place in each issue. Such practices set a dominant pattern for the narration of filmic experiences that, for Tina Mai Chen, reflected "the CCP vision of the power of film to produce new people."[46] As she analyzes, the standard narrative often goes: one watches a film and is emotionally affected. The film viewing then becomes a turning point for the individual, causing a change of heart or renewed determination. The viewer not only identifies with model film characters psychologically, but also vows to emulate them in his or her own everyday life, transforming the emotional impact of film into concrete actions. Chen calls this "the mimetic model of spectatorship." Such a narrative then provided readers with images of an ideal viewer they were called upon to imitate, as well as the political language they could use to describe their own filmic experiences.[47]

It would be wrong to assume that the ideal viewer was merely a textual construction that existed on paper. In retrospect, many viewers remember their younger selves as being deeply inspired by films. I have interviewed a retired engineer who attended Tsinghua University from 1953 to 1958. According to him, Soviet films had a significant impact on how he and his high school classmates chose majors when they applied for colleges:

> Some students applied for the major of agricultural mechanics in their college applications. That was because of the movie *Tractor Drivers* (*Traktoristi/ Tuolaji shou*, 1939). In the movie *Cossacks of the Kuban* (*Kubanskie kazaki / Xingfu de shenghuo*, 1950), we saw people driving tractors, singing and dancing on trucks, and we felt uplifted, since "Today's Soviet Union is our tomorrow!" So a lot of students chose to learn about tractors. There were a few others who chose geology, also under the influence of Soviet films. . . . How come I decided to study hydraulic engineering? It was because I saw a Soviet documentary about the "Dubuqieke" hydroelectric power station.[48] Large-scale hydraulic projects were important for constructing communism. I was inspired by the movie to study hydraulic engineering.[49]

There is no denying that the transformative potential of film was realized in viewers' lives. Among the people I interviewed, many also indicated that the values acquired by their younger selves through films have stayed with them over the years, such as patriotism, hard work, and devotion to collective causes, as well as the moral vision that good films should teach audiences how to be better persons.

However, the pedagogical function of moviegoing by no means encompasses the entirety of cinematic experiences. A large portion of audience memories cast a brighter light on routines, rituals, anecdotes, interactions, and feelings that seemed irrelevant, if not contradictory, to the goal of learning from films. It is these memories that have mostly escaped scholarly attention because of their deviation from the film text and will take center stage in this book. Of course, this does not mean that audiences' engagement with films is negligible. Some readers may be interested in finding out more about how viewers, even under the pressure of political education, found ways to assert their agency as critics of films, evaluating and comparing the artistic achievements of Chinese and dubbed foreign films. Others may be interested in the phenomenon of viewers repeating lines or reenacting scenes from well-known films. These topics are unfortunately outside the scope of this book and deserve extended treatment elsewhere.[50] What the book does focus on in its second half is recurring themes in audiences' retrospective accounts that exceeded textual reception and challenge us to rethink what cinema is.

From 2013 to 2014, I conducted interviews with sixty people that had personal experience with film exhibition and moviegoing during the four decades covered by the book.[51] Three of my interviewees were film projectionists; the rest were moviegoers. Although the majority of the interviews took place in Beijing and Shanghai, I took advantage of the rich life trajectories of the interviewees, many of whom have relocated across regions and the rural-urban divide over the years and can recall multiple exhibition contexts. I also strived as much as possible for diversity in interviewees' social identities to include people of different genders, age groups, education levels, and professional backgrounds (see the appendix). Although these interviews obviously only capture the moviegoing experiences of a tiny fraction of the Chinese population, I take comfort in the fact that they reveal noteworthy patterns to serve as a starting point for future studies of Chinese socialist film spectatorship.

Moreover, my interviews are supplemented by publicly available testimonies, memoirs, and creative works such as fictions, songs, and films. One useful source I draw from is *Childhood Flashback*, the television show in which Cui Yongyuan offered the description of "projecting cinema." Transcripts of interviews from the show's first four years (2004–2007) were published as a four-volume book in 2007.[52] Whereas about two thirds of my own interviewees were born before the founding of the PRC, with the oldest born in 1926 and the youngest born in 1957, guests interviewed on *Childhood Flashback* tend to belong to younger generations born in the 1950s and '60s. Because of its focus on childhood, the show presents a rather narrow and highly consistent set of collective memory about watching movies as kids. The reminiscence of the child-self has also become the predominant lens in popular cultural representations of socialist moviegoing. Film directors Zhang Yimou (b. 1950) and Chen Kaige (b. 1952), writer Su Tong (b. 1963), and singer-songwriter Yu Dong (b. 1972) are a few of the most well-known creators behind such works, some of which will be analyzed in this book.

FORGETTING, REMEMBERING,
AND POSTSOCIALIST NOSTALGIA

While memory discourses enable new understandings by articulating private thoughts, desires, and experiences that cannot be found in archival sources, they also present challenges for those courting historical truth. As Andreas Huyssen reminds us, the temporal status of any act of memory is always the present and not the past itself.[53] Recent studies in neuroscience and cognitive psychology also confirm that memory is unstable, subject to factors from the neurological process of reconsolidation to the influence of language and collective memory.[54] To evoke memory as a research source thus requires grappling with forces at psychological, social, and cultural levels that shape what audiences remember, what they forget, and how they remember.

One way to understand what is currently available in testimonies of socialist moviegoing is to examine the dynamics of forgetting and remembrance. On one end of the spectrum, there are audience members who can recall very little about their past moviegoing experiences; on the other end, there are those who speak with detail and nostalgia. These two tendencies largely correspond to two groups of viewers. Those who forget tend to be older, who experienced post-49 film screenings mainly as working adults. Those who remember tend to be younger, post-49 generations, who remember most vividly and express strongest nostalgia for moviegoing experiences that occurred during their childhood and adolescence.

The intergenerational differences can in part be explained on an individual level. We do not remember everything that happens in life and even fewer episodes stick with us for years. Researchers have discovered that for an episode to become memorable in the long term, it needs to fulfill certain criteria: it needs to involve either physical sensations, powerful emotions, or direct and dramatic impact on the individual; moreover, the event needs to be recast in a memorializing form, usually a story. As the story is repeated in conversations, writings, or in our heads, an experience is consolidated into long-term memory.[55] For many people, moviegoing is forgotten because it simply did not register as important in the first place, and as such, it was less likely to be talked about later and remembered. People could choose not to frequent film screenings due to a lack of interest, or they simply did not have time for films. The latter was true for many working adults, especially women. Facing the double burden of paid work and unpaid domestic labor, married working women were probably a social group that spent the least amount of time watching movies. In one telling interview I did in 2014 with a couple who was almost in their nineties at the time, the husband, who used to work for a city government, suggested several times that his wife, a retired textile worker, did not like watching movies. She, however, made it very clear that the reason why she did not watch a lot of movies was because she did not have time. After an exhausting twelve-hour or eight-hour shift, she still had to cook and take care of chores, which left her with no time for leisure activities.[56] By contrast, a male steel factory worker from Shanghai (b. 1936) used to attend screenings several times a week at the factory assembly hall (*da litang*). He recalled with amusement that he loved watching movies so much that people came to find him in the auditorium when his wife went into labor.[57] Nevertheless, this worker remembered little about the films he watched. By and large, he and other members of the older generations tend to describe moviegoing with fewer words and a more matter-of-fact tone than the younger generations.

In comparison, the post-49 generations, represented by some of my interviewees, most guests on *Childhood Flashback*, and cultural figures who have shaped much of the public discourse on socialist moviegoing, are more likely to retain robust memories of their moviegoing experiences as children and adolescents. If, as mentioned above, an event becomes more memorable in the long run because of its impact on an individual, then films and cinematic experiences are more likely to influence and then be remembered by younger viewers who are still developing a sense of self. In her study of female film viewers in 1940s–50s Britain, Jackie Stacey discovers that what many women recall most passionately is how female Hollywood stars, who embodied ideals of femininity, played an important role in the transformation of their identities during adolescence.[58] Similarly in the Chinese socialist context, films provided role models, revolutionary heroes, values, and worldviews, which all had a significant impact on young viewers, who also enjoyed moviegoing as a fun, exciting activity outside of their normal routines. What their older selves remember can be further divided into three categories based on a scheme developed by Annette Kuhn.[59] The first and least frequent type is remembered scenes or images from films. Viewers generally do not speak about films with more details than a rough synopsis. This is true even with films that have deeply impacted them. The exception is when a film became the object of repeat viewing. During the first few years of the Cultural Revolution, only a handful of films were allowed to be shown, including *Lenin in 1918* (*Lenin v 1918 godu/Liening zai 1918*, 1939), *Lenin in October* (*Lenin v oktyabre/Liening zai shiyue*, 1937), *Tunnel Warfare* (*Didao zhan*, 1965), and *Zhang Ga the Soldier Boy* (*Xiaobing Zhang Ga*, 1963), which popularized some lines and scenes that many can still recall years later. The second type is situated memories of films, where films are remembered in the context of the subject's own life. This kind of memory often takes the form of anecdotes, involving first-person narration of specific, one-off events. The third and most prevalent type is memories of the social activity of moviegoing. Discursively, this kind of cinema memory is characterized by what Kuhn calls "repetitive memory discourse," which describes events in the habitual mode and often features first-person-plural narrators "we" or the generic pronoun "you." As Cui Yongyuan's narration of "projecting cinema" exemplifies, this type of memory discourse is particularly significant in the formation of collective memory, as it generates "scripts" that are perceived as shared and fundamental.

Moreover, collective memory is not only formed from an aggregation of individual memories but maintained through public symbols and discourses. A crucial background for the remembering of socialist moviegoing is the ongoing collective efforts to make sense of the socialist past in postsocialist China. Since Arif Dirlik used the notion of postsocialism to describe a condition of ideological contradiction and uncertainty in 1980s China, scholars generally agree that postsocialism marks a stage of development that both departs from and yet maintains deep connections with the socialist past.[60] But the starting point of postsocialism in China has been a subject of debate. Chris Berry argues that films made as early as in the years immediately following the Cultural Revolution, between 1976 and 1981, already constituted the first cinematic site for the construction of postsocialist Chinese culture.[61] Yingjin Zhang similarly locates the beginning of Chinese postsocialist cinema in the late 1970s, coinciding with the beginning of "reform and opening" (*gaige kaifang*).[62] For other scholars, although "reform and opening" marked the entry into the New Era (*xin shiqi*) or the Reform Era, postsocialism needs to be associated more closely with cultural developments since the early 1990s. For Jason McGrath, the fundamental logic of Chinese cultural production did not go through a market-driven rupture until the 1990s.[63] Xudong Zhang treats the Chinese 1990s (beginning with the student protests in 1989 and ending with China's entry into WTO) as an independent chapter in Chinese history distinct from the "modernist" and idealistic 1980s. He links postsocialism with the condition of postmodernism, both of which point to bewildering contradictions in economic, social, political relations in the inescapable context of global capitalism.[64]

These different positions not so much contradict each other as identify multiple locations and historical points where ruptures occurred. It thus makes sense to understand postsocialism not as a singular historical period, but as a multifaceted phenomenon that has varied manifestations and a layered temporality. By situating my investigations of socialist film exhibition in the years between 1949 and the early 1990s, I do not suggest that there were not wide variations across this period. To get a sense of the differences between the earlier Mao period and the 1980s, one only needs to look at the changing references of the Chinese word *xuanchuan*, which can mean either "propaganda" or "publicity." In archival sources from the earlier period, *xuanchuan* predominantly referred to political propaganda; however, this usage almost entirely disappeared from the journal *Film Popularization* in the 1980s, which instead discussed *xuanchuan* in the context of promoting films. While acknowledging such changes, my periodization is closely associated with the shared scripts that several generations of Chinese moviegoers use to describe moviegoing of the previous decades. Often glossing over both the politicization of the early socialist period and the increased market activity that was permitted in film exhibition in the 1980s, these scripts foreground continuities that were primarily grounded in the configurations of exhibition (notably open-air cinema) and the centrality of moviegoing in the everyday cultural life of ordinary Chinese people. Although there were new developments in film exhibition in the 1980s, such as the emergence of "township cinemas" (*jizhen yingyuan*) and the contracting of projection teams to private owners, it was in the early 1990s that a more significant rupture occurred as audiences transitioned to television and newer channels of consumption in the newly established market economy, forcing old exhibition institutions either to close doors or fumble with innovative ways to increase attendance.

It was also in the 1990s that the socialist era became the subject of a memory boom. If the 1980s saw attempts to make sense of the immediate traumas of the Cultural Revolution, what rose in the 1990s and the early 2000s was widespread, commodified nostalgia for life under the socialist planned economy. This nostalgia is widely understood as a by-product of market reforms. In Ban Wang's rather broad terms from the mid-2000s, "the general wind of intellectual and aesthetic trends in contemporary

China tends either toward an uncritical embrace of globalization and commodity form, or toward a moralistic rejection of Westernization in a nostalgic throwback to the socialist good old days."[65] This nostalgia can be seen in the so-called "Mao-craze," epitomized by small portraits of Mao dangling as talismans from the rearview mirror of taxi drivers.[66] It was behind the popularization of retro restaurants, old posters, remakes of "red classics," fueled by groups like the former "educated youths" (*zhiqing*), urban youths who were sent to the countryside for reeducation during the Cultural Revolution.[67] In films and TV dramas of the '90s and 2000s, socialism, as Sheldon Lu observes, conveniently signifies values that are putatively absent in the market era such as idealism, egalitarianism, self-sacrifice, and innocence. Notable examples include Zhang Yimou's film *The Road Home* (*Wo de fuqin muqin*, 1999) and the popular TV drama *Years of Burning Passion* (*Jiqing ranshao de suiyue*, 2001).[68] Nostalgia was also evoked in depictions of "red childhood" by the so-called post-60 generation, such as best-selling writer Wang Shuo (b. 1958) and film directors Zhang Yuan (b. 1963), Jiang Wen (b. 1963), and Wang Xiaoshuai (b. 1966), who offer depoliticized and romanticized representations of childhood and adolescence against the backdrop of the Cultural Revolution.[69] Most of these nostalgic expressions belong to what Lingchei Letty Chen recently calls "national collective memory lite," which consists of either "superficial nostalgic fads" or representations that only touch on positive experiences or personal suffering without probing underlying causes.[70]

From the mid-2000s onward, memory discourses of the socialist past became increasingly contentious and fragmented. The Chinese state began to play a more active role in shaping memories of the socialist past. One of its most successful tools is red tourism, which the state began to promote in 2004. By turning entire historical sites into immersive red experiences, national and local governments seem to have found a way to not only control narratives of the past, but also bring the past into the lives of Chinese citizens for the sake of building a harmonious society in the present.[71] Meanwhile, as Jie Li and Enhua Zhang observe, while the state selectively taps into the socialist past to "construct a spectacular façade of power," alternative understandings of the past are also possible, mobilized by different cultural producers and communities.[72] For the increasingly noticeable neo-Maoists, Mao is not merely an image to be printed on tourist souvenirs in a tongue-in-cheek fashion, but a symbol of resistance against the current political system that embraces capitalism. "The socialist good old days" are not only something to be missed but provide the blueprint for what some see as a radical political movement in today's China. Popular memories that critically reexamine the Mao era in the forms of unofficial testimonies, oral histories, investigative studies, and documentaries are equally prominent. As Sebastian Veg notes, these recent works often focus on the everyday lives of ordinary people as a way to generate new historical knowledge outside of official history.[73]

Socialist moviegoing has occupied a relatively small but stable corner through the changing waves of this memory boom. Without ambivalence, publicly available discourses of socialist moviegoing, especially open-air screenings, have been tinged with a strong sense of nostalgia. Chinese scholar Liu Jian observes in an article published in 2016 that "as a historical memory and a nostalgic symbol, open-air cinema has become an object of rumination in both folk oral history and academic discourse." He identifies people born in the 1960s and 1970s as the generation most nostalgic for open-air cinema. This generation was the first beneficiary of "reform and opening," but as they reap the benefits of market economy and urbanization, they also suffer the pressure and anxiety of urban dwelling. Open-air cinema thus becomes alluring as an emblem for the amalgamation of traditional rural life and the socialist planned economy.[74] Liu's observation echoes my own findings of younger, more nostalgic viewers. But it is also important to note that such nostalgia is not entirely spontaneous. A TV show like *Childhood Flashback* actively encouraged collective nostalgia. In the interview transcripts, one can clearly see the show's regular host Zhang Zequn, who was also born in the 60s, skillfully uses his questions and responses to integrate individual stories into a collective narrative, drawing out commonalities and shared sentiments. As the common link among all guests, Zhang holds the power of what psychologists call a dominant narrator, whose narration has a higher chance of shaping collective memory.[75] Another popular show dedicated to memories of "old films" with a similar tone of nostalgia was produced by none other than Cui Yongyuan himself. Broadcast on China Central Television from 2004 to 2009, *Film Legend* (*Dianying chuanqi*) offered viewers behind-the-scenes looks at many popular films from the 1950s and '60s. Filling each episode with original footage, interviews with filmmakers, and reenactments of classic scenes performed by Cui Yongyuan himself and other actors, it portrays the socialist past as one of integrity, sacrifice, and optimism in the face of material shortage and technical challenges. Although *Film Legend* pays much less attention to the activity of moviegoing, by paying respect to old films, it encourages audiences to remember their own encounters with these films.

Although my own interviews have generated narratives of socialist moviegoing that are much terser and more matter-of-fact, pointing to more diverse experiences than what has been publicly articulated, my analysis does rely heavily on nostalgic discourses, which might magnify some aspects of audiences' experiences while ignoring others. As a result, readers are encouraged to keep in mind the incompleteness of the picture this book draws. Not only are there aspects of socialist moviegoing that await to be explored, but what is revealed about everyday life under socialism through the lens of moviegoing is also limited. The fact that socialist moviegoing can be romanticized in retrospect does not mean that Maoist political campaigns did not cause oppression, violence, and trauma. It would also be problematic to assume that nostalgia is only a defense mechanism against the present and has nothing to do with historical reality. After all, the complexity of lived socialism is attested by the continuing efforts to unearth new materials, produce oral histories, and revise existing narratives. With an incomplete picture of socialist moviegoing, this book might only be able to supply a small missing piece to the puzzle of Chinese socialism. It is nonetheless a crucial piece sitting at the crossroads between ideology and everyday life, between official institutions and grassroots practices, between socialist ideals and postsocialist marketization. Connecting all of these is precisely cinema's potential for enabling a multitude of interfacing relations.

THE CHAPTER INTERFACES

Each chapter of the book is organized around one "off screen" interface associated with film exhibition and moviegoing in socialist China. Readers will notice that there is an asymmetry between the two parts of the book. While the first three chapters detail strategies for mobilizing and inscribing extra-filmic interfaces in film exhibition, readers will be disappointed if they look for audiences' direct responses to these strategies in the second half of the book. There is little information in my sources to help determine, for example, how audiences received projectionists' lecturing or their slideshows. But what is significant is precisely the silences in audience testimonies, which are otherwise vocal about interactions that largely escaped ideological control. It is these interactions that I foreground in chapter 4 through 6.

Chapter 1 uses space as the focal point to provide an overview of the socialist film exhibition system. To the PRC state, where films were shown was not only a practical matter but also highly symbolic. In the development of a national exhibition network, two processes became prominent: the relocation of cinema from the urban, commercial movie theater to workers' cultural halls/clubs and remote rural areas; and the active design and inscription of these spaces as propaganda interfaces. Both processes, I argue, were driven by the cardinal principle of "serving workers, peasants, and soldiers." Chapter 2 focuses on the physical labor of rural projectionists as another interface. As couriers, projectionists literally connected film reels to audiences in remote areas, urging us to recognize the role of human labor in the cinematic apparatus. Meanwhile, the projectionist's body, now an object of audiences' gaze, was actively deployed by the cultural establishments as a locus of meaning and propaganda, mediating a socialist ethos of labor that celebrated hard work, sacrifice, and the malleability of the human body. Chapter 3 continues to decenter the film in socialist "film" exhibition, which is shown to be a multimedia institution. Situating this institution in the longer history of audiovisual education (*dianhua jiaoyu*) in modern China, this chapter explores the roles of two additional media interfaces—slide projection (*huandeng*) and projectionists' live performance.

The second half of the book examines three aspects of cinematic experiences that were most closely associated with open-air cinema. Chapter 4 argues that as a long-existing and yet overlooked paradigm in film history, open-air cinema foregrounds the interface of atmosphere, encouraging what I call "atmospheric spectatorship"—a mode of cinematic experience characterized by embodied presence in a porous, disruptive environment, which is distinct from the dominant theatrical mode that favors sustained attention on the screen in a darkened room. In postsocialist memories of open-air cinema, the atmosphere is foregrounded either in terms of "*kan renao*" or through an association of open-air cinema with nature and community. Chapter 5 examines memories of seemingly negative experiences of moviegoing that involved extreme cold, heat, mosquito bites, and fatigue. Treating physical discomfort as a result of audiences interfacing with the material conditions of film exhibition, I relate the positive attitude toward discomfort to the socialist structure of feelings, in which struggle, even in the extreme form of torture, is seen as a source of spiritual elevation. By investigating discomfort, I also broaden the scope of what is typically considered embodied spectatorship. Finally, chapter 6 focuses on audiences' tactile interactions with the screen as a tangible material object, which include acts from physically touching the screen to casting hand shadows and moving from one side of the screen to the other. I push against a reading of rural viewers and children as naive and make sense of these interactions through the lens of play. Together chapters 4, 5, and 6 explain why against ostensibly negative factors, either political or material, socialist moviegoing can still be remembered as an activity of fun and uplift.

The narrative of the book thus begins with the design and implementation of film exhibition as a state institution and then moves on to the experience of moviegoing and its remembrance. It provides aerial views but also zooms in for close-ups of individual projectionists and viewers as they labored, performed, endured, and enjoyed themselves. I will end with a cut to the present, contemplating what this past means for our continuing reimagination of cinema.

CHAPTER 1

Space

"Film is the most important of all arts." Attributed to Lenin, this slogan was reportedly posted in movie theaters across China. It is hard to say if film was in fact more important than literature, theater, and other visual arts to the CCP. But party investment in film production and exhibition began early on. While based in Yan'an, a remote town in Shaanxi Province, during the War of Resistance against Japan (1937–1945), the CCP began its initial foray into cinema with the creation of the Yan'an Film Group (*yan'an dianying tuan*) in 1938. As part of the General Political Department of the Eighth Route Army, the Yan'an Film Group shot documentary films and managed three projection teams. In 1946, during the Civil War (1945–1949) with the Guomindang, the CCP founded its first film studio, the Northeast Film Studio, which was followed by the establishment of the Beijing Film Studio and Shanghai Film Studio in 1949. The Central Film Bureau came into being under the party's Central Propaganda Department in February of the same year and then became part of the Ministry of Culture in October. The bureau would remain the official government organ that oversaw the production, distribution, and exhibition of films, around which what Yingjin Zhang calls a "sprawling bureaucracy" took shape.[1] Another key player in the system was China Film Corporation (*zhongying gongsi*). Founded in February 1951, it was the central agency overseeing all film distribution in China. Despite minor institutional changes, the overall distribution mechanism remained largely the same over the next five decades: the China Film

Corporation purchased film copies from state-owned film studios for a flat rate, shielding the studios from both market pressure and incentives; it then distributed the films to its regional branches, which rented copies to various exhibition outlets.

As the end point of a film's life cycle, exhibition was the interface between the nascent socialist film industry and its audience. In the first years of the PRC, there was a consensus among both high-level administrators and exhibitors on the ground that a new nation required not only new films and new aesthetics but also new kinds of spaces to show these films. They treated exhibition space not as a neutral background to other objects of attention, but a semiotic field that actively interpellated viewers—in other words, an interface that carried its own message. This chapter provides a historical overview of the socialist framework of film exhibition by showing how the state and its agents at the grassroots level purposefully tried to find and produce the "right" exhibition space. Two intertwined processes were involved: the expansion of film exhibition from commercial movie theaters in urban centers to communal spaces in work units, rural areas, and military camps, and the active inscription of the exhibition space as a communication interface. Most of the chapter focuses on the early socialist period or the Seventeen Years, during which both processes were guided by the cardinal principle of "serving workers, peasants, and soldiers." A brief discussion of new developments in the 1980s is also included, showing how ideological shifts at a time of transition were reflected in the spatial configurations of film exhibition.

MOVIEGOING IN "OLD CHINA"

When the CCP seized control of existing film infrastructures from the Guomindang, films had been shown and produced in China for half a century. Although the domestic film industry that grew large during the Republican era (1911–1949) was influenced by diverse interests, practices, and audiences, the dominant post-49 narrative portrayed film culture of the "old society" as commercial, bourgeois, capitalist, and imperialist. In *A History of the Development of Chinese Cinema* (*Zhongguo dianying fazhanshi*), a canonical text first published in 1963, Cheng Jihua summarizes that after being introduced to China as "a novel plaything," cinema has been "a tool used by imperialist countries to achieve both the economic and cultural invasions of China." Except for a small number of films that reflected the pursuits of capitalist democratic culture, Republican cinema, for Cheng and many others, embodied the "semi-colonial and semi-feudal" nature of Chinese society.[2]

Such a characterization of pre-49 Chinese cinema is not entirely without basis. Cinema was indeed imported as a commodity for entertainment. Some of the earliest venues for exhibiting films in China around 1900 were teahouses and amusement gardens, where cinema was shown as a novelty among other attractions such as magic shows, traditional opera performances, fireworks, and displays of antiques and rare flowers.[3] In the first decade of the twentieth century, film exhibition began moving into purposely built movie theaters. Cities including Harbin, Jinan, Kunming, Guangzhou, Wuhan, Beijing, Tianjin, and Shanghai all reportedly had their first dedicated movie theaters built by 1910.[4] Domestic film production began around the same time, allegedly first in Beijing and then in Shanghai.[5] Early short films offered entertainment to a growing urban audience with genres such as slapstick comedies, urban sceneries, and current affairs. As long narrative films became more standard, crime, romance, martial arts (*wuxia*), and the supernatural (*shen-guai*) emerged as some of the most popular genres until the Guomindang government passed the Film Censorship Law (*dianying jiancha fa*) in 1930, tightening censorship of content deemed superstitious, immoral, or unpatriotic. Although the 1930s saw the emergence of leftist films, working out of Shanghai—the center of Chinese film industry at the time, socially conscious filmmakers had to negotiate their political vision with commercial demands.[6]

What Chinese filmmakers also faced was a film culture that remained heavily Westernized. Although domestic films gradually gained more market share in the 1930s and in the few years after the beginning of World War II, foreign imports, especially Hollywood films, dominated the Chinese market for most of the time before 1949. Some first-run theaters exclusively showed foreign films, which were considered superior to domestic productions. Movie theaters were also Westernized places. In Shanghai, most of the movie theaters built between the 1910s and 1949 had Western-sounding names, such as Empire (*Enpaiya*, opened in 1921), Carlton (*Ka'erdeng*, 1923), and Odeon (*Audi'an*, 1924).[7] Aspiring to be like movie palaces in Europe and America, many theaters built in the 1920s and '30s boasted grandiose façades, Western architecture and equipment, large seating capacity, comfortable sofa-chairs, air-conditioning, and luxurious interiors. The famous Grand Theater (*Daguangming yingxiyuan*)—first opened in 1928 and remodeled in 1933—featured architecture that was so impressive that the Chinese press gave it the title of "the only grand architecture in the Far East."[8] Nanking Theater (*Nanjing daxiyuan*), which opened on March 25, 1930, reportedly had an interior modeled after the Italian renaissance style with bricks imported from Britain and expensive fabric decorating the whole place.[9] Spatial design within the movie theater and services provided to customers also betrayed Western influences. In luxurious first-or-second-run theaters, signage was often in English; it was standard to have smoke rooms for the gentlemen and makeup rooms for the ladies; theaters also employed non-Chinese ushers to further boost their prestige.[10]

All that was deemed desirable about a movie theater became reasons for denouncing the Republican film culture after 1949. Take the Roxy Theater as an example. When the Roxy Theater opened in Shanghai in December 1939, its opening announcement touted it as the pinnacle of progress: "In Shanghai today, population density has reached the highest level. It has become obvious that the city needs the most scientific, most up-to-date modern movie palace. By rebuilding on the site of the former Olympia Theater, the Roxy stands at the forefront of the new age."[11] With an exclusive contract with the Hollywood studio MGM, the Roxy Theater was seen as the "epitome of the glamour, sophistication, and cosmopolitanism of modern urban life."[12] By 1951, an article in *Mass Cinema* describes the theater in completely changed terms: "No one in Shanghai did not know about the Roxy Theater. But before 'liberation,' very few people had the right to enter the theater. It was because its entry fee was too high, which was also why it was famous. This theater was initially established by a Chinese person with the surname Pan, but . . . it exclusively served imperialists. Hence English was spoken in the theater and English signs were everywhere."[13] Attacking the old Roxy on the grounds of class and foreign connections, this passage exemplifies the dominant CCP criticism of pre-49 Chinese cinema. Such criticism deliberately overlooked the Republican history of education cinema, which actually provided precedents for many of the practices of socialist film exhibition (see chapter 3), so that the stage could be set for the new regime as the harbinger of radical change, a revolutionary that would rid China of "harmful" capitalist culture that dominated the "old society." But what principles should the "new society" adopt for its cultural production and consumption? In Western discourses, the new socialist logic is often dismissed as "propaganda." The label is not unjustly applied; in fact, the CCP never shied away from publicly acknowledging cinema as "an instrument of propaganda" (*xuanchuan gongju*). But merely calling socialist culture "propaganda" does not tell us much about how it worked, what messages it tried to convey, and what forms or mediums it employed to convey those messages. I will instead turn to the notion of "serving workers, peasants, and soldiers," which was first advanced by Mao Zedong in his 1942 "Talks at the Yan'an Forum of Literature and Arts" ("Talks" hereafter). Following the principle of "serving workers, peasants, soldiers," film exhibition was reorganized not just as an institution of propaganda, but to serve the goals of both political education and mass entertainment.

BETWEEN MASS CULTURE, EDUCATION, AND PROPAGANDA

In May 1942, a forum on literature and arts was held in Yan'an, in which Mao gave speeches at two separate meetings, which became known as "Talks at the Yan'an Forum of Literature and Arts." At the All-China Congress of Literary and Arts Workers, held in Beijing in July 1949, Zhou Yang (1908–1989), a prominent literary theorist who also held multiple high-level positions within the CCP cultural establishments, declared that the artistic direction laid down by Mao's "Talks" would be the only correct direction for literature and arts in the new regime, namely, that literature and art should serve the masses, especially workers, peasants, and soldiers.[14]

Frequently evoked by artists, critics, and party authorities, the mandate of "serving workers, peasants, and soldiers" was not as straightforward as it first seemed. On one hand, the "Talks" demanded that literature and art be subordinate to politics. Against the backdrop of the War of Resistance against Japan, Mao called on writers and artists to be a cultural army in the revolutionary machinery ("we must also have a cultural army, which is absolutely indispensable for uniting our own ranks and defeating the enemy"[15]). It follows that political criteria should always take priority over artistic criteria in the evaluation of art. In Ban Wang's view, it was this interpretation of the "Yan'an principle" that led many in the West to dismiss Communist art as mere propaganda lacking aesthetic value.[16] On the other hand, the "Talks" has also been seen as the culmination of a trend toward popularization in literature and art since the 1920s. The expectation that Mao had for writers and artists was to produce works welcomed by the worker-peasant-soldier masses. Recent studies of Maoist culture have increasingly called attention to the link between the "Talks" and popular culture. Barbara

Mittler sees "serve the people" as an ideology that demands propaganda art to be popular.[17] Krista Van Fleit Hang argues that according to "Talks," providing accessible entertainment to the masses is a task of equal importance to the education of the masses, which Mao describes respectively as "popularization" (*puji*) and "elevation" (*tigao*).[18]

I agree with Van Fleit Hang that the "Talks" advances not one, but two imperatives for writers and artists. But how should mass entertainment and education relate to each other? It is important to note that the "Talks" did not view entertainment and education as separate goals, but as different stages in the same dialectical process known as the "mass line" (*qunzhong luxian*). The "mass line" policy required leadership to be "from the masses to the masses." For literary and artistic workers, it meant that they "must serve the people with great enthusiasm and devotion, and they must link themselves with the masses, not divorce themselves from the masses."[19] In David Holm's words, writers and artists were instructed to "massify" themselves by gaining "a first-hand knowledge and sympathetic understanding of the local worker, peasant and soldier audiences."[20]

The purpose of getting to know the masses, however, is not just to create works that appeal to them. After being the pupils, writers and artists are supposed to become the teachers of the masses. The notion of "the people" in Maoist discourse is an ambivalent one. According to Maurice Meisner, Mao identifies "the people" primarily with the peasantry and attributes to them an almost inherent revolutionary spirit.[21] In the "Talks," "the people" are the object of lavish praise. Talking about his own transformation as a youth, Mao opposes workers and peasants against intellectuals. Initially, as a student himself, he thought intellectuals were clean, whereas workers and peasants were filthy. After he joined the revolution, his perception was reversed. Unreformed intellectuals became in his eyes the filthy ones. Despite the dirt and feces on their bodies, workers and peasants were in fact clean. Showing how the young Mao progressed from superficial impressions to an understanding of the underlying truth, this narrative fundamentally validates the moral character of "the people." For Mao, not only should their entire way of life and their spontaneous artistic expressions be studied, but their hard work and struggle should also be praised. At one point, Mao asks passionately, "Why should we not eulogize the people, the creators of the history of mankind?"[22] Meanwhile, the masses are not without flaws. Mao calls on writers and artists to learn from the masses, but also to educate them. Chinese scholar Wang Hui believes that a bifurcated view of the peasantry was at the root of the internal paradox of the Chinese revolution. In Maoist discourse, he suggests, the peasantry was the agent of revolution, and yet the "enemies" inside their consciousness—illiteracy, superstition, and ignorance—were also the targets of revolution.[23] In Mao's wartime analogy, "it is often more difficult to combat the enemies inside people's minds than to fight Japanese imperialism."[24]

What adds yet another layer of complexity to the Maoist "people" is that the people are construed as desiring to be educated themselves:

> The problem facing the workers, peasants and soldiers is this: they are now engaged in a bitter and bloody struggle with the enemy but are illiterate and uneducated as a result of long years of rule by the feudal and bourgeois classes, and therefore *they are eagerly demanding enlightenment*, education and works of literature and art which meet *their urgent needs* and which are easy to absorb, in order to heighten their enthusiasm in struggle and confidence in victory, strengthen their unity and fight the enemy with one heart and one mind.[25]

In this revealing passage, Mao describes workers, peasants, and soldiers as political agents actively demanding their own education. Rather than passive objects to be educated and mobilized by the party, they themselves desire to use literature and art to enhance their struggle. As Mao emphasizes, "When we say that literature and art are subordinate to politics, we mean class politics, the politics of the masses, not the politics of a few so-called statesmen."[26] The people's demands and revolutionary politics are mutually legitimating. Although the party occupies the position of leadership, the desires and the legitimacy for revolution are seen as ultimately coming from "the people." Without close connection with "the people," party politics would lose its authority. The demands of "the people" are justified because they are believed to be inherently progressive. Positioned in between the mass audience and its politics, literature and art find a proper place and a sense of purpose as instruments that aid the people in their self-mobilization and self-liberation. The subordination of art to politics is thus integral to the principle that literature and art should serve workers, peasants, and soldiers. In other words, by acting in accordance with the needs and wishes of the masses, cultural workers also serve the demands of revolutionary politics. According to the "Talks," therefore, the tasks of creating popular culture for the masses and enlightening them politically ultimately converge.

Interestingly, although Mao emphasizes educating and elevating the masses, he never uses *xuanchuan*, the Chinese term for propaganda in the "Talks." Strictly speaking, what is implicit in the concept of *xuanchuan* is a top-down relationship between the party and the masses that would be rejected by the Maoist "mass line" politics. *Xuanchuan* literally means "to announce" (*xuan*) and "to transmit, disseminate" (*chuan*). According to Chinese scholar Liu Hailong, *xuanchuan* first appeared as a compound word in the third-century historical text *Weilüe* written by Yu Huan (239–65).[27] Its premodern usage mainly referred to the dissemination of ideas from the ruling class. In its original sense, *xuanchuan* not only did not carry the kind of negative value judgment that has become associated with propaganda in the modern West, it even derived a profound ethical legitimacy from the superior positions from which it emanated.[28] In the early twentieth century, *xuanchuan* acquired a broader usage and could be applied to the dissemination of religion, knowledge, information, and thought for educational, commercial, political, and military purposes.[29] In other words, the modern meaning of *xuanchuan* is much broader than the English word *propaganda*, as it can also refer to advertising, promotion, or publicity depending on the context.

The CCP was particularly influenced by theories and practices of propaganda from the Soviet Union. As Peter Kenez observes, the Bolshevik approach to propaganda was premised on a Leninist view of the working class as incapable of developing class consciousness or understanding their interest on their own. Because of its superior knowledge of the process of history, the party was supposed to lead the Russian people to a successful revolution. Such a condescending attitude on the part of the Bolshevik leadership led to, for example, a distinction between "propaganda" and "agitation": the propagandist explains complex ideas to an elite audience; the agitator mobilizes the masses by arousing their emotions.[30] The two terms, translated into Chinese as *xuanchuan* and *gudong*, were adopted into the CCP vocabulary. In a 1941 guideline for party propaganda work, Zhang Wentian (1899–1976), a Soviet-educated intellectual and the head of the Ministry of Propaganda at the time, emphasizes the importance of both propaganda and agitation. While agitation is supposed to build the foundation for propaganda among the masses, propaganda should consolidate and deepen the achievement of agitation. Zhang instructs party members to make use of all possible tools for propaganda and agitation, including various modern technological media such as radio and film.[31] For Mao, political authority comes ultimately from the people. Although the party, equipped with superior theoretical knowledge, should educate the masses and help them improve; it is supposed to do so in accordance with the masses' demands for self-education. By contrast, to speak of *xuanchuan*, either in its premodern sense or as a concept influenced by Leninist thought, implies an elitist, top-down model of politics, which contradicts the dialogic relationship between the leader and the led pursued by "mass line" politics.

What faced cultural workers of the new regime after 1949, therefore, was not one, but two sets of proposals for the organization of culture in a socialist society, although their different theoretical origins tended to be ignored as new overlaps and fissures were drawn in a period of cultural experimentation. On one hand, both the Maoist and Leninist lines of thought foregrounded education as part of the political process. One common feature that could be found in both Bolshevik and CCP propaganda was the frequent conflation of propaganda with education. Since the Russian people were considered generally backward, in order to build socialism, it was deemed necessary to not only teach them communist ideas, but also promote literacy and scientific knowledge among them. For example, one type of propaganda material that was disseminated by the many agitational trains that went to the countryside during the Russian Civil War (1917–1922) was short didactic films known as *agitki*. These films not only depicted stories that aimed to arouse class consciousness and garner war support among peasants, but also promoted modernization through topics like how to combat diseases with modern medicine.[32] Similarly, in the PRC, it was difficult to distinguish propaganda (*xuanchuan*) from education (*jiaoyu*), which often appeared hand in hand in a compound term "*xuanchuan jiaoyu*." The content of propaganda and education could be major political and economic campaigns. But it could also concern subjects that, upon first look, appeared apolitical and mundane. From 1949 to 1950, for example, there were propaganda campaigns focusing on the theft of electricity, the cause of lunar eclipse, summer epidemic prevention, and the new Marriage Law.[33] The inclusion of everyday issues in party propaganda indicated that to become a citizen of a modern socialist nation, it was not enough to possess the correct political consciousness. One must also be equipped with modern scientific, moral, and legal concepts.

On the other hand, cultural workers positioned themselves in a more subordinate position toward the "worker-peasant-soldier" masses, who were now considered the rightful consumers of culture. In literary and artistic circles, one practice that was institutionalized was "delving into life" (*shenru shenghuo*). Writers, artists, and intellectuals were expected to spend time living in the countryside or in factories so that they could gather source materials, study folk arts and ways of expression, and eventually produce works that the people would love. The influential writer Zhao Shuli (1906–1970), for instance, continued to spend a large portion of his time in rural Shanxi Province even when he held a number of official positions in Beijing.[34] Zhao came to be known for his realistic and nuanced portrayal of peasant characters and for his command of a down-to-earth, dialect-inflected language. For film projectionists, the demand of "serving workers, peasants, and soldiers" was equally imperative. One of their most important tasks as people's servants was to make cinema available for the people, especially rural and remote populations that had no previous access to cinema. In order to achieve this goal, projectionists were expected to overcome a series of obstacles posed by the lack of infrastructure and material shortage.

However, education and entertainment were difficult goals to reconcile. In the mid-1950s, for instance, didactic films that portrayed workers, peasants, and soldiers were received poorly by audiences. One theater manager complained that moviegoers would turn away from the movie theater as soon as they saw a poster with a lathe or a factory. One worker-subject film, *The Great Beginning* (*Weida de qidian*, 1954), sold only forty-nine tickets at his theater on International Workers' Day.[35] The fact that many domestic films underperformed at the box office prompted the editors at Shanghai-based newspaper *Wenhui Daily* (*Wenhui bao*) to organize a debate near the end of 1956 about why domestic films had failed to attract audiences. The conflicting demands of "Talks" can best be illustrated by "The Gongs and Drums of Film" (*Dianying de luogu*), one of the most famous articles emerging out of this debate, and the subsequent backlash against it. Written by film critic Zhong Dianfei (1919–1987), this article questions whether the principle of "serving workers, peasants, soldiers" is truly at work when films are rejected by the very audience they are supposed to be serving. Zhong is especially critical of the practice of categorizing films into rigid genres such as "industrial films," "agricultural films," and "military films."[36] He explains elsewhere that such categories not only sow divisions among the masses, but also deprive the audience's cultural life of diversity. In his view, it would not be appealing to workers and peasants if they have to revisit the factory after a day's work or relive their day in the field on a film screen.[37] However, despite his own emphasis on Mao's "Talks" as a source of authority, Zhong was soon criticized for giving too much weight to film's entertainment value at the expense of political standards

and for "garbling the words of Lenin and Mao."[38] Did Zhong misinter-
pret Mao's words? The "Talks" indeed gives support to Zhong's prioritizing of audience preferences, but the challenge facing him and other
cultural workers was that unlike Mao's original conception, in reality,
mass tastes did not always converge with political demands.

This tension contributed to much of the policy vacillations in the
early socialist period. After the Anti-rightist Campaign (1957–1959)
silenced critics like Zhong Dianfei, the 1961 campaign to promote "four
goods" (sihao) in domestic films—good story, good acting, good cinematography, and good music—reenvisioned filmmaking from the point of
view of the audience. As famous director Cai Chusheng (1906–1968)
explained, unlike party officials and film professionals, audiences experienced films intuitively. The "four goods" reflected how audiences watched
and thought about films.[39] To demand that filmmakers achieve the "four
goods" thus reaffirmed the official recognition of the critical power of
the audience. On the eve of the Cultural Revolution, however, almost all
literature and arts of the Seventeen Years period were branded as under
the influence of an "anti-party, anti-socialist black line" which stood in
opposition to Mao Zedong Thought. To truly "serve workers, peasants,
and soldiers," according to Mao's wife Jiang Qing (1914–1991), the only
correct way was to create and praise heroic worker-peasant-soldier characters.[40] Jiang's instructions soon led to the production of model operas
during the Cultural Revolution. Speaking of the exhibition of model
opera films in a newsletter in 1972, one exhibition worker from Jiangxi
Province states that "to serve workers, peasants, and soldiers, the goals
of exhibition work is exactly to let the great worker-peasant-soldier
masses watch and understand revolutionary films so that they can be
educated."[41] By this point, "serving workers, peasants, and soldiers" was
completely aligned with political education. In short, "serving workers,
peasants, soldiers" should not be seen as an empty slogan merely paying
lip service to the needs of the masses. While it was a powerful rhetoric
that legitimated the party's rule, it also had tangible effect in producing
a new socialist mass culture, which, ideally, was supposed to at once
entertain and educate the masses.

FROM ROXY TO NEW CHINA: SOCIALIST REFORMS
OF MOVIE THEATERS

If "serving workers, peasants, and soldiers" made demands on literary and artistic creators in terms of the content and aesthetics of their

works, in film exhibition, it manifested first and foremost as spatial practice. In Henri Lefebvre's theory of the social production of space, spatial practice refers to the organization of physical space within a given social formation that follows logics that are cohesive but not necessarily coherent.[42] In this sense, film exhibition can be seen as part of a broader movement to reorganize space according to socialist principles, which also included land reform in rural areas and the restructuring of urban governance around work units and neighborhood committees (*jiedao*). Within film exhibition, "serving workers, peasants, and soldiers" led to changes in the locations of film screenings. While the urban movie theater soon ceased to be the primary venue of moviegoing, two other kinds of exhibition outlets rose in number and prominence: so-called film clubs (*dianying julebu*)—fixed nontheatrical exhibition venues that included workers' cultural palaces (*gongren wenhuagong*), workers' clubs (*gongren julebu*), and assembly halls within work units; and mobile film projection teams (*liudong dianying fangyingdui*), which offered traveling film shows mainly in rural and suburban areas. The spreading of these exhibition outlets into universities, factories, government institutions, mines, and the countryside was responsible for the rapid growth of film attendance. National film admissions tripled from 1949 to 1950. Except for a few years during the Cultural Revolution when exhibition statistics were unavailable, the size of film audiences in China continued to be on the rise until it entered a period of decline in the mid-1980s, reaching a historic high in 1979 with 29.31 billion admissions per year (figure 1). Beyond the formulation of new screening spaces, film exhibition also involved everyday spatial practices in the usage of another French theorist, Michel de Certeau. For de Certeau, it is important to emphasize the potential for improvisation, tactics, and individual agency against institutional planning and rules.[43] Socialist film exhibition, too, was sustained by the daily efforts of grassroots agents to inscribe and control the exhibition space through concrete actions and objects. The three types of exhibition spaces can thus be examined from two levels: how the location itself symbolized the state's dedication to "serving workers, peasants, and soldiers"; and to what extent exhibition workers could further transform a space to enhance its messaging.

According to different sources, there were between 596 and 678 movie theaters in China at the birth of the PRC, more than half of which were concentrated in large cities such as Shanghai, Tianjin, Beijing, Guangzhou, Wuhan, Shenyang, Chongqing, and Kunming.[44] While

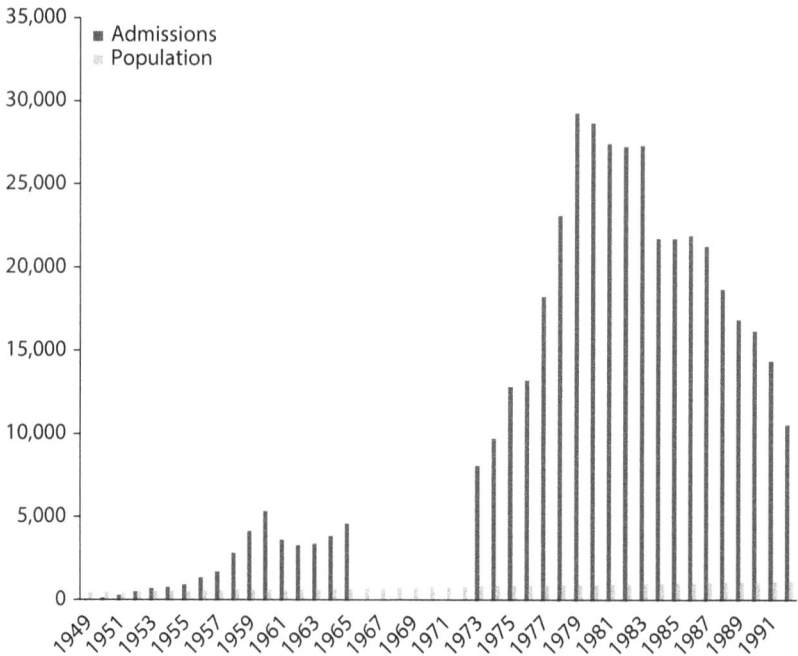

FIGURE 1. National film admissions 1949–1992 (in millions). Source: Chen Bo, *Zhongguo dianying biannian jishi: faxing fangying juan* [Chronicles of Chinese cinema: Volume on distribution and exhibition]. Beijing: Zhongyang wenxian chuban she, 2005.

the new regime relied on these theaters as ready infrastructure for film exhibition, it also asserted the need to de-associate moviegoing from its former connections to luxury and foreign domination. In the early 1950s, a series of reforms was carried out with the goal of redefining the movie theater as a space for the people.

The reduction of entry fees was at the forefront of the reforms. Chinese movie theaters had followed Hollywood's tier model for film distribution, which sequenced the showing of a film from the most lavish and expensive theaters to smaller, cheaper ones through multiple runs. This strategy, as William Paul points out, was based on principles of exclusivity that assigned a special stature to first-run theaters, where patrons paid more to gain the privilege of seeing a film first.[45] In 1950, the most expensive tickets at first-run theaters in Shanghai cost up to 9,000 yuan (equivalent to 0.9 yuan in the new currency series adopted in 1955) whereas entry fees at a fourth-run theater cost 2,000–4,000 yuan.[46] In addition to the discrepancy, audience members complained in letters to *Mass Cinema* that the overall price range was too high.[47] In order to increase mass access, Shanghai cultural administrators enforced three consecutive price reductions between November 1950 and 1952. After the price reduction in April 1952, a film only needed to go through two runs, with a price range from 1,000 to 3,000 yuan.[48] In 1954, China Film Corporation issued an announcement stipulating that all movie theaters across the nation should charge between 500 and a maximum of 4,500 yuan.[49] By 1959, watching a feature film cost 0.3–0.5 yuan at the Grand Theater, the most expensive first-run film theater in Shanghai, while the same film could be seen for only 0.1–0.3 yuan at many other places or at early morning shows.[50] In the same year, the average monthly wage for workers in Shanghai was 63.4 yuan. In comparison, entrance to Grand Theater in the early 1930s cost at least 0.6 yuan, when factory workers only made about 14–15 yuan a month.[51]

In order to create a space where the worker-peasant-soldier masses could feel at home, efforts were also made to sinicize the theater space. Naming might be a small issue, but it was highly symbolic. In Shanghai, the theaters whose original names were Paris, Queen, Hollywood, and Empire were respectively renamed as Huaihai, Heping ("peace"), Shengli ("victory"), and Songshan (Mount Song) after they were taken over by the government.[52] Roxy Theater, which was mentioned earlier, was given the new name of Xinhua, meaning "new China." In Republican Shanghai, where the West held tremendous power in the cultural imaginary, exotic names and a theater front splashed with English words signaled to patrons the prestige to which the movie theaters aspired. To the new regime, however, such foreign influences were a reminder of the humiliation that the "old China" suffered under Western imperial powers. A new era required new signage. The new names chosen for movie theaters conjured up the greatness of the Chinese nation, particularly a history of revolution and resilience. "Peace" and "Victory" commemorated both the War of Resistance against Japan and the Civil War between the CCP and the Guomindang. The name Huaihai referred to a key battle fought between the CCP and the Guomindang in the vicinity of the cities of Huaiyin and Haizhou in 1948–1949. Mount Song is the central mountain in the Five Great Mountains of China. Xinhua proudly announces the birth of a new nation. Collectively, these new names reinscribed the geography of moviegoing in Shanghai with patriotic sentiment. The change of signage did not stop at the exterior of movie theaters; foreign languages that were visible inside movie theaters were also removed. As mentioned above, Xinhua Theater, formerly the Roxy, used to have only English signage. According to journalist Yao Fangzao, when staff members first tried to make a Chinese sign for restrooms, they wrote the word wrong (rendering *guanxishi* as *xiguanshi*). When they realized their mistake, they felt ashamed and became more determined to eliminate any traces of American imperialism from the theater.[53]

At a movie theater, the area between the front entrance and the auditorium may be seen as a transitional space. Since visitors cannot avoid spending time in this space, either waiting for the auditorium to open, buying snacks, or using restrooms, this space not only sets expectations for visitors' subsequent engagement with films, but may also offer stand-alone pleasures that have little to do with cinema. The American drive-in theater, for example, used to include an array of amenities from playgrounds to dance floors that turned the establishment into an entertainment center, in which watching movies constituted only one activity among others.[54] Contemporary Indian multiplexes, similar to their counterparts in the West, featured spacious lobbies, vibrant interiors, and a wide range of food and beverage options to produce a cosmopolitan, middle-class space of safety, comfort, and entertainment distinct from the outside world.[55] A movie theater's additional offerings are not part of an experience of the film image, but they contribute to an overall package, drawing connections between moviegoing and other kinds of sensory and cognitive experiences.

In post-49 Chinese press, this transitional space easily evinced the double meaning of "serving workers, peasants, and soldiers." On one hand, new amenities and services were praised as indications that the movie theaters no longer catered to upper-class ladies and gentlemen but served the practical needs of the working-class masses. From northern China to the south, theaters reportedly created reading areas, offered free books, magazines, water, and tea, and established service stations that provided free bag check and medicine.[56] One reader of *Mass Cinema* found it worthwhile to praise a server at the International Theater (*guoji daxiyuan*) in Shanghai for being particularly nice to visitors.[57] Movie theaters also catered to specific groups of film audiences. In 1954, *Guangming Daily* reported the opening of the first children's movie theater in China, located in the city of Changchun, which tailored their amenities to the needs of young patrons. According to the report, the waiting room of the theater was equipped with soft chairs designed for children. There were fresh flowers on every table and various toys to keep the kids comfortable. In addition, the theater also had a reading room and a service desk, which would allow children to read books and buy candy when they took breaks from watching movies.[58]

On the other hand, theater managers did not forget about their mission to propagate political messages and educate audiences. It became imperative for theaters to decorate lobbies and hallways with propaganda posters, slogans, and educational drawings. During campaigns such as the Resist America and Aid Korea movement (*kangmei yuanchao*) and the Campaign to Suppress Counterrevolutionaries (*zhenya fangeming*), theaters in Beijing and Tianjin reportedly displayed slogans and propaganda materials everywhere. Loudspeakers were also installed to broadcast news and party policies.[59] In this way, the theater space was not only visually redefined but gained distinct aural and temporal dimensions that made sure a viewer's entire visit to the theater could be politicized from the moment they arrived at the front entrance. Combining such strategies with the screening of "propaganda" films, the socialist movie theater was transformed into a propaganda space. Meanwhile, the emphasis on propaganda should also be viewed in the context of mass access and mass entertainment. For the socialist reformers, it was not a question of whether movie theaters propagated ideas to audiences, but whose ideas and which audience. As Yao Fangzao concludes at the end of her observation of the new Xinhua Theater: "from Roxy to Xinhua, what was changed was not just the name, but the theater itself from a strong hold for disseminating the poisonous thought of American imperialism to a lecture hall for educating the people."[60]

WORKERS' CULTURAL PALACES AND WORKERS' CLUBS

Workers, especially industrial workers, enjoyed a special status as vanguards of revolution in the communist epistemology. What was referred to as "film clubs" in official film exhibition statistics—some open to public and some internal—offered both a way to meet the cultural needs of this specific group and a category through which their film consumption could be made statistically visible, distinguished from the rest of the worker-peasant-soldier masses. The most common types of film clubs were workers' cultural palaces and workers' clubs. Both were designed to be all-in-one destinations for workers' spare-time needs and to provide a wide range of cultural and recreational activities, differing only in scale. While a workers' cultural palace was usually a large establishment managed by municipal workers' unions, a workers' club served workers in an urban district or a specific work unit. In January 1950, only months after the founding of the PRC, the All-China Federation of Trade Unions (*zhonghua quanguo zong gonghui*) instructed that every city with more than fifty thousand workers must build city-level workers' clubs and that every factory that had more than two thousand employees should also have their own internal clubs.[61] In Beijing, the Working People's Cultural Palace (*laodong renmin wenhuagong*) was converted from the Imperial Ancestral Temple a few months later. The various halls of the temple were turned into a library, an auditorium, and rooms for reading newspapers, entertainment, music, dance, and drama.[62] Cultural palaces and workers' clubs with similar facilities soon appeared in all parts of China. By September 1954, there were more than 840 workers' clubs in Shanghai.[63] In January 1955, *Guangming Daily* reported that a total of 12,376 workers' clubs could be found across the country, which was fourteen times more than the number of workers' clubs in 1950. These clubs, the report writes, have organized studies of politics, current affairs, and science and technology, as well as diverse cultural, recreational, and sports activities. They have become favorite places for workers to spend their spare time.[64]

For Chang-tai Hung, the emphasis on workers' clubs being places that belonged to the people was more of a rhetorical nature than a description of reality. The Working People's Cultural Palace in Beijing, he suggests, was hailed by the official press as "a paradise of the working people in the capital" from the beginning. Officials of the Beijing Federation of Trade Unions also described the place as gearing "to the needs of grassroots units and the masses." However, Hung argues that the Working People's Cultural Palace was never simply a recreational area but a political park for the party to conduct state activities for the advancement of socialist policies. It was used for holding various exhibitions such as exhibitions about model workers, political campaigns, and industrial construction in other socialist nations, as well as for state funerals and diplomatic activities. In Hung's view, this meant that the government's original promise that the Cultural Palace would be a place where common people could come for amusement was often unfulfilled, and that people's private recreational needs were ignored.[65]

However, political education did not need to be incompatible with recreation. What characterized the goals of cultural production and consumption in socialist China was precisely the integration of these two functions. A set of regulations issued by the Beijing Federation of Trade Unions in 1958 explicitly stated that the missions of district-level workers clubs were to "educate workers and their families about Communism and organize their cultural life and spare time."[66] The press also did not only present one side of the story as Hung implies. A 1951 *Guangming Daily* article, for example, suggests blatantly that workers' clubs constituted the best venues for conducting propaganda and mobilizing workers. And yet at the same time, it tells readers that according to the requirements of the All-China Federation of Trade Unions, a factory-level workers' club should have facilities for entertainment and exercise.[67]

More specifically, relocating film exhibition into mixed-function clubs was an effective strategy to reframe moviegoing in terms of "serving workers, peasants, and soldiers." If the movie theater had a commercial, "imperialist" legacy that needed to be purged, the workers' cultural palaces and clubs, by default, constructed a new type of space where education and recreation could blend in. Consider this description of the Shanghai Workers' Cultural Palace found in the Shanghai-based English-language journal *China Monthly Review*: "A worker can enjoy himself here at little or no cost. For instance, he or she can join group dancing and singing in the music hall which seats 500 people. *Organized study* and discussions of literature, arts, drawing and *current events* are held regularly. Free movies are shown daily in the 400-seat theater; on occasion popular operas are staged in the evenings either by local professional troupes or workers' own groups."[68] What is remarkable in this passage is how the author is able to smoothly reference politically charged events, such as organized study and discussion of current events, in the same breath as leisure activities such as dancing and singing without hinting at any possible contradictions between them. In the socialist framework, one should not separate propaganda-education from entertainment, the divergence of which was rather a sign of failure. A club that had mixed functions thus situated cinema at the precise location of where it needed to be that is, at the intersection of politics and leisure.

Moreover, a direct result of film exhibition moving into workers' clubs in work units was easy access. Going to the cinema often literally implies "going out"—leaving the routinized space of one's everyday life to enter a ritualistic space of public gathering. The allure of luxury movie theaters in the Republican era in part depended on this separation. But the work unit introduced a new spatial logic. By 1957, an estimate of 90 percent of the Chinese urban population were within the work unit system.[69] Under this system, social services and grassroots political activities were all organized around the workplace. A factory, for example, was a unit of production subject to the central economic planning of the state. Meanwhile, with party organs embedded in it, the factory effectively functioned as "a branch of government," overseeing the local enforcement of policies and organization of campaigns.[70] A work unit was also a social welfare institution that provided its employees with services (housing, day care, school, medical care, dining, recreation, etc.) and permissions for civil activities including marriage and travel. Spatially, this meant that workplace, residence, and social facilities typically existed in close proximity to one another within walled and gated compounds, which also included workers' clubs or assembly halls where movies were shown.[71] For workers, employees, their families, and sometimes residents in the nearby areas, moviegoing could be a very convenient activity to participate in on a daily basis. A worker could easily return home for dinner after work and then head to the workers' club for film screenings, crossing between different quarters within a work unit in a matter of minutes. The convenience was further enhanced by the arrangement of show times around work schedules. According to a retired projectionist from a steel factory in Suzhou, since workers rotated on three eight-hour shifts, she showed films at the end of each shift, including at midnight, so that every worker had the opportunity to watch films.[72] In addition to workers' clubs, open-air screenings provided another common way whereby moviegoing entered the everyday space within a work unit. One viewer recalls that there used to be three locations for open-air screenings in his work unit in the Western suburb of Beijing: one was a basketball field; the other two were open areas next to a cafeteria and a bath house.[73] Cinema thus extended further into nonspecialized spaces, routinized as one element that made up the fabric of everyday life.

MOBILE FILM PROJECTION TEAMS

In tandem with descriptions of pre-49 Chinese film culture as commercial and imperialistic, official discourse also portrayed the vast countryside of China, especially areas distant from coastal economic centers, as virgin land untouched by cinematic technologies. A short article published in the trade journal *Film Projection Resources* (*Dianying fangying ziliao*) in 1956 illustrates this narrative. The author Jin Lisheng, a film projectionist from rural Inner Mongolia, talks about how things have changed: before "liberation," peasants in Inner Mongolia had barely enough to eat. They could not afford to watch films. Many had not even heard of the word *dianying* (film/cinema). As living conditions improved, their demands for a better cultural life became more urgent. Jin feels happy and proud to be able to serve them as a mobile film projectionist. He wants to keep increasing the numbers of screenings and viewers in his area. After summarizing the achievements of his projection team in 1954 and 1955, he pledges to accomplish as many as twenty-eight screenings per month (at least three at each screening location) in 1956.[74]

With numbers, Jin offers a linear narrative of progress in which the past was a blank slate and the future promises continuing, quantifiable growth. The institution that could enable such growth was the mobile film projection team. In December 1949, the Central Film Bureau set the goal to increase the number of film projection teams to seven hundred the next year to serve the military, factories, rural areas, and various governmental bodies.[75] In August 1950, the Bureau organized a three-month program in Nanjing that trained over eighteen hundred projectionists from around the nation, who later played instrumental roles in developing exhibition networks in their home regions. Among all film projection teams, the majority were managed by cultural bureaus at various administrative levels. These teams concentrated their work primarily in the countryside and have so far received the most scholarly attention.[76] From the 1950s to the '70s, there was a tendency to increasingly localize the administration of rural projection teams, which moved from provincial level to county and then to the commune (*gongshe*) and even the production brigade (*shengchan dadui*).[77] Projection teams were also organized by workers' unions (the second largest commissioner of projection teams), the People's Liberation Army (PLA), and various institutions like the Sino-Soviet Friendship Society. According to one official report, from 1950 to 1960, the number of film projection teams nationwide (including both 35 mm and 16 mm teams) increased from 522 to 11,151, while national film attendance grew from 150 million in 1951 to 537 million in 1960 (see table 1).[78] The increasing availability of film in the countryside was a major factor contributing to the growth of film attendance in general. Whereas most film audiences were found in cities upon the founding of the PRC, by 1960 rural audiences made up 60.5% of all audiences.[79]

Mobile film projection teams, especially those serving rural areas, received prominent attention in the Chinese press. Tina Mai Chen suggests that rural film projectionists were attributed an important role to play in the creation of a unified nation. As she observes, media coverage of film projection teams described their work in both geographical and temporal terms. The delivery of film to remote rural areas or

TABLE 1   EXHIBITION OUTLETS IN THE PRC (SELECT YEARS)

	Movie Theaters	Film Clubs and Others	Film Projection Teams
1950	674	67	522
1955	594	1,577	3,698
1960	1,767	3,931	11,151
1965	2,528	3,828	13,997
1970	Unavailable		
1977	2,683	22,585	77,945
1980	2,729	103,072	19,639
1985	9,663	148,690	25,081

SOURCE: Chen Bo, *Zhongguo dianying biannian jishi.*

ethnic minorities was particularly celebrated. As marginalized social groups were targeted as film audiences, they were seen as being included into the national community as part of "the people." Film also came to signify modernization. The arrival of film projection teams at a village, sometimes juxtaposed with the availability of tractors and other machinery, often suggested the dawning of a new era where agents of the party brought modern technologies and progress to the hinterland.[80]

While Chen emphasizes the link between the showing of film and nation building, the ideological significance of film projection teams should also be seen in the ways they embodied the ideal of "serving workers, peasants, and soldiers." Similar to reformed movie theaters and workers' film clubs, mobile film exhibition generated new spatial interfaces. Like theater workers, rural projectionists would use wall posters, photos, or comic drawings to turn everyday space into space for propaganda. Projectionists often tried to respond quickly to the so-called "central tasks" (*zhongxin gongzuo*)—important issues that commanded the most resources and attention of party cadres at a given time. The timely responses to current events of an all-female projection team from Shuangcheng County, Heilongjian Province was especially praised in an issue of *Film Projection* in 1959. It was reported that the team stayed in close contact with local party authorities to receive the latest instructions and propaganda materials. "When the General Line of Socialist Construction was announced, they exhibited images related to the General Line of Socialist Construction. When American and British imperialists invaded Lebanon and Jordan, they exhibited images showing how Chinese people supported the just struggle of the people in Lebanon and Jordan." Altogether they organized eighty-eight image exhibitions for more than thirty thousand viewers.[81]

But because screenings organized by mobile film projection teams frequently took place in the open air, projectionists were unable to control the semiotics of the environment to the same degree as one could in an enclosed architectural space. In this situation, what was more important became the location of screening itself. Browsing through newspapers and magazines from the socialist era, one can easily encounter titles such as "Raising the Screen on Big Ba Mountain," "Bringing Movies to Wuzhi Mountain," and "Our Only Purpose Is to Deliver Movies to the Island."[82] Even for readers who were not familiar with the geography of these specific locales, the words "mountain" and "island" evoked remote spaces that testified to the far extent of the benefits of the new nation. A similar logic can also be found in visual representations. A photo on the cover of the second issue of *Film Projection* from 1957 is especially telling (figure 2). In this black-and-white photo, what occupies the center space is a large rectangular screen hanging over grassland. On top of the screen, against its dark edge, there is a single bright star, signifying the presence of the party. Behind the screen lies a high austere mountain ridge that spans the entire background of the photo. On both sides of the screen there are people looking and pointing at the screen with smiles on their faces. Some of them wear headscarves and are dressed in a style of clothing that distinguish them as non-Han ethnic minorities. Even without caption, the meaning of this photo is rendered apparent by its easily legible parts. If, as the official narrative goes, moviegoing used to be a privilege accessible only for a small population of urban bourgeoisie, the composition of the photo highlights the relocation of cinema to the frontier. In this unprecedented screening space, there is no need to reinscribe the environment to convey any messages. The natural landscape itself speaks volumes about the extent to which the regime sought to bring culture to its people, including ethnic minorities and those in remote rural areas.

Film exhibition, therefore, was as much a matter of ideology as a problem of spatial practice. As a principle of cultural production, "serving workers, peasants, and soldiers" complicated the widespread belief that Chinese socialist cinema was a propaganda tool, which at best tells half of the story. From movie theaters to film clubs and mobile film exhibition teams, these exhibition outlets, while striving to create propaganda spaces, were also public interfaces that mediated socialist ideals

電　影　放　映

第　二　期

一 九 五 七 年 二 月 十 日 出版

FIGURE 2. Film screen in the mountains. Magazine cover, photograph, *Dianying fang-ying* [Film Projection] 2 (1957).

of mass access and mass culture that were supposed to be balanced between education and recreation, politics, and entertainment.

CODA: THE RETURN OF THE MARKET

The tensions within these complicated demands, however, partly led to the collapse of "serving workers, peasants, and soldiers" as a cultural ideal after the Cultural Revolution. To end this chapter, I will briefly discuss how changing ideological emphases in the early reform era of the 1980s led to the reconfiguration of exhibition spaces, proving again that space is an important interface of film exhibition that requires ongoing production.

One dramatic change in the journal *Film Popularization* (*Dianying puji*), the reincarnated version of *Film Projection*, in the 1980s was the lack of reference to "serving workers, peasants, and soldiers." Instead, the Maoist slogan was updated and echoed in two new discourses. One was the discourse of the primary stage of socialism. According to the Sixth Plenary Session of the Eleventh Central Committee of the CCP that took place in June 1981, China was currently in the primary stage of socialism, during which the main contradiction of society was between the growing material and cultural needs of the people and the backwardness of production.[83] The second was the discourse of socialist spiritual civilization. In a speech made on December 25, 1980, Deng Xiaoping emphasized that in order to build socialism, it is important to obtain both high degrees of material civilization and spiritual civilization; the latter includes not only education, science, and culture but also ideology, ethics, and interpersonal relationships.[84] Both discourses were frequently evoked in *Film Popularization* as contributors affirmed the need to develop film exhibition networks to satisfy the growing cultural needs of the people and the ability of cinema to participate in the building of socialist spiritual civilization.

At the same time, the market became more and more accepted as an organizing principle for film exhibition. A 1981 article from *Film Popularization* states that "the fundamental goal of developing the exhibition network is to satisfy the growing cultural needs of the people to the greatest degree while increasing revenue and accumulating capital for the country."[85] In 1987, an editorial by an author named You Ming explicitly addresses whether it is appropriate to refer to rural film exhibition as a market: "Some people worry that by using the notion of market, one commodifies cinema which is supposed to be a tool of spreading spiritual civilization; some people say that film screenings in the countryside in the 1950s were not free, and therefore there has long been a market. Cinema is consumed through the circulation of commodities. The fact that it has the nature of a commodity is clear. Therefore, it is the commodity form that determines marketization, not the market that makes cinema a commodity."[86] What You Ming alludes to is that even under the mandate of "serving workers, peasants, and soldiers," film exhibition did not stop being an economic activity. Indeed, in the early 1950s, the state exerted pressure on the film exhibition industry to fulfil screening quotas and generate revenue. According to a work report of the Shanghai Municipal Cultural Bureau, after a decision that film projection teams should be managed as enterprises (*qiye*) was made at the National Film Administration Conference in October 1952, the Shanghai Cultural Bureau began trying out a new system of managing projection teams in March 1953. In addition to listing concrete measures taken by projection teams to cut cost and increase revenue, the report emphasizes the need to continuously reform one's thinking. On one hand, one must not think projection teams could rely on government subsidies. On the other hand, the report warns against the danger of falling into a "pure economic standpoint" at the expense of propaganda and education.[87] Despite the warning, theater managers in Shanghai were repeatedly admonished by cultural administrators for pandering to audiences to increase revenue while ignoring proper propaganda work. In 1954, several Shanghai film theaters were criticized for their promotional strategies for the film *Taking Mount Hua by Strategy* (*Zhiqu huashan*, 1953), which supposedly put too much emphasis on cinematic spectacles without mentioning the ingenuity and courage of the PLA soldiers.[88] Five years later, a Director Li from the Shanghai Municipal Cultural Bureau launched a new round of criticism against theaters for using sensational and popular films, such as the British film *The Thief of Baghdad* (1940) and the Hong Kong film *A Widow's Tears* (*Xingua*, 1956), to attract audiences at the expense of political education. In his words, some theaters had fallen into a "capitalist mode of business," conducting propaganda as advertising: "in their promotional materials there was no correct consciousness. They'd rather attract audiences by using words such as 'thrilling' and 'shocking.'"[89] Such incidents support You Ming's claim that market considerations were never eliminated during the early socialist period. The affirmation of the commodity nature of cinema then laid conceptual groundwork for a full-on marketization that would be realized in the 1990s.

All these changes led to new developments in the spatial practice of film exhibition. If the demand of "serving workers, peasants, and soldiers" initially opened up new screening spaces in rural China, mobile projection was increasingly seen as inadequate in the 1980s. To improve viewing conditions for rural viewers, rural exhibition infrastructure was seen as needing upgrades in three respects: to allow viewers to attend screenings indoors, to allow them to watch films while seated, and to transition from 16 mm or 8.75 mm film projection to bigger formats. While mobile teams continued to be run by counties, communes, and brigades, as well as individual contractors, the distinct innovation of this period was the rural "township cinema" (*jizhen yingyuan*). Since 1981 when this model was first promoted nationally, more than 10,000 township cinemas were recorded in 1984, and 13,200 in 1992.[90] Although township cinemas were often cheaply built with very basic equipment and amenities, they were lauded for providing rural viewers with better conditions and more choices in screening times and programs. In urban areas, efforts to renovate existing movie theaters became more widespread in the second half of the 1980s. In 1987, there were more than 400 movie theaters nationwide that underwent renovation, the most since 1949. In addition to upgrading seats and installing air conditioning to make viewing more comfortable, a prominent trend was to diversify the offerings of movie theaters. A multifunctional movie theater would not only show films but operate a variety of businesses such as cafés, dance halls, and video halls. For an exhibition worker from Shen Yang, this new model had two advantages: by creating the opportunity for a range of cultural activities, it could better satisfy the cultural needs of the people and potentially increase the revenue of the theater.[91]

If vocabulary such as *revenue, market,* and *economic benefits* became more and more visible among exhibition practitioners, it was partly because the 1980s witnessed a steady decline of film attendance due to the competition of television and VHS tapes. The need to win over audiences thus acquired extra urgency, which drew attention to the issue of *xuanchuan*. In a dramatic shift from the pre-reform era, mentions of *xuanchuan* in *Film Popularization* rarely referred to political propaganda but to the promotion of films to attract audiences. Exhibition workers used *Film Popularization* as a public forum to share tips on best strategies to bring audiences into movie theaters, one of which was the use of outdoor display boards or windows to promote films. Such displays often involved elaborate designs with both images and texts, visible to anyone who passed by. With promotional materials rather than propaganda posters as what first greeted visitors, a movie theater could be redefined as a welcoming space that promised narrative fulfillment and entertainment.

There is no denying that the early reform era from late 1970s to the early 1990s saw innovations in the organization of film exhibition spaces, which registered evolving conceptions of socialism. But similar to other areas of cultural production, film distribution and exhibition of this period continued to rely on existing socialist administrative structures, which shielded exhibitors from the full force of the market. While the intricacies of everyday cultural consumption in the 1980s remain to be fully explored, what is significant in the context of moviegoing memories is how nostalgic discourses often flatten the past. Township cinemas, which captured much attention in the film industry throughout the '80s, almost entirely disappeared from publicly shared memories, which instead lavish tender feelings upon open-air cinema. Similarly, although the older framework of "serving workers, peasants, and soldiers" was paramount for cultural workers in the early part of the socialist period, it is rarely mentioned in audiences' memories of moviegoing, which are marked more by lived experiences of material shortage, community, and the *dispositif* of cinema—that is, where and how films were shown, than by political rhetoric and campaigns. In other words, a history of socialist film exhibition and the memories of socialist moviegoing do not converge. The 1980s is a testament to their divergence.

CHAPTER 2

Labor

There is a small black-and-white drawing in the CCP official newspaper *People's Daily* on June 13, 1960. Appearing in the upper right corner of page 8, it shows a somewhat familiar scene of moviegoing: in a darkened space, rows of motionless spectators face the screen, seemingly absorbed by the narrative unfolding there. But it would not be hard to notice a few "anomalies": the projector, instead of being kept out of the audience's sight in the back, is visible in the middle of the audience, shooting a bright ray of light at the rectangular screen on the left. And instead of a room, we see contours of brick houses, slanted roofs, trees, mountains, and open sky, which indicate that this is a scene of open-air cinema somewhere in rural China. "Raising the Screen on Big Ba Mountain," the news article accompanied by the drawing tells yet another story: The Number Three Film Projection Team of Pingli County, Shaanxi Province, has to make a challenging journey to bring cinema to remote mountain villages that can only be accessed on foot. Fired up by the determination to reach their destinations, the projectionists endure cold weather, rain, fatigue, and hunger. They walk across freezing rivers carrying heavy equipment as their lips turn blue. According to the article, the worst part of the trip to one village deep in the mountains is an area locals name "leech slope." Blood-sucking leeches had stopped several previous attempts of the projection team to go to the village. It was not until the Great Leap Forward (1958–1961) that the projectionists were encouraged to try again and succeeded.[1]

In a word, the drawing does not *illustrate* the writing, but extends it, infusing the dream of a classical cinema of narrative absorption into a new *dispositif*.[2] If the editors who decided to pair up this image with the news story thought this was a good choice because it conjured up some general sense of "cinema," the discrepancy was precisely the point, as it challenged readers to think about how we could reconcile the words and the image. How do we situate a narrative about the rural projectionist's travel in discourses of cinema?

The more familiar status of the projectionist in film history is someone hidden in the projection booth that does not draw attention to themselves. By contrast, film projectionists in socialist China, especially during the early Seventeen Years period, were prominent public figures. Some became nationally renowned role models. The Three Sisters Projection Team from Laishui County, Hebei Province, likely the most well-known projection team in the country, was the subject of a newsreel film in 1963 and became the focus of a small museum that opened in Laishui in 2016.[3] Stories similar to the one I just described also proliferated in the press in the form of articles, poems, drawings, and photographs. Celebrating rural film projectionists on the road, they insisted on a gaze at the inner working of the socialist cinematic apparatus. Readers of the newspaper and potential film spectators were instructed to "look at" the projectionist's body at work and appreciate the physical labor that went into the delivery of cinema (see figure 3).

The cultivation of this gaze is the focus of this chapter. As a unique mini-genre with its own narrative conventions, tales of the projectionist on the road reveal how the projectionist's laboring body functioned as an interface in the socialist cinematic apparatus. As the PRC state tried to expand rural film exhibition in a widespread state of underdevelopment, the projectionist was called on to be the logistical solution to problems of transportation and infrastructure deficiency. As couriers, projectionists delivered cinema into villages and remote areas. Their labor functioned as an interface, an indispensable link in the cinematic apparatus, that connected films to their intended audiences. Meanwhile, the projectionist was not only a precondition of spectatorship; his or her laboring body was constituted as an object for the spectator's gaze. Extending the discussion from exhibition space to the agents of exhibition, this chapter reiterates that it was not solely in the filmic text that the PRC state saw the space for propaganda and moral instruction. To the extent that the visible body of the projectionist personified an assemblage of socialist ideals, particularly the validation of manual

FIGURE 3. The Three Sisters Projection Team on the road. He Shiyao, "Ba dianying songshang shanqu" [Take cinema into the mountains], photograph, *Renmin huabao* [China pictorial] 11 (1965): 19.

labor, it became an interface of ideology constantly foregrounded for attention and celebration.

CINEMA WITHOUT INFRASTRUCTURE

As discussed in chapter 1, under the guidance of "serving workers, peasants, and soldiers," rural film exhibition soon became a widespread reality after 1949. While the press celebrated the expansion of cinematic technology as part of the nation's modernization, what complicated this process was the manner in which cinema traveled. In China, the railroad never became associated with the dissemination of cinema as it did in the Soviet Union, where agit-trains were dispatched to spread propaganda messages during the Russian Civil War (1917–1923).[4] Instead, projection teams, typically made up of two to five people, traveled by tractors, tricycles, hand-drawn carts, and horse-drawn carts. In mountainous areas, they might be forced to travel on foot and use mules or carrying poles for transporting projection equipment that included at least a projector, a power generator, a slide projector, an amplifier, and film reels. Such manual means of transportation were necessitated by the slow progress of infrastructural building that left large territories inaccessible by trains or automobiles. To quickly build what Brian DeMare calls a "cultural infrastructure" against this backdrop of underdevelopment, the state could only rely on its millions of cultural workers and their human agency, without much infrastructural support.[5]

The tension between cultural and infrastructural development was already a prominent theme in Republican-era experiments with rural film exhibition. In his study of the Zhenjiang Mass Education Center, Hongwei Thorn Chen looks at how the center's mobile film screening activities from 1933 to 1937 were mapped onto infrastructural development around Zhenjiang as a new regional center in the Province of Jiangsu. According to Chen, the center's transportation solution was a van that could move educational films, posters, a projector, a generator, an amplifier, and instructional staff over newly developed regional highways. The van must have achieved considerable success, as it was seized by the Ministry of Culture and became "National Projection Team One" upon the outbreak of the War of Resistance against Japan. However, as Chen notes, educators and projection workers often had to confront the uneven development of infrastructure and use alternative means to access areas connected only by older networks of small roads, alleys, footpaths, and canals. In a 1937 report, the center's director recognized "logistic inconvenience"—the slow pace of travel on foot and the difficulties of getting food and lodging—as the greatest challenge of ambulatory teaching work.[6]

Similar difficulties faced film projection workers after 1949 to an even greater degree. Whereas the Zhenjiang Center was located in the economically more developed Jiangsu Province, the CCP had the ambitious plan of making cinema available across the entire nation, regardless of how challenging it could be for projection teams to reach a remote village. In many regions, the challenges of the complex terrain were so great that reports about film projection teams failing to arrive in certain areas could be found in the press from time to time. In 1953, for example, *People's Daily* published a letter from the cultural bureau of Yunxi County, Hubei Province. The letter explained that automotive transportation to Yunxi county was unavailable and the only way to reach the county was by boat. To satisfy the cultural demands of its people, the county had requested the projection teams from the Xiangyang special district (*zhuanqu*) to come and show films, but their requests had been denied because "transportation is inconvenient, and equipment might get damaged." Pointing out that another projection team from the nearby Shaanxi Province had visited Yunxi County upon invitation, the letter urged the Xiangyang projection teams to strengthen their determination and overcome the difficulties in transportation.[7]

As the letter implies, rural film projection teams at the time were managed by the "special district," a level of administration between the province and the county.[8] From the early 1950s onward, there were repeated attempts to further localize the administration of film projection teams, which were at least partly motivated by the need to solve the problem of transportation and make film more readily available in rural areas. Take one Jiangjin County of Sichuan Province for example. Chinese film historian Liu Guangyu identifies four stages of development in rural film projection in Jiangjin: before 1956, there were three 16 mm projection teams managed by the special district; from 1956 to the beginning of the Cultural Revolution, the county managed its own projection teams, which increased from three to seven; beginning in the 1970s, domestic production of 8.75 mm projectors allowed projection teams to be housed in communes and production brigades; from 1981 to 1989, nine township cinemas were built within the county while more projection teams were organized by brigades and individual contractors.[9] The more projection teams appeared at lower administrative levels, the less frequently they needed to travel. Therefore, rural projection teams faced the most challenges in transportation before the early '70s. From the late '50s to the early '60s in particular, an emphasis was put on further expansion of rural film exhibition (*puji fangying*), creating extra demands on projection teams to chart larger territories and create more screening locations.

Another way to recognize the long distances projectionists had to travel during this period is to look at how audiences perceived the arrival of projection teams. According to "Raising the Screen on Big Ba Mountain," peasants made up a song to praise the deeds of the Number Three Projection Team of Pingli County: "Cinema comes to our village; everybody is so happy. Thanks to the leadership of Chairman Mao, what an unusual sight to see films at one's door."[10] The excitement of the villagers was tied to the fact that cinema was something foreign that came from afar. Meanwhile there was a slight sense of powerlessness, as the villagers had no control over when cinema would be available, and they could not go *to* the movies like urban audiences. This reliance on mobile projection teams intensified the responsibility of rural projectionists as the agents that made spectatorship happen. Before they could project films, they first had to be a part of the film distribution infrastructure.

CINEMA AS A POSTAL SYSTEM

While film distribution is often thought about in terms of market strategies and box office performance, the spatial practice of distributing film copies to physical locations rarely enters conversations in film studies. Whether in André Bazin's emphasis of cinema's indexicality, psychoanalytical concerns with spectator inscription, Jean-Louis Baudry's division of the cinematographic apparatus into production and projection, Seung-hoon Jeong's notion of cinematic interfaces, or inquiries into cinematic affect and embodied perception, the cinematic medium is seen as directly connecting two processes: the making of the film and the spectator's experience of the finished product. Baudry famously speaks of a "work"—operations "between 'objective reality' and the camera, site of inscription, and between the inscription and the projection"— that is concealed by the finished film on screen.[11] His account of the cinematographic apparatus, however, glosses over important steps along these operations such as the printing of the film onto multiple copies and the distribution of film copies to screening sites. If these operations are easily ignorable when they pose no problem to the delivery of film, material shortage and infrastructural lack in the early PRC threw them into sharp relief.

The availability of film stock, for example, could not be taken for granted. The Chinese domestic film industry in the 1950s relied heavily on foreign import of film stock, a situation that was only slightly improved with the opening of China's first film stock factory—the Baoding Film Factory (baoding dianying jiaopian chang)—in 1958. As a result, the number of copies released for films was typically low. According to one official statistics report, from 1949 to 1960, there were only twenty domestic feature films that had over seventy 35 mm copies struck.[12] The White-Haired Girl (Baimao nü) released in September 1951, enjoyed the highest number of 35 mm prints, which was 117. This record was not broken until 1960 when For Sixty-One Class Brothers (Weile liushiyi ge jieji xiongdi) came out with 139 35 mm copies.[13] In comparison, what may be considered "modest" for domestic films would already be a large-scale release in the case of dubbed foreign films, which were typically released with between ten and forty 35 mm copies.[14] Movie theaters, which projected 35 mm prints, were thus forced to frequently share reels by having theater workers shuffle them back and forth between theaters on bicycles—a practice known as "running the film" (paopian).[15] Most film projection teams instead relied on the smaller

16 mm format. Although there were considerably more 16 mm film copies printed for films that were considered of interest to rural audiences,
these prints tended to be of lower quality and in black and white (even
when the 35 mm version of the same film was in color), and they often
had delayed release schedules compared to 35 mm prints.[16] When the
Soviet Union pulled their supply of film stock in 1960 due to the sever-
ance of ties between China and the Soviet Union, it immediately sent the
Chinese film industry into crisis, forcing a reduction in production and
distribution capacity.[17] Combined with the lack of automotive transportation, such material shortage made the threat of film not reaching its
target audience real and constant. For the CCP, therefore, if cinema was
to function as a medium of political education, the problem of delivery
must be prioritized.

Once we recognize delivery as a necessary operation of the cinematic
apparatus, then we can reconceptualize cinema as a postal system. An
illuminating text that can shed light on rural film exhibition in socialist
China is *Postmen in the Mountains* (*Nashan, naren, nagou*), a 1999 film
directed by Huo Jianqi (b. 1958). The film follows two postmen, a father
and son duo, on a trip to deliver mail to villages in a mountainous area.
The trip is the father's last one before retirement and the son's very first.
Set in the 1980s, Huo's postsocialist film exudes bittersweet nostalgia
for the Maoist notion of "serving the people" by focusing on the labor
of the two postmen. Throughout the film, extreme long shots of green
mountain sceneries, combined with close-ups of the bodies in motion
shot with a handheld camera, paint a dynamic picture of the postmen
walking on their route with heavy bags on their backs. The retrograde
ethos of the film is particularly felt in one scene where the father rejects
the notion that they can now deliver mail by automotive travel, which
has actually become available in the area. Walking the old mail route on
foot, for the father, is the only correct and honest way.

In their role as courier, the rural projectionists' job was almost iden-
tical to that of the postmen: both professions required long hours of
travel in areas with limited transportation, both required carrying heavy
loads, and both aimed at the delivery of content to isolated communities. The postal system, as Weihong Bao points out, exemplifies a linear
model of the medium that emphasizes the relationship between the
sender, the receiver, the message, and the channel.[18] In this model, the
central tension is between transmission and interference, or what information theory refers to as signal and noise. In the cases of both *Postmen*
and the rural projectionists, the delivery journey constitutes a channel

of transmission, and a particularly precarious or "noisy" one, as nature and geography pose constant threats to the successful delivery of the message. In *Postmen*, the long and intimidating mountain paths often extend across the screen. At one time, the father, son, and their family dog come across a shallow but wide river that they need to cross on foot, with fast currents and slippery stones adding extra challenge to the trek. Later, when they take a moment to rest, a gust of wind almost blows away the letters that need to be delivered. Similarly, rural projectionists faced many obstacles, such as the cold weather, wind, frost, snow, hunger, and fatigue mentioned in "Raising the Screen on Big Ba Mountain." Similar challenges from different parts of the nation were documented meticulously in newspapers, magazines, and trade journals. Natural forces such as rain and cold weather not only threatened the health and comfort of projection workers but also might cause damage to the celluloid film and screening equipment. In the absence of more efficient means of storage or transportation, transmission could only be secured by the courier. As they relied on their own body and physical labor to ensure the delivery of cinema, the projectionists became a channel, a medium, and, if we agree with Jeong that "the interface can be generalized as any mediating form that assures the principle of connectedness," an interface.[19]

THE PROJECTIONIST AS COURIER: LABOR AND TECHNIQUES OF THE BODY

One telling scene from *Postmen* shows how the laboring body engages in active problem solving as it moves in a challenging environment. In the beginning of the scene, the father and the son are walking up a narrow footpath when two peasants come down from the opposite direction. Being ahead of his father, the son comes face to face with a man carrying long branches on both ends of a shoulder pole. Trying to figure out how to get pass him, the son, carrying a big backpack, fumbles, loses balance, and finally falls against the hill on the right side, letting the peasant pass first. When the camera cuts to the father, he smiles warmly and instructs his son to always lean sideways to the right when he comes across people again. In the next shot, a low-angle full-body shot focusing on the son, the son does not speak, but stops and then turns sideways with his back slightly bent toward the hill. He bends his right knee and places his right foot on the slope to steady himself. Unlike earlier when he is caught off guard, this time the actions appear intentional and precise, as if he is doing a gymnastic stretch. Next, he takes a few steps, and repeats the same movements—even more swiftly this time—before carrying on with his journey.

What is most significant about this sequence is that by showing how the young first-time postman learns and practices a specific bodily movement, it implies that sheer determination is not enough to guarantee delivery, which must involve an active body that has its own intentionality and techniques. By intentionality, I do not simply mean desire or consciousness, but more specifically embodied tendencies in a phenomenological sense. Questioning the Cartesian mind-body dualism, phenomenology emphasizes the body as the basic condition for our being-in-the-world. As Maurice Merleau-Ponty illustrates with the phenomenon of the phantom limb in amputees, the psychological and the physiological cannot be entirely separated.[20] The subject cannot experience the world outside of its body. The body is not a passive object; it is lived and has its own purpose and intelligence that do not necessarily derive from a separate mental realm. When the son first comes across the other traveler, his body has not yet formed a clear intention, which results in him stumbling. But he quickly gains control of the body after the more experienced father teaches him how to handle the situation. With more practice, he probably can perform this action without consciously thinking about it, while it remains an intentional action.

Meanwhile, this action constitutes a particular technique of the body. Marcel Mauss uses the notion of "techniques of the body" to refer to mechanical schemas of the body that are embedded in social relations. Because techniques of the body are passed down from one generation to another and are unique to every society, Mauss believes, they should be studied as fundamental constitutive elements of society.[21] The trick of "leaning to the right" is a great example of techniques of the body. Passed down from the father to the son, it is also indicative of broader material and social relations. On the one hand, the technique is born out of the body's interaction with a natural environment yet to be mapped by large-scale modernization. Shaun Gallagher and Dan Zahavi's description of how the environment directly or indirectly regulates the body can be applied to what is going on here: "The environment calls forth a specific body style so that the body works with the environment and is included in it. The posture that the body adopts in a situation is its way of responding to the environment. The body finds itself already with feelings, drive states, kinesthetic sensations, etc., and they are partially defined by the environment in which it must function."[22] With the body as their only means of transportation, there is no intermediary between the father/ son duo and the hilly, dangerous environment that surrounds them. They must respond to the environment in a bodily manner. From the father's tone, it can be inferred that the particular posture probably has emerged from years of experience. The know-how is already ingrained in the father's identity, while it is only beginning to define the son's body. On the other hand, the specific body style adopted by the father and son is also underpinned by the spirit of "serving workers, peasants, and soldiers." It is significant that the two postmen wait for other travelers to pass first. As people's servants, they are supposed to put the people first. The fact that the father and son take it for granted that they should be the ones to lean to the side serves as a strong indication of their uncorrupt dedication to the people. The investment of the film in delineating such an ethics thus sets it apart from other postsocialist works of nostalgia that tend to set aside the political in favor of personal stories of socialism.

Similarly, the rural projectionist also employed techniques of the body that centered on the body's interaction with the underdeveloped environment. Techniques of endurance were perhaps the most important. Long journeys in remote areas entailed many kinds of bodily discomfort such as hunger, fatigue, cold, and bodily aches from long hours of physical labor. As mentioned earlier, the director of the Republican-era Zhenjiang Mass Education Center had recognized food and lodging as the greatest difficulties for mobile teaching work. Whereas he tried to explain how the lack of clean restaurants and hotels in rural areas was detrimental to his employees' health and their work, the socialist projectionists were expected to endure through the precarious conditions presented by rural travel. Take cold weather for example. In 1956, the Heilongjian Provincial Culture Bureau made the "exciting" decision that film exhibition should continue during the coldest months of the year. The decision reportedly motivated ninety-two rural projection teams to look for suitable venues to screen films for peasants in −20°C (−4°F) weather (one of the films they showed, incidentally, was called *The Story of Summer* [*Xiatian de gushi*]).[23] Around the same time, another projection team was praised for traveling to an exhibition site in the mountains in the coldest months of the year against extremely strong wind.[24] While endurance was constant and habitual, the projectionist also needed to be capable of improvising in the face of unexpected challenges. One projection team from Shandong Province reportedly reached some mountain villages that had never seen a film before. The challenges they faced included having to carry projecting equipment uphill on stairs built on a cliff. At first, four projectionists carried the equipment together, but the stairs were too narrow for four people to go through at the same time. They then had to figure out other ways to move forward and ended up using rope to hoist the equipment.[25]

Moreover, when they were on the road, projectionists had to make sure that neither the projection equipment nor film reels were damaged so that they could be put into prolonged use against the backdrop of material shortage. *Aiji hupian*—"caring for machines and protecting film reels"—became such a prominent tradition in the PRC film exhibition community that special booklets dedicated to experiences in this area were published.[26] One projection team from Yunnan Province, for example, would carry important parts of the equipment separately. When walking across rivers, they would take the equipment off of pack animals and carry it themselves.[27] Another projection team from Xinjiang that worked in the Pamir Mountains was reported to be hit by a blizzard one night. The first thing that crossed the minds of the three Tajik projection workers was to protect the equipment. They moved all the equipment next to their three yaks and huddled together through the night to make sure the equipment stayed intact. It was not until the next morning that they realized that their food was gone.[28] The situation this projection team faced was quite extreme, of course, but bad weather was frequently a challenge. A more common technique was to take off one's clothes and use it to cover the equipment when it rained. Frequently mentioned in the press, this technique became a hallmark of the rural projectionist identity. In a four-panel illustrated poem that appeared in the journal *Film Projection*, the first of the four drawings captures this technique in motion: a projectionist is trying to put her coat over equipment on a hand-drawn cart while a coworker continues to pull the cart (figure 4). A poem below declares: Dark clouds roll, and storm is coming; one hurries to take off clothes; rather shivering in the rain, than letting the equipment hit by a drop.[29]

What was common to all of these stories was how projection workers chose to prioritize the needs of the projecting equipment over the needs of their own bodies. As one projectionist explained in *Mass Cinema*: "Machines are dead and do not know how to talk. We must take good care of them. If the magnetic parts get wet and cannot generate electricity, we won't be able to show films. We human beings are alive. If it's windy, rainy, or cold, we just need to carry more loads or run faster. We are failing the party and the people if we do not work

FIGURE 4. Taking off clothes to cover the equipment. Li Ruidong, drawing, *Dianying fangying* [Film Projection] 1–2 (1966): 22.

hard."[30] In this and other techniques of the body, we see the dismissal of the body's need for comfort. Lu Xiaoning recently suggests that projectionists' care for the cinematic apparatus illustrates what Tina Mai Chen calls the human-machine continuum, a close association between humans and machinery that was crucial for effecting qualitative social change and the formation of a liberated subjectivity.[31] In Chen's analysis, emphasis is given to discourses and representations where human bodies are fused with tools like guns, hammers, and pickaxes. As tools become extensions of the body, the body becomes machinelike, heralding a future subjectivity that is ultimately enlivened and empowered by the human-machine continuum.[32] In stressing physical endurance, the projectionist may indeed be seen as functioning like a machine: they are expected to ignore their bodily needs to achieve machine-like consistency. But what is missing from both Lu's and Chen's discussions is how the human body can be seen as superior to machines, the latter described as fragile, easily damaged, and requiring the protection of humans who are more malleable and adaptive. In line with Mao's voluntarism, which recognizes human actors as the ultimate decisive factor of history, the view expressed here is that the projectionist, rather than the mechanical apparatus, is the motive force of the exhibition system.

Given the crucial role the projectionist played in securing transmission, their techniques of the body may also be seen as cultural techniques in the sense defined by German media theory. As Bernhard Siegert suggests, the notion of cultural techniques has been used to refer to "inconspicuous technologies of knowledge" that constitute the basic conditions of discourse and meaning.[33] Activities such as reading, writing, making music, and counting, as well as seemingly insignificant tools from index cards and typewriters to blackboard and alphabetization have all been examined through the lens of cultural techniques. Broadening this concept to include corporeal practices, Markus Krajewski understands domestic service as a cultural technique as it contributes to cultural efficacy through "the interplay of purposeful bodily gestures and the use of aids such as tools, instruments, or other medial objects."[34] By securing the physical transmission of cinema over unstable channels, the bodily techniques employed by the rural projectionists proved no less essential for the development of culture than other types of cultural techniques. They created conditions for accessing the cinematic, which, in the forms of feature films, newsreels, science education shorts, and so on, constituted a basic mode of communication between the country's political and creative elites and the rural masses.

THE POLITICS OF VISIBILITY

While the crucial role of rural film projectionists in the nationwide distribution of films is undeniable, what is equally significant is that such a role was not merely acknowledged, but also widely publicized and reiterated with detail in narratives of projection teams' travels that could be found in both specialized journals and publications for the general public. What messages did such narratives communicate to readers and potential film audiences? In what ways can they be seen as an interface of the socialist film exhibition system?

The emergence of film projectionists as protagonists, and very often heroic ones, in cultural representations should first be viewed in the context of their newfound visibility in the PRC. After all, it is the effacing of the projectionist from the production process and the spectator's mind that has characterized the institutionalization of cinema since the 1910s. Timothy Barnard gives a detailed account of the once shaky importance of the projectionist in the storefront cinema era (c. 1905–1912) in the United States and Europe. As he reveals, before motor-driven projectors appeared on the market in 1908, the operator of the hand-cranked projector had a significant role to play in determining the final product shown to the audience: they could vary the speed of projection to achieve desired effects and were therefore very much participants in the production of films. Early cinema, Barnard reminds us, was often filmed with varied speed. Filmmakers like D. W. Griffith (1875–1948) were likely to anticipate the intervention of the projectionist to finish the final look of their films. It was based on this unique role that projectionist unions, with varying degree of success, advocated for higher wages and better working conditions for the machine operators, who, many argued, were not ordinary mechanics but skilled artisans.[35] However, if the creation of the projection booth in the 1900s marked the moment when the operator's labor began to be hidden from the public, standardization in the film industry further erased traces of their labor. The institutional mode of representation, also known as classical Hollywood cinema, "presents itself as natural and thus unalterable to an audience absorbed in its narrative and undistracted by signs of its production."[36] In other words, the classical mode encourages the spectator to focus on the diegesis, and discourages attention to the process of production, including the work of the projectionist.

The projectionist was not only invisible in the classical Hollywood system, but has been largely left out of film studies.[37] Baudry's apparatus theory again provides a telling example. Baudry discusses projection and its positioning of the viewing subject and yet is able to avoid mentioning the projectionist altogether.[38] While he recognizes how cinema functions by concealing its own construction and thus appearing to the spectator as perceptions of reality, his descriptions of cinematography and projection also efface human labor as a force of production. In his account, the camera and the projector seemingly run by themselves as self-sustained operations whereas human participation does not warrant attention in itself, as it only aids the mechanical processes, which alone constitute meaning.

As digital technologies threaten to eliminate the projectionist's job entirely, it is tempting to accept a teleological history of the projectionist as one of decreasing visibility and utility since the early twentieth century. The history of cinema in China, however, disrupts this neat progression. There has been little research into the work of projectionists in Chinese film history, especially during the Republican era. But it is not an exaggeration to suggest that 1949 marked a new period of public attention for projectionists in China when the invisible status of projectionists in Western movie theaters was increasingly stabilized. Cinema's expansion and relocation to new environments entailed reconfigurations of the screening *dispositif*, which included the disappearance of the projection booth. As cinema moved outside of purpose-built movie theaters into work units, parks, village squares, and other outdoor or indoor venues within communities, the projectionist literally became visible as an object of interest for curious audience members. As a new locus of attention, the projectionist could then be turned into an effective signifier for larger societal changes.

A 1951 article from *Mass Cinema* vividly illustrates the new relations formed between the projectionist and the spectators in open-air cinema. Written by a sixteen-year-old female projectionist named Li Shukai, the article recounts Li's experience at her first public screening at a park in Shanghai. Nervous about completing her task for a large audience that gathered both in front of and behind the screen, Li is surprised to find herself becoming the object of attention: "Strangely, audiences all looked toward me. One old lady asked how old I was, and I told her I was sixteen years old. She looked at me with envy. I guess they also found me strange. How come even a woman can be a film projectionist nowadays? And she is only sixteen! Well yes, this is indeed strange, because they have never heard of anything like this in the old society!"[39]

Being out in a park, the projectionist is literally visible to the audience, who not only can direct their gaze on her but interact with her. The novelty of this exchange of looks and words between the older woman and the young projectionist is a direct result of the cinema's relocation. While projectionists used to be hidden in the booth, it was also unlikely for an older woman to visit movie theaters, which tended to target the young and Westernized middle class (her presence was thus indicative of the CCP's drive to popularize cinema). Although Li seems oblivious to the significance of the gender and age of her interlocuter, she is well aware of how her own visibility serves as a public display of female empowerment. What is evoked is politics in the sense of what Jacques Rancière terms "the distribution of the sensible," which concerns the delimitation of what is visible and invisible, what is included and excluded in the common space of a community.[40] Contrasted with the past where a female projectionist was unseen and unheard of, the visibility of Li thus marks a new system of distribution where women are allowed entry into the public arena as female tractor drivers, female pilots, female hairdressers, and so on. A sketch accompanying the article further reinforces the spectator's gaze at the projectionist (figure 5). Drawn from a slightly lower angle mimicking the perspective of a seated

FIGURE 5. A Projectionist
standing next to her projector.
Unknown Author, drawing,
Dazhong dianying [Mass
Cinema] 26 (1951): 23.

spectator, the sketch shows Li standing next to a projector with one
hand resting on top of it, eyes looking forward as if totally absorbed
in her work. Covering one side of her body, the bulky projector almost
becomes a part of her. What is depicted here is the human-machine
continuum: more specifically, the projectionist operates the projector,
which in turn defines her liberation.

In rural areas, the first sight of "cinema" was often not a film being
shown or even a screening venue, but the projection team. In "Raising
the Screen on Big Ba Mountain," the projection team is met by villagers miles outside of the village, who then walk together with them
for several hours to reach the destination. The sense of fascination felt
by many toward the projectionist is wonderfully dramatized in a short
story by Yi Xiangdong (b. 1964) originally published in 2005 in *Fiction Monthly* (*Xiaoshuo yuebao*). The story's first-person narrator is an
eleven-year-old village boy passionate about watching films:

> In the late afternoon, the projectionist carried the projector to the middle
> of the field with the help of an electrician from the village. Cheers erupted
> as children gathered to stare at the projectionist—how his mouth whistled
> beautiful tunes, how his eyebrows blinked, and how his hands and feet

moved. Ears, nose, mouth, and eyes that would look ordinary on another person became so worthy of observing once appearing on a projectionist. The projectionist became a little irritated and yelled: "Step aside, step aside! What is there to look at? You can't get it out once it goes into your eyes!"[41]

Instead of marveling at the projector or the modern technology it stands for, the children focus their attention on the projectionist. Mimicking their gaze, Yi's writing dissects his body, each part of which appears to exude magic on its own. For the young narrator, the projectionist, who enjoys a level of mobility and political privilege unusual for the rural world, is a figure of allure and mystique that he aspires to be when he grows up. This story thus makes clear that with the arrival of cinema there also emerges a public role model available for mass admiration and identification.

Interestingly, Yi's short story goes beyond offering a nostalgic look at the socialist past by revising and thus critiquing some of the familiar socialist narratives of rural open-air cinema. As the story goes on, the projectionist ironically turns out to be a corrupt and morally suspicious figure who retaliates against the narrator's aunt after she rejects his advances. The revelation of true character may be seen as foreshadowed in the above passage in his discomfort at being the object of scrutiny. By contrast, in the earlier narrative by Li Shukai, her surprise at the audience's interest in her evolves into a historically informed understanding of the spectator's gaze. In fact, her writing further invites the reader's attention by offering her backstory: her father was a GMD official who had fled to Taiwan, abandoning her mother, who had since become mentally ill, and herself. Taking readers "behind the scenes," Li's narrative reinforces the recognition of the projectionist as a symbol of liberation. Moreover, in accepting and encouraging the spectator's attention, Li then "returns the gaze" by vowing to work harder and serve the people loyally.[42] This warm reciprocal interaction demonstrates Mao's "mass line" whereas Yi Xiangdong's reconstructed projectionist, in refusing to be looked at, hints at its failure. The latter thus reminds us that the visibility of the projectionist has no inherent meaning. Visibility simply provides another possible interface for the articulation of ideology.

THE PROJECTIONIST AS MODEL LABORER

In the broader context of visibility, travel narratives showing rural projectionists on the road belonged with a large body of literature describing the projectionist's labor, which also included technical, political, managerial, and performance aspects. Why was there a need to publicize this particular segment of the projectionist's work? Tina Mai Chen locates the significance of the projectionist's travel in its mapping of the territory of a new nation. The emphasis on inclusion and access explained why projection teams that reached the most remote areas were particularly celebrated.[43] But the detailed manner in which the journeys were described also suggests that something else was at stake: these narratives drew the public's attention, specifically, to manual labor.

Early film projectionists in the United States and in Europe, as Barnard suggests, tried to distance their work from manual labor. To earn a better living for themselves and the respect of the industry, they emphasized their contribution to cinema as skillful artisans.[44] A divide between manual labor and projection work also seemed to have been sustained in the activities of the Zhenjiang Mass Education Center in Republican China. Hongwei Thorn Chen discusses a copper plate illustration in which bare-legged laborers pulling a cart of equipment were juxtaposed with educational staff dressed in black carrying suitcases. While an inscription next to the illustration urges the "comrades" to "pull hard" and "push hard" as it is "our great educational responsibility," Chen expresses his confusion about whom the poem is referring to, the laborers or the instructors.[45] By casting projectionists as laborers who carried loads and pulled carts, Mao-era narratives of the projectionist's journey thus alluded to a radical ideological transformation under socialism: instead of being disparaged, manual labor, as well as the proletariat, was now celebrated as a source of moral virtue.

A reevaluation of the traditional hierarchy between intellectual and manual labor was central to Mao's theory of literature and arts. If we recall Mao's "Talks," what provided the moral foundation for the ideal of "serving workers, peasants, and soldiers" was precisely the validation of manual laborers. Consequently, intellectuals, writers, and artists must humbly bring themselves closer to the worker-peasant-soldier masses, gain firsthand knowledge of their lives and their spontaneous artistic expressions, and produce works that appeal to them. The lowered status of intellectual and artistic work and the elevated status of manual labor was reflected in the use of terms such as "literary and artistic worker" (*wenyi gongzuozhe*) and "cultural worker" (*wenhua gongzuozhe*) that entered official discourse after 1949. Rather than suggesting a special class of creators, the notion of "worker" designated equal participants of a larger community. It also had the function of blurring the line between different types of labor involved in cultural production. The wording of a 1983 report on national film exhibition is telling of this leveling effect: "Our country now has a cultural army of a million. In this grand army, there are 440,000 people in the film system, 260,000 people in the theatrical arts system, 220,000 in the publishing system. . . . The film system has the largest number of people in the entire cultural army, and 90 percent of personnel of the film system work in distribution and exhibition."[46] In addition to evoking the metaphor of the cultural army from the "Talks," this passage makes no distinction between screenwriters, directors, actors, distributors, or projectionists. If actors and directors are privileged as stars and auteurs elsewhere, they enjoy no special status in the socialist cultural system. Instead, treating everyone inside the cultural army equally allows the speaker to recognize the contributions of distribution and exhibition workers to the entire film industry.

In tandem with the ascendance of socialist cultural workers over elite artists, there rose the moral status of laborers. Visually, images of laborers, especially peasants and industrial workers, proliferated in propaganda posters, magazines, and films, appearing as monuments and statues.[47] Institutionally, model laborer campaigns recognized those with exceptional dedication to labor. Influenced by the Soviet Stakhanovite movement from the 1930s, the CCP first began promoting labor heroes during the Yan'an era in the middle of the War of Resistance against Japan. The First Conference of Model Laborers, held in 1943, awarded 185 model workers.[48] Campaigns to recognize model laborers continued in the 1950s when economic development became a top priority for the new socialist nation. Three national conferences were held in 1950, 1956, and 1959, and a total of 5,286 people received the title of "national industrial model worker" during this period.[49] Some of these recipients became "star" workers whose deeds were widely publicized in national media and through study sessions organized by governments and work units.[50] Among the qualities of model worker, high productivity, self-sacrifice, loyalty to the party and Chairman Mao, patriotism, as well as willingness to help those who were ideologically backward were often mentioned.

Travel narratives of projectionists on the road foregrounded precisely their identities as laborers who mobilized their bodies in the transmission of cinema. There were many similarities between these narratives and the rhetoric surrounding the model laborer. One notable theme concerned how a strong determination stemming from revolutionary or patriotic consciousness could enable one to overcome tremendous difficulties. The author of "Raising the Screen on Big Ba Mountain" made sure to tell readers that the projection team derived sources of energy from "the party's education" and "the people's expectations."[51] For the official from Yunxi County who wrote a letter to *People's Daily* to complain about the absence of local projection teams, the reason why another projection team was able to reach challenging mountainous areas was mainly because of their "courage and resolution to overcome difficulties."[52]

Mao's voluntarist philosophy attributed to human consciousness the power to drive history more or less independently from stages of socio-economic development. As Maurice Meisner observes, such strong faith in human agency has led to constant concerns with correct ideological consciousness and "thought reform" since the Yan'an era.[53] Chinese model laborers were also distinguished from the Soviet Stakhanovite-type heroes: while the latter were praised for their high productivity and technological innovations, the former had to demonstrate extra degrees of ideological commitment on top of their productive output. As Rachel Funari and Bernard Mees suggest, the earliest Yan'an labor heroes, such as Zhao Zhankui (factory worker, 1896–1973) and Wu Manyou (peasant, 1894–1959), were noted for their conscious efforts to educate fellow villagers and workers about the Communist ideology and revolution.[54] After 1949, the emphasis on subjectivity continued to be widely present in politics, education, arts, and public discourse. Model laborers, including several highly publicized People's Liberation Army soldiers in the early 1960s (most notably Lei Feng), were known for their devotion to revolution, the communist ideology, the party, and eventually to Mao himself. In fact, scholars have noticed the increasing weight of Mao Zedong Thought in defining a model figure in the years leading up to the Cultural Revolution. As Mary Sheridan points out, a major innovation in model promulgation in the '60s was the use of diaries. Heavily edited, these diaries shifted focus from deeds to thought, indicating that to perform heroic deeds one must constantly engage in self-examination and reflection following the guidance of Mao.[55] For the rural film projectionist who had the responsibility of propagating party policies and interpreting films for a rural populace, political study was a regular component of their training and day-to-day work. More than being a mouthpiece for the state, the projectionist was also supposed to derive a strong work ethic from revolutionary teachings, particularly Mao's call for cultural workers to serve the people. After one projection team from Pingdu County, Shandong Province, stayed at the headquarters of a commune for twenty-five consecutive days, leaving 100 among the 170 villages they served to go without a film screening for a long time, local authorities instructed them to study Mao's "Talks" again. As a result, they reportedly gained a better understanding of what it meant to serve the people and were able to overcome their fear of hardship.[56] The increasing centrality of Mao Zedong Thought in the model rhetoric can be seen in the title of an article from *Film Exhibition* from 1966, which simply reads "Mao Zedong Thought gives them the power to charge forward."[57]

It may seem like political consciousness was sometimes presented as the only thing projectionists needed to succeed in delivering film to remote places. But the amount of detail contained in accounts of the projectionist's journey also affirmed the importance of concrete techniques in problem solving. The projectionist thus exemplified for the public a mode of embodiment in which political consciousness was constantly transformed into purposeful and skilled bodily actions, and where the strengthening of the mind was integrated with the training of the body. Consciousness itself may not have delivered films, but it was supposed to empower the body to endure, improvise, and deliver.

Another common theme in the descriptions of model laborers is the effort to protect collective property even at the cost of one's own life.[58] This was a uniquely socialist virtue produced by the combination of material shortages and the prioritizing of the collective over the individual. Xu Xuehui, for example, was known for protecting 50,000 RMB at the bank she worked for against a group of burglars at the age of eighteen. She lost her two hands as a result of the fight and was rewarded the title of "national model laborer" in 1959. People even sacrificed their own lives so that damages to collective property could be avoided. One widely publicized case was female textile worker Xiang Xiuli (1933–1959), who died trying to prevent a fire at her factory. Such prioritizing of collective property over human life paralleled the practice of "caring for machines and protecting film reels" in the film industry. The projectionist's labor in protecting screening equipment, which I discussed earlier, was thus crucial not only for the transmission of cinema to a particular destination, but for the sustainability of the entire industry.

In summary, situated in a broader discursive context, narratives of projectionists' journeys not only constructed an essential figure in the operation of the socialist cinematic apparatus, but also participated in the larger campaign to produce the so-called Socialist New Man (*shehuizhuyi xinren*) by offering projectionists as models for emulation. What these narratives also implied was that the Socialist New Man must be an embodied subject, with both moral and physical dimensions. The body itself has been seen as an object of reform in modern China. For Denise Gimple, the Chinese state has been engaging in what she calls somatic engineering, seeking to incorporate sociocultural values in the body.[59] Interested in the Chinese penal procedures, Michael Dutton describes the "reform-through-labor" (*laojiao*) system as a disciplinary project in the Foucauldian sense that "acts upon" the body and the mind to produce "active, committed, and useful socialists."[60] Nevertheless, the mechanisms Gimple and Dutton describe would not apply to narratives of the projectionist's travels. Whereas the notion of somatic engineering implies totalizing control and "docile bodies," the projectionist exerted only exemplary influence, the efficacy of which depended on the reader-spectator's own willingness to learn from them. In this sense, the projectionist was not different from film characters. Mao-era film administrators often urged filmmakers to portray positive, heroic characters so that they could serve as role models for audiences. While completion of this task was uneven at best, travel narratives undoubtedly constituted an effective genre through which a collective image of the rural projectionists as precisely "active, committed, and useful socialists" took roots.

Ideological effects, according to Baudry, depend on the concealment of the process of production.[61] This is a typical view of ideology in Western leftist criticism. If ideology, as Louis Althusser suggests, is the imaginary relationship between individuals to their real conditions of existence, a critique of ideology is believed to be achievable through acts of unmasking, denaturalizing, or rupturing what appears to be reality.[62] Counter-cinema à la Jean-Luc Godard (b. 1930) is a prime example of this approach to ideological critique. By deliberately going against cinematic conventions, it seeks to foreground the cinematic apparatus and lay bare the construction that is behind illusions of realism.[63]

Chinese narratives of the film projectionist on the road also exhibited an urge to unmask. Relocating cinema to open-air venues has exposed the projectionist to the public eye. In contrast to practices at most commercial movie theaters, there was no attempt to conceal the projectionist's labor. Instead, audience attention to the projectionist was encouraged. Media representations of projection teams trying to deliver film to remote areas that lacked basic infrastructure further invited the audience to observe the process of transmission that was an inherent part of the cinematic apparatus. What Chinese socialist cinema came to rely on in these circumstances was the projectionist's manual labor. If Western commercial cinema seeks to erase labor from its final products, the importance of corporeal practices and bodily techniques in building a national film exhibition network was fully acknowledged and celebrated in socialist China.

The twist, of course, is that the unmasking in this case is not really a critique of ideology, but an articulation of the dominant ideology of socialist China. One might say that by celebrating labor as virtue, socialism is inherently a critique of capitalism. In that case, what we need to do is to revise the equation of ideology with concealment, because what the Western critics' universalist assumptions gloss over is that it is always a particular ideology (e.g., capitalism) concealing some particular aspects of power relations (e.g., work). Socialism has another set of concealments and transparencies—a redistribution of the sensible. In cinematic matters, the projectionist's body became a signifying body on the condition of its newly gained visibility. As an object of the spectator's gaze, it expanded cinema: the "message" now came not only from the film, but also from the body that delivered the film.

CHAPTER 3

Multimedia

A projection team arrives and gets ready for a screening. Then what happens? In one instance, a projection team from Xinjin County, Liaoning Province, decided to incorporate physical objects before their screenings as a way to introduce new productive technologies to audiences. They demonstrated how to burn pests with fire. They burned three hundred pests in ten minutes while performing clapper talk (*kuaiban*)—a traditional oral form performed over rhythmic beats produced by bamboo clappers. As a result, it was said that "from schools to the production team, everyone was mobilized. They burned countless pests, which played a positive role in ensuring a big harvest."[1] In this case, the projectionists assumed the roles of grassroots science educators, who put on a multimedia performance involving objects, percussion instruments, and their own bodies—all at an event known as "film exhibition."

From the early 1950s to at least the mid-'70s, film exhibition in China, especially rural China, was purposefully run as a multimedia institution that employed noncinematic media technologies to achieve the dual goals of propaganda and education. Slide projection (*huandeng*), live performance in various traditional and local styles, and the use of lecturing (*jieshuo*) to accompany film screenings were some of the most common tools adopted by film projectionists. By examining official guidelines, journalistic reports, and reflections of exhibition practices found in film journals and other kinds of archival materials, this chapter demonstrates how the showing of films was decentered, and sometimes completely marginalized, by other media practices in socialist film exhibition. In this sense, socialist film exhibition in China is better situated in the tradition of audiovisual education or "electrified education" (dianhua jiaoyu) that dates back to the last decade of the Qing Dynasty (1644–1912). As an established academic field in the PRC, the study of dianhua jiaoyu concerns how technologies can serve as instruments for education. To examine film exhibition as a "branch" of dianhua jiaoyu thus implies broadening the perspective of film studies to look at how cinema was deployed alongside other mediums for pedagogical purposes. In fact, cinema was not always seen as adequate for successful political communication and therefore had to be supplemented by other interfaces.

AUDIOVISUAL EDUCATION BEYOND CINEMA

With its explicit focus on propaganda and education, socialist film exhibition can be seen as a continuation of practices of education cinema in the Republican era. A history of education cinema in China might begin with the early showing of films by missionary organizations. In the 1910s, a surprisingly active exhibitor of cinema in Shanghai was the Shanghai branch of the YMCA founded in 1900. The organization held screenings as "healthful entertainment" and used films as visual aids for lectures on a variety of topics from brain health and individual hygiene to farming and Christianity.[2] The domestic production of science education films began in 1918 after the Shanghai Commercial Press (shangwu yinshu guan) established a Motion Pictures Department (huodong yingxi bu). Under the influence of the international education movement, the Motion Pictures Department together with foreign agencies, university cinematographers, and private film companies produced hundreds of science education films from the 1920s to the 1940s.[3] A parallel development was state-sponsored cinema produced through both collaboration with private film studios and the film section of the Central Propaganda Committee of the Guomindang, established in 1929. As Weihong Bao points out, education cinema and state cinema were often conflated during this period, both functioning as vehicles for state policy, mass literacy, and state modernization projects.[4] The beginning of the War of Resistance against Japan further brought these two cinemas together. Driven by the urgent need for war mobilization, mobile film projection teams were organized by the Political Department of Guomindang's Military Committee and several film studios based in Chongqing, Guomindang's wartime capital. Guomindang's

Chief Film Projection Team (*dianying fangying zongdui*) (made up of 104 projectionists and ten groups), for instance, held 493 screenings between 1939 and 1941 for twenty-seven million audiences. Religious and educational institutions were also among those that organized mobile or open-air screenings during the war.[5] Scholarship on education cinema naturally takes cinema as their primary object of study. Matthew Johnson focuses on science education film as a genre.[6] Bao, while consciously investigating intermediate relations, is concerned with how other media—television, wireless technology, and so on—impacted the articulation of cinema as a distinct medium. Although she observes that wartime mobile film projection also employed slideshows, live performance, music record playing, and radio broadcasting, acknowledging that in the end "the media ensemble prevailed over any singular medium," her analysis centers on cinema without going into detail on how other media technologies functioned on their own and in relation to each other.[7]

Cinema, however, would lose its status as a privileged medium in the context of audiovisual education. In the PRC, audiovisual education was officially established as a university curriculum and an area of academic research, as the Ministry of Education directed universities to offer *dianhua jiaoyu* (*dianjiao* for short), as electives in 1951. The journal *E-education Research* (*Dianhua jiaoyu yanjiu*) was founded in 1980, with Nan Guonong (b. 1920) as its editor in chief.[8] Having studied for a master's degree in education at Columbia University in the late 1940s, Nan is widely regarded as one of the pioneers, if not *the* leading figure, in the field. In audiovisual education studies, which examines broadly the relationship between education and technology, cinema is weaved into a diverse array of media, institutional, legislative practices around the subject of education. An example of this approach can be found in Chinese scholar A Lunna's survey of audiovisual education history before 1949. While the production of education films and film exhibition for educational purposes were prominent components of this history, what emerges from A Lunna's account is a broader picture in which cinema was but one of many tools employed by the different actors involved.[9]

Beginning her account in the late nineteenth century, A Lunna observes how education institutions played a crucial role in the early adoption of modern audiovisual technologies in classroom instruction. Missionary schools were the earliest formal education institutions in China to utilize photography, posters, miniature models, and film as pedagogical tools. The Dengzhou Literary Association School (*Dengzhou wenhui guan*), a missionary school founded by Calvin W. Mateer (1836–1908), imported a film projector for educational uses as early as 1898. According to A Lunna, the Chinese term for cinema, *dianying*, was allegedly coined by Sun Xisheng (1868–1932), who was a pupil of the school at the time. Later the most impactful institution in the field of audiovisual education was Jinling University. As early as 1915, the university designated a special area for open-air screenings. As one of the first domestic institutions to produce education films, it established a Film Education Committee in 1930 and a Department of Education Film under its School of Sciences in 1936. By the time of the War of Resistance against Japan, *dianhua jiaoyu* had not only been integrated into the curriculum of Jinling University but also had become one important way for the university to participate in civic affairs. Under the leadership of Sun Mingjing (1911–1992), head of the Education Film Department, who also happened to be the son of Sun Xisheng, Jinling University engaged in a wide range of *dianjiao* activities during the war, such as producing education films, organizing outdoor and indoor screenings, conducting training sessions for the Ministry of Education, publishing the journal *Cinema and Radio Broadcasting* (*Dianying yu boyin*), and operating a radio station.

Outside of formal school settings, another line of development that A Lunna traces was mass education (*pingmin jiaoyu*). An early practitioner in this field was Yan Yangchu (1893–1990), who first started using slides to teach characters to Chinese laborers in France during World War I and then continued with similar work in China. From the 1920s onward, mass education centers emerged across the country. Similar to the Zhenjiang Mass Education Center studied by Hongwei Thorn Chen, these centers relied heavily on audiovisual means considered accessible for the general population, including radio, photography, slides, and film. By 1936, 121,713 mass education centers had been established in the nation.

Among all the educational tools, A Lunna gives special attention to radio and film exhibition. According to her, Guomindang's Ministry of Education actively promoted radio by distributing radio receivers to schools and mass education centers. By 1938, more than twenty-five hundred radios had been distributed. And by 1942, the Central Broadcast Station, established in 1928, had developed a variety of educational programs, covering topics ranging from civic education, science, and hygiene to art, Mandarin, geography, and law. Meanwhile, film exhibition was institutionalized as a part of state-sponsored audiovisual education with the demarcation of 81 film education touring zones across the nation in 1933, which increased to 149 in 1941. By the end of 1943, the Ministry of Education had opened Audiovisual Education Offices in eighteen provinces and maintained fifty-two mobile audiovisual education in nineteen provinces. These teams screened education films and played radio broadcasts to local audiences and were expected to participate in other social education affairs according to the abilities and interests of their members. The CCP similarly invested in radio broadcasting and film exhibition, albeit on a smaller scale. On December 30, 1940, CCP's first radio station, the Xinhua Radio Station, began broadcasting in Yan'an, where the Yan'an Film Group was established in 1938. Moreover, A Lunna briefly surveys the pre-49 production of education films and legislations that contributed to the official recognition of audiovisual education as an administrative category, such as the drafting of "A Proposal for Education during a Time of National Calamities" (*Guonan shiqi jiaoyu fang'an*) in 1936, in which both film education and radio education were promoted as official state policies.

Cramming much information into the space of two journal articles, A Lunna's account does not go beyond a summary of historical facts, but what is instructive about her approach is the framing of such a diverse range of educational and media practices under the rubric of audiovisual education. From this angle, she foregrounds aspects of Chinese cinema that are often ignored in film studies due to the conventional bias toward feature films.[10] By drawing attention to the role of the Guomindang state in sponsoring audiovisual education, she challenges the early PRC rhetoric that presented mass education as an innovation of the socialist state (see chapter 1). It is thus important to consider to what extent socialist film exhibition continued earlier practices of audiovisual education.[11] A Lunna's account also makes clear that reframing film exhibition through the lens of audiovisual education entails that one goes beyond merely acknowledging the existence of a "media ensemble" while retaining the focus on cinema. Instead, it is imperative to set aside cinema to investigate other media technologies, practices, and interfaces co-present with cinema.

In socialist film exhibition, two such media interfaces were particularly prominent: slide projection and live performance (figure 6). Both of these forms supplemented the films being screened, offering introduction, interpretation, and guidance for viewers. But it would be wrong to treat them merely as accessories in socialist film exhibition. Rather, both

FIGURE 6. Two projectionists preparing slides and practicing rhymed talk. Li Ruidong, drawing, *Dianying fangying* [Film Exhibition] 1–2 (1966): 23.

could serve educational purposes on their own, producing interfacing relations that hinted at the potential failures of cinema as a shared political horizon.

DISCOVERING *HUANDENG*

As a neologism borrowed from Japanese, the Chinese word *huandeng* (pronounced *gentô* in Japanese) originally referred to the magic lantern, which arrived in China not long after its invention in Europe in the seventeenth century. The lantern was initially known by a number of other names such as *jingying deng* and *fangzi jing* before *huandeng* was stabilized as a translation in the early twentieth century.[12] By the early 1950s, slide projection technologies had evolved significantly beyond the magic lantern while the meaning of *huandeng* had also expanded to include slide projection of all kinds (it can refer both to the projector, also called *huandengji*, and the slide, also called *huandengpian*). It would thus be inaccurate to translate references to *huandeng* in post-49 sources as "magic lantern" or "lantern slides." In fact, projectors and slides available in 1950s China were fairly diverse. In a 1953 handbook written by Wu Dinghong, an author of several books on slide projection and optical technologies published in the '50s and '60s, eight different kinds of

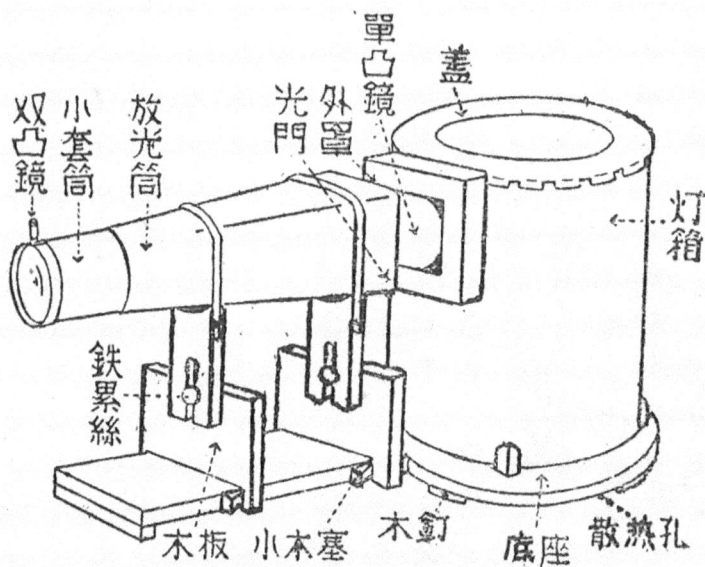

雙凸鏡　小套筒　放光筒　光門　外罩　單凸鏡　蓋　灯箱　鉄累絲　木板　小本塞　木釘　底座　散熱孔

圖五十一　昔陽式幻燈機

FIGURE 7. A "Xiyang"-style slide projector from the early 1950s. Wu Dinghong, *huandeng gongzuo shouce* [Handbook for slide projection] (Beijing: wenhua xueshe), 71. Drawing.

domestically produced slide projectors are discussed in detail, including some resembling magic lanterns that use small oil lamps as light sources and project individual glass slides, some that can project slides printed on 35 mm filmstrips, and one overhead projector (figures 7 and 8). Wu also lists up to ten common types of slides, including single slides of six different sizes, three formats of filmstrips, and one "long format" used mainly in rural areas.[13]

To get a sense of how *huandeng* was situated in relation to film exhibition in the first years of the PRC, we can look at two short articles from *Mass Cinema*. The first one, published in the magazine's fourth issue in 1950, offers a general introduction of *huandeng*. The article begins by dating the underlying principle of *huandeng* to Aristotle but attributes the invention of *huandeng* to a "Kechina" in 1640—probably referring to the publication of Athanasius Kircher's *Ars Magna Lucis et Umbrae* in 1645. It then discusses the mechanism of slide projection and how it is used in the present day: "When we go to the movie

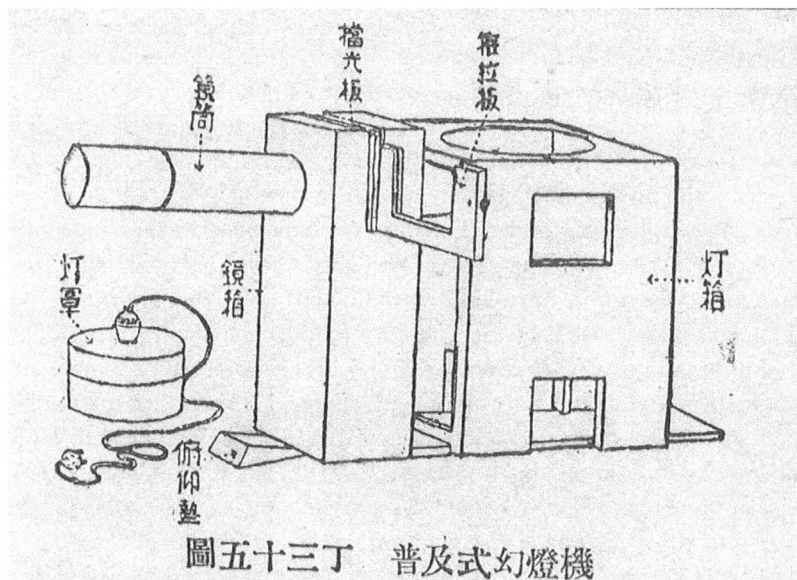

檔光板　窗拉板

鏡筒

燈罩　鏡筒　　　　　　　　　　灯箱

俯仰墊

圖五十三丁　普及式幻燈機

FIGURE 8. A "universal" (*puji*) -style slide projector from the early 1950s. Wu Ding-hong, *huandeng gongzuo shouce*, 75. Drawing.

theater to watch films, there are always commercials before the main feature starts. Those commercials are projected with slides. Some movie theaters use slide projectors to show Chinese subtitles. In school instruction or public lectures, slides are sometimes projected to show pictures, photos, or illustrations from books on walls or screens so that everyone present can see." Since the issue came out in early 1950, it is reasonable to assume that the practices the author describes were established before 1949. In this older model, *huandeng* was deployed in both commercial theaters, where it served a commercial purpose and complemented films, and in educational contexts where it provided visual aids to classroom instruction. Moreover, the article affirms the shared mechanism between cinema and *huandeng*: although film projectors are more complex, they are adapted and improved from the principles of *huandeng*.[14]

This article can be contrasted with a reader's letter to *Mass Cinema* published a year later, which prescribed a new context and a new usage for *huandeng*. The author first acknowledges that both film and huandeng have become "weapons" in political campaigns such as the Resist America and Aid Korea movement and the Campaign to Suppress Counterrevolutionaries. But their usage has not been widespread (*puji*) enough. *Huandeng*, the author suggests, should play a bigger part, especially in rural areas. This is because slides are easier to make, so they can closely speak to the needs of ongoing campaigns. They are also more accessible to audiences that do not understand Putonghua, the official language of the PRC in which all films were required to be shot.[15]

From the previous article to this letter, a clear shift had taken place. Not only was the commercial function of *huandeng* elided and its political potential elevated, but also its preferred spaces changed from theaters, schools, and lecture halls to the countryside; *huandeng* was no longer assigned a supporting role in relation to cinema. Recognizing *huandeng* and cinema as equally useful tools of propaganda, the second author also points out two unique advantages of *huandeng*: its timeliness and ability to adapt to local audiences (cinema, by implication, is limited by its long production cycle and standardization). Unlike the first author, who considers cinema as a more complex and evolved form than *huandeng*, it was the second approach, which viewed *huandeng* as a separate medium with distinct functions, that would become more dominant in film exhibition in the following years.

How slide projection technologies continued to shape culture, politics, and education in the twentieth century is a topic that has received little scholarly attention. In Western contexts, more attention has been paid to the magic lantern from the disciplines of visual studies, Victorian studies, art education, childhood studies, and film and media studies. Most of this research concentrates on the period from the late nineteenth century to the early twentieth century, when a full-blown media culture had developed around the lantern, a culture that also nourished the initial development of cinema.[16] Although scholars like Ine van Dooren have tried to dispel the myth that cinema more or less replaced the lantern, there is limited research into the continuing evolution of projection technologies and how they were used in different contexts from the 1910s onward.[17] The neglect of a long "middle" period between the early twentieth century and the arrival of digital technologies can be illustrated by Jennifer F. Eisenhauer's study of discourses surrounding slide projection technologies in art education. Having demonstrated how the shift from magical to scientific conceptions of the lantern lent the medium to the emerging discipline of art history in the late nineteenth century, Eisenhauer immediately shifts to the early twenty-first century and argues that digital projection technologies like PowerPoint bring into education a corporate visual epistemology of persuasion, management, and entertainment.[18] The missing "middle" period is left unexplored also because of the minor status of slide projection compared to other education technologies. Historians have investigated the roles played by film, radio, television, and computers in the American classroom more extensively, whereas slide projection technologies tend to either receive brief mentions or be subsumed under the notion of visual instruction.[19]

Similarly, scholarship on slide projection in China and Sinophone areas is sporadic and centers on the magic lantern. Research published in English has focused on a few historical moments and cases, such as Chinese pastor and educator Yen Yung Kiung's 1885 lantern show "A Tour Round the World," the use of lantern slides as visual aids in lectures by the Shanghai YMCA, and magic lantern shows in colonial Taiwan.[20] Among PRC scholars, Sun Qing traces the many different Chinese translations of magic lantern from the late seventeenth century to the early twentieth century and investigates archival materials to document diverse uses of the lantern in entertainment, religious, and educational contexts.[21] Influenced by new film history and media archeology, Tang Hongfeng is interested in understanding the intertwining relations between film and magic lantern in turn-of-the-century China. She emphasizes the shared exhibition apparatus and virtuality (*xuni*) of the two mediums. To early Chinese film audiences, Tang observes, the experience of watching projected moving images was very similar to the experience of attending a magic lantern show.[22] Lantern projection also appears in historical scholarship of audiovisual education. It is shown that Western missionaries not only laid down some of the groundwork for audiovisual education in China but were also the first to recognize the educational potential of the lantern both in their writings and through their practices.[23] Most of these studies, however, do not go beyond the first two decades of the twentieth century. It may be tempting to assume that once film became the more popular medium, slide projection lost much of its appeal as a unique visual medium.

This may have been true in the entertainment world, but in the field of mass education, an interest in slide projection persisted. Martin Loiperdinger observes that in Western countries the use of slides and films began to separate after World War I: "The educations sector preferred slides to films, whereas in the entertainment business of commercial cinemas the use of slides became more or less limited to announcements and local adverts."[24] Although more research is needed to determine the exact usages of slide projection in commercial settings during the Republican period, the general trend was similar in China.

Two articles from the 1930s can illustrate how educators perceived the unique advantages of slide projection in mass education before 1949.

In a 1930 issue of the journal *Education and the Masses* (*Jiaoyu yu minzhong*), an author named Li Qiongzhi penned a detailed introduction of why and how to use slide projection in the pedagogy of mass education. A central principle of mass education, Li explains, is efficiency, that one should be able to invest the least amount of funds, labor, and time to achieve maximum effect. Slide projection fulfills this principle, as it can project words or images to a large audience of a hundred to three hundred people at the same time. It is particularly suitable for places of dense population, such as in factories and in the military, but if the audience size is small, it is not as economical. Li instructs readers on the mechanism of *huandeng* and methods of operation. It is mentioned that educators could purchase slide projectors from organizations like the Shanghai Youths Society (*Shanghai qingnian hui*) and the Beiping Association of Mass Education (*Beiping pingjiao zonghui*), as well as individual makers (someone named Lu Wanrong is mentioned). Their projectors range from 5 to 85 yuan, with varying degrees of complexity, but all of them share the use of convex lenses and a light source. Li then gives detailed instructions on how to organize a slide lecture and even offers a sample lesson plan for a Chinese literacy class. Compared to traditional pedagogy that relied on textbooks, Li summarizes, pedagogy with slide projection has many merits: it can spark students' interest, hold their attention, make it easier to illustrate ideas and memorize knowledge, and, most important for him, allow the lecturer to address a large audience, which is particularly desirable for educating the Chinese population, the majority of which remained illiterate.[25]

Some of the same points made by Li were reiterated two years later in a journal dedicated to the education of peasants. In addition to confirming *huandeng's* potential mass appeal, Jin Liangbi, a regular contributor to the journal, emphasizes two more advantages. First, Jin compares *huandeng* with other educational technologies, including film, specimen, models, pictures, and texts. A film projector is expensive, cumbersome, difficult to transport, and complicated to operate. The other tools can be rigid and dull. A slide projector, on the other hand, is cheaper, easier to carry and operate. Moreover, slides can be easily made as demanded. As Jin instructs, one only needs a few things to make slides—a glass cutter, a pen, ink, a ruler, a sample slide, and other pictures for reference. As for the glass needed to make slides, one can use any kind of ordinary glass or remnants from doors, windows, and household items. This is not only more economical than purchasing slides from professional makers, thus particularly suited for mass education agencies that have limited funds; making one's own slides also allows more variety and freedom.[26]

Written to persuade and provide guidance to other educators, these two articles allude to a situation in which the pedagogical use of slide projection was not yet widespread, thus giving rise to the need to promote this particular medium on the basis of its economic efficiency, portability, and adaptability. These were characteristics that would later be encapsulated in a common nickname people had for slide projection: "*tu*-cinema" (*tu dianying*). The Chinese character *tu* has been translated as "indigenous," "native," "rustic," or "crude." *Tu* contrasts with *yang*, which means "foreign" or "Western." Sigrid Schmalzer has suggested that in Mao-era scientific discourse, the *tu-yang* binary was central in articulating the vision of a socialist science produced by the people with more emphasis given to *tu* and its associated values of self-reliance, mass mobilization, and practical application.[27] The notion of "*tu*-cinema" affirmed similar qualities for slide projection. But in this case, slide projection was not opposed to cinema through the terms of "Chinese vs. non-Chinese" but as a medium that could be made locally and employed locally, unlike cinema, which required institutional and infrastructural support on a national scale and addressed a national audience.

THE VICISSITUDES OF *TU*-CINEMA

The evolving relationship between slide projection and cinema in socialist film exhibition can be examined through the changing weight assigned to the *tu* aspects of slide projection. To put it simply, the more the *tu* aspects of slide projection were celebrated the more importance was given to slide projection over the showing of films. In the early '50s, when little attention was paid to the *tu* potential of slide projection, it more or less remained a supplement to the screening of feature films, sharing similar status as other activities that may be included in the "pre-screening propaganda" portion of a screening. The PLA reportedly invented the three-part screening procedure that would become a standard among exhibition workers: in addition to pre-screening propaganda, projectionists were instructed to lecture during screening (*yingjian chahua*) and organize post-screening discussion (*yinghou taolun*).[28]

Pre-screening propaganda typically involved three kinds of content: the propagation of policies and political campaigns, the dissemination of scientific or practical knowledge, and the introduction of the feature film to be screened. Sources from the early-to-mid '50s show the use of *huandeng* being discussed mainly in the context of the first and third categories. For example, a 1952 work report by the Shanghai Movie Theater Guild mentions that in the process of reforming existing movie theaters in Shanghai, slides were shown to make announcements on behalf of government agencies.[29] Around the same time, contributors to *Mass Cinema* discussed ways to introduce a film before the screening. A projectionist from the PLA shared the experience of replacing plot sheets (*shuomingshu*) with slides: as the former was costly and time-consuming to reproduce, they began to copy excerpts from plot sheets onto slides, which would be shown and read to the audience before screenings. The slides not only fulfilled the same function as plot sheets; but since they were read out loud, they also helped those who could not read to understand the films.[30] But not everyone found slide projection to be the most efficient way to introduce films. Another contributor, also an exhibition worker, found playing recordings to be a better solution since recordings were less complicated to make and could be easily reused.[31]

Toward the second half of the 1950s, the use of *huandeng* in pre-screening propaganda became more stabilized, while the balance between political propaganda and introduction of the main feature film tilted slightly more toward the latter. A representative document from this period is a guideline issued by the Guangdong Provincial Cultural Bureau on propaganda work by rural film projection teams. The guideline specifies that for film projection teams, propaganda work should mainly center on the promotion and explanation of film content, on the basis of which they should conduct appropriate propaganda work with regard to the "central tasks" of a given period. Accordingly, the guideline offers a formula for pre-screening propaganda, which includes the following steps that should be completed within forty minutes: playing music records, oral performance or announcements by local leadership, and two kinds of slideshows. The first kind of slideshow focuses on "central tasks," major national events, and local news. As preparation, a projection team is expected to either gather slides from relevant authorities or make their slides based on their own research in the local area. This part should usually feature no more than fifteen slides. Afterward, projectionists are supposed to use slides to introduce the feature film. The guideline instructs projectionists to prepare and design these slides with reference to local events and make sure to show images of film characters so as to strengthen audiences' impressions.[32]

What can be inferred from the guideline is that projection teams were expected to devote a significant amount of their time researching and preparing their own slides. Meanwhile, slides produced by professional art workers were also available. The Beijing Slides Manufacturing Factory (*Beijing huandeng zhipian chang*), for example, was reformulated from the former Central Manufacturer of Tools for Audiovisual Education (*Dianhua jiaoyu gongju zhizao suo*) in 1951.[33] By 1958, it had published slide sets in a variety of subjects, such as science and technology, biography, classic stories, children's stories, and news, including popular titles such as "Dong Cunrui," "Liang Shanbo and Zhu Yingtai," "Give Everything to the Party," "An Outline for Agricultural Development," and a children's story called "A Smart Monkey."[34] Slides such as these would be purchased by government and educational entities. Among others, the China Artists Association (*zhongguo meishujia xiehui*) and People's Fine Arts Press (*renmin meishu chubanshe*) both had slide projection units that toured the countryside.[35] Institutions from children's palaces in urban areas and agricultural cooperatives in the countryside were also reported to use slideshows for educational or recreational purposes.[36] However, although the sales of professionally manufactured slides were growing in the '50s, according to a 1956 article from the *Fine Arts* (*Meishu*) journal, they were not meeting demands. The author of the article notes that there has been resistance to the slide medium among art workers: some people think it is an outdated art form that would be replaced by film; others disdain it for being a popular, lowbrow form similar to serial picture books and New Year pictures. The article urges artists to overcome these obstacles to produce more slides, as slides are well liked by the people as an educational tool and an attractive entertainment.[37]

Another article published in the same journal in 1958 further articulates the merits of *huandeng*:

> Slides and film each have unique features. The advantages of slides cannot be replaced by film. *Huandeng* is portable, convenient, more adaptable to audience demands. One can lecture in different ways for audiences of different levels and needs. If the audience still does not understand after going through a slide once, one can go over it one more time. When necessary, the projection unit can design and draw slides to serve political tasks in a timely way. Building slide projectors does not cost much, and they are easy to operate. Rural governments, factories, and schools have the conditions

to build their own. For example, among the 132 slide projectors in Xiyang County, Shanxi Province, 80 percent are made by people at the village or township level.[38]

Like Republican-era educators, this author recognizes the unique advantages of *huandeng*, particularly the flexible pace it offers instructors and the ease with which one can make both slides and slide projectors manually—the "*tu*" qualities. The low output of slides by professional manufacturers is again noted, but is it a true impediment if slides can be easily made and can address local needs better when they are self-made?

This grassroots, do-it-yourself, "*tu*" ethos became the driving force behind developments in the 1960s when slide projection temporarily occupied the center stage in film exhibition, taking up the bulk of projection teams' daily work to the extent that some teams devoted themselves entirely to slideshows. Reaching a high point around the years 1964 and 1965, the elevated status of *huandeng* was associated with several new developments, including the foregrounding of slide projection as a local communal medium, the movement to build triple-lens slide projectors, and the emergence of regional slide showcases and competitions.

These trends can be illustrated with the case of Jiangjin County, Sichuan Province. According to Liu Guangyu, although slide projection had already appeared in Jiangjin county in the 1950s, it did not thrive until the Socialist Education Movement (*shehuizhuyi jiaoyu yundong*), a campaign to fight against capitalist tendencies, launched in 1963. With intensified need for propaganda, the movement led projection teams— seven in the county at the moment—to shift the focus of film exhibition from screening films to directly propagating political messages, a task that fell heavily on slide projection. During this period, county projection teams created more than thirty sets of slides that instructed peasants on local history and the importance of class struggle.[39] However, although the Socialist Education Movement pushed a turn toward slide projection, Liu discovers that as a whole, there were more slides of content closely related to the daily life and agricultural production of the local communities. Many slides promoted admirable deeds by real people. For instance, a 1961 work report mentions slides that praised one man for plowing five *mu* of land (about seven thousand square feet) a day. In Degan Commune, a film projection team held recurring slideshows of commune news, which, by 1965, had run for four years with thirty-two installments. Members of the commune were quoted saying that "it is more exciting to watch commune news than watching films" or "I have watched the film already, and I bought the ticket just to watch commune news." These slideshows thus constituted what Liu describes as "news that belong to the people." In addition, projectionists also used slide projection to provide peasants with weather forecast and agrarian knowledge, offering practical guidance such as what to plant and how.[40]

Liu speculates that the reasons why slide projection could be diverted onto local topics were because of both projectionists' inability to handle abstract political rhetoric and the need to communicate to a peasant audience.[41] It can be further argued that the realization of slide projection as a communal medium was predisposed by its *tu* qualities. Since slides could be made by projectionists themselves, they were less restrained by propaganda demands from above, thus acquiring a degree of freedom outside of state control. Slide projection may also be seen as performing the function of local broadcast media. The Chinese television industry was in its nascence in the 1960s. It was not until 1958 that the first television station in China—Beijing Television Station— was established. Until after the Cultural Revolution, television was basically nonexistent in the Chinese countryside.[42] Bao has suggested that film exhibition during the War of Resistance against Japan aspired to achieve the speed and coverage of broadcast media through mobile projection in conjunction with other media.[43] Socialist film exhibition was similar. But more precisely, as the case of Jiangjin County demonstrates, it was slide projection, which could more easily respond to current events and local needs than films, that brought "film exhibition" closer to television.

While slide projection became embedded in local communities, its lack of movement was increasingly perceived as a limitation. Many film projection teams thus turned to the triple-lens projector, which was believed to be a more engaging and effective propaganda tool, as it could produce movement and other special effects. From the beginning, the popularization of this coveted object was built on "*tu*" ideals of self-reliance and grassroots initiatives. Almost all the archival sources I have encountered talk about how projection teams built or modified projectors themselves. In Jiangjin county, projectionists were sent to a different county to learn the construction of triple-lens projectors. In 1965, they managed to modify one two-lens projector and seven three-lens projectors in two months.[44] Similar efforts can also be found in Yongcheng County, Henan Province. As the county gazetteer documents, a projectionist named Lü Zichen was credited for modifying the first three-lens projector in 1964. In the 1970s, the county promoted the use of double-lens projectors, which were all locally designed and manufactured.[45]

In the midst of grassroots enthusiasm and technological innovation, regional showcases and competitions further fueled investment in slide projection. The archival sources that Liu Guangyu has found suggest that in Sichuan Province, there were competitions organized at the provincial, regional, and county level.[46] A slide program created at the grassroots level could work its way up these competitions and even get attention at the national level. In the case of Yongcheng County, in 1965, the slide performance of their Number One Film Projection Team entered competitions first in the Shangqiu region and then in Henan Province. In May, the team was selected to perform at a five-province showcase organized by the CCP South-Central Bureau in the city of Guangzhou in conjunction with a conference on rural film exhibition and slide projection. At the conference, the first secretary of the CCP South-Central Bureau, Tao Zhu, instructed propaganda departments at all government levels to strengthen the development of slide pro-jection.[47] According to *Yongcheng Gazetteer* (*Yongcheng xianzhi*), Tao Zhu met with the Number One Film Projection Team; the photo of this meeting was published by a local magazine. Later, the team continued to tour the country. In June and September, it traveled to Beijing twice to perform for the Ministry of Culture and the China Film Corpora-tion. During its second stay in Beijing, the projection team performed a slideshow called *Bad Wolf Li Laoyao* (*E lang Li Laoyao*) seventeen times for government ministries. Peng Zhen (1902–1997), the mayor of Beijing at the time, also attended their performance and met with the projectionists.[48]

Although a more comprehensive history of slide projection in China is yet to be written, these scattered records offer a glimpse into the pres-tige enjoyed by slide projection in the mid-1960s. However, this peak moment did not last long. In *Yongcheng Gazetteer*, which was pub-lished in 1991, only two more activities are mentioned in the *huandeng* chapter: in 1972, projection teams from several other provinces came to Yongcheng to study the construction and operation of triple-lens pro-jectors; in 1982, Yongcheng's Number Three Projection Team partici-pated in a joint performance in Hebei Province, showcasing several sets of slides on the topic of family planning, which were to be adapted into a TV program by the Shangqiu Television Station.[49] If slide projection was used to present local news, then it is not surprising that as television became more available, slide projection became obsolete. In an issue of *Film Popularization* from 1983, an employee of the Zhuzhou County (Hunan Province) branch of the China Film Corporation called for relevant agencies to manufacture more portable slide projectors because most rural projection teams in the area no longer had slide projectors.[50] However, judging by the rare frequency with which *huandeng* was mentioned in the journal in the next few years, the wish of this reader was likely not granted.

PERFORMING "PRE-SCREENING PROPAGANDA"

It can be misleading to separate slide projection from the projectionist's live performance during film exhibition. In fact, slide projection was already intermedial, as the projected images were always accompanied by the vocal and bodily performance of a lecturer, who not only controlled the narrative and pace of the presentation but could play a decisive role in how audiences experienced the images emotionally. Charles Musser's emphasis on screen practices as what provided continuity between early cinema and magic lantern shows offers one way to recognize the importance of the lecturer's presentation strategies.[51] The connection between performance and spectatorship can also be illustrated by magic lantern shows in late nineteenth-century Japan. According to Ryo Okubo, there existed two popular forms of lantern shows from the 1870s to the 1890s—educational lantern shows and shows about the First Sino-Japanese War (1894–1895). In the first case, audiences were expected to sit silently while an instructor stood beside the screen, explaining slides and directing audience attention with a pointer. In the second case, by contrast, a narrator called *benshi* would intentionally excite the spectators with skillful performance, as a result of which spectators would shout, clap, sing, and turn the occasion into a public airing of patriotic sentiments.[52] In this case, it was the *benshi* rather than the slides themselves that was the focus of the lantern show. As an attraction in themselves, *benshi* performances would continue to become a staple of Japanese movie theaters until the 1930s, long after live narrators disappeared in other early cinemas.[53]

There is no evidence suggesting Chinese projectionists of the socialist era were explicitly given the task of arousing audience emotions through slide projection. Rather, their role was seen more in terms of provoking audience interest and providing information. For this purpose, projectionists advocated accompanying slide projection with a simple and lively style of speech or traditional oral forms. An actor, for instance, urged projectionists not to read from a script, since it would deprive the narration of authentic emotions. They should instead speak in a way that is "clear, smooth, natural, vivid, and with feelings."[54] Speaking from experience, Qian Zhengzhuan, a projectionist from Jiangsu Province, emphasized avoiding formulaic language in introducing characters and plots.[55] He gave an example of how his team introduced the film *Undying Fire* (*Pu bu mie de huoyan*, 1956) during "pre-screening propaganda." While a slide of the protagonist Jiang San was projected, the projectionists performed rhymed clapper talk:

> Dear audience please be quiet. Let me tell you what this film is about.
> Once there was an anti-Japanese hero named Jiang San, who was the
> bravest and the best shot.
> First an Eighth-Route Army soldier, then a leader of guerrilla war
> fighters,
> All the devils and traitors were afraid of him while the people called him
> a hero.

As a result of these combined methods, Qian reported, "everyone paid full attention, and at the end of the introduction, they were able to grasp the plot, the characters, as well as the film's educational value."[56]

Clapper talk and other folk forms were also stand-alone performances that could be incorporated into film exhibition. Situated in the tradition of CCP propaganda and education, such incorporations built upon earlier multimedia practices. As David Holm observes, as early as during the Northern Expedition (1926), the Red Army of the CCP was already employing a wide range of propaganda mediums, such as pictorial magazines, cartoons, revolutionary songs, propaganda leaflets, public announcements, declarations, wall newspapers, and costumed propaganda—many of which originated from the Soviet Union.[57] In the 1930s and '40s, party propagandists began to pay more attention to folk cultural forms as the need to communicate effectively with the peasantry became urgent. Among regional operas, songs, and oral performance traditions, the *yangge* opera and dance from Northern China became perhaps the most successful, giving rise to influential revolutionary performances like *The White-Haired Girl* (*Baimaonü*), which was later adapted into a film and a ballet opera.[58] During the same period, the party also engaged in what was known as worker-peasant education (*gongnong jiaoyu*), which would provide the model for peasant education in the early years of the PRC. As Glen Peterson notes, by 1949 the

CCP had already developed a wide range of popular educational techniques, including lectures, opera, and traditional storytelling.[59]

Once "pre-screening propaganda" became formalized as a part of film exhibition in the early '50s, the intertwined traditions of employing folk forms for political communication and mass education of the CCP, as well as the audiovisual education practices led by the Guomindang, could be seen transplanted into film exhibition. For many projectionists, this meant that they needed to acquire new performance skills. Liu Guangyu has found an archival source that describes the challenges facing the Number One Film Projection Team of Jiangjin County in the late 1950s. Initially, none of the three projectionists of the team was prepared for "doing propaganda work": one of them only had a primary school education; one was trained as an electrician, with no experience in writing or singing; one could sing but was very shy. But they worked hard to train themselves in the arts of lyric writing and calligraphy. Eventually they were able to use more than fifteen folk and traditional operatic forms in their propaganda activities.[60] Projection teams also invited local opera troupes to perform at screenings. Such was the case of two projection teams from Jiading County, Jiangsu Province. In order to promote state monopoly over the purchase of grain, these teams reportedly adopted a variety of strategies. In addition to showing newsreel films, exhibiting comics, posters, and banners, and projecting slides, they invited amateur troupes to perform political scripts accompanied by local operatic tunes.[61] In the example I give at the beginning of this chapter, the modern pedagogical method of demonstration was combined with clapper talk for the purpose of practical science education. In all these cases, the projectionists were essentially grassroots innovators, improvising according to a functional approach to traditional oral media.

THE ART OF LECTURING

Following "pre-screening propaganda," rural film projectionists were expected to accompany screenings with the practice of lecturing. Film lecturers or narrators were regular presences in early cinemas. In Europe and America, lecturers initially supplied contexts and explanations during screenings to help audiences appreciate the new medium; they were typically associated with genres like travelogues, scenics, topicals, and actualities.[62] Around 1908–09, with the rise of fictional narrative films, the lecturer's role, as Tom Gunning points out, changed into one that "consisted in aiding spectator comprehension of, and involvement with, the more complex stories."[63] For Miriam Hansen, the lecturer of this moment was ambiguously situated in a transitional period. While there was a move toward narrative absorption and a more middle-class mode of reception, the lecturer remained outside the diegesis, thus maintaining connections with an earlier mode of exhibition where non-filmic activities, such as live acts and music performances, were very much integral to the "show." Rather than a part of the mass distribution strategy of national production and distribution companies, the presence of the lecturer suggested local variability, which, for Hansen, was closely related to the potential of early cinema to be an alternative public sphere.[64]

When cinema was first introduced into China, it also depended on lecturers to cultivate a new audience. Since foreign films dominated the Chinese market, major responsibilities of Chinese lecturers included translating intertitles, explaining stories, and supplying background information on foreign cultures. According to Zhen Zhang, it was very likely that in their attempt to accommodate local audiences, much of what the lecturers said actually deviated significantly from what was "intended" by the images.[65] The effort to localize an imported medium can also be seen as lecturers appropriated the performance style of the traditional storyteller. They were reported to use stock descriptions, questions that intensified audience anticipation, and sometimes exclamations to punctuate key scenes.[66]

If early Chinese film lecturers, like their Western counterparts, contributed to local variances in film reception through their oral performances, their reincarnation after 1949 in the figure of the mobile film projectionist was premised on different concerns. Although projectionists had to respond to local conditions and the needs of particular audiences, their lecturing was motivated by a need to control the reception process and to reduce unpredictability. A prevalent view in the early PRC years was that film was too difficult for rural audiences to understand. It was reported that peasants complained that images moved too fast and that they could not keep up with what characters were saying.[67] For dialect speakers and ethnic minority audiences, the standard Putonghua constituted another barrier for comprehension. The authorities were also concerned that audiences could not interpret films properly. One problem that film projection teams working in the suburbs of Shanghai noticed was that children had trouble telling the different armies apart when watching war films. They applauded even when the enemy (the Japanese, the Guomindang, etc.) was winning.[68] The first goal of *jieshuo*, as the guideline by Guangdong Provincial Cultural Bureau stated, was to "help the audience better understand difficult shots and film plots."[69] In this sense, *jieshuo* was essential for the goal of making culture more accessible for rural audiences. Urban audiences were considered more sophisticated and therefore did not need such assistance. At the same time, *jieshuo* served the purpose of political education. "It should guide peasants to reflect on the reality of their consciousness with the help of film stories so that they can receive profound education through these films."[70] In other words, beyond understanding film plots, projectionists were in charge of connecting the audience to larger political discourses that may not have been obvious otherwise. They were required to constantly study party policies and stay in touch with local authorities—both were sources substantiating their interpretative authority.

These goals translated into a style of lecturing that focused on interpreting signs, both linguistic and cinematic ones. Projectionists sometimes needed to read aloud written words appearing in films for audiences presumed to be illiterate. In the film *Li Shuangshuang* (1962), for instance, there is a scene showing the character Xiwang returning home and seeing a note left for him on the door. At this moment, the Fourth Film Projection Teams of Hai'an County, Jiangsu Province, would explain that the note was written by his wife, Li Shuangshuang. It tells him that the key was left at the usual place, their daughter is with her aunt, and that he should heat up the stove once he is home.[71] Projectionists could assume the role of an interpreter between native tongues and the national language, sometimes narrating entire films in a different language. Film projection teams in Yanbian Autonomous County, Liaoning Province, for example, were applauded in *People's Daily* for narrating films in Korean.[72] In other cases, it was not the dialect but the nature of discourse that caused confusion. The reception of science education films, in particular, depended on projectionists to translate formal, scholarly expressions into vernaculars that were familiar to rural audiences. Projectionists were also expected to explain cinematic techniques such as flashbacks, dream sequences, and symbolic images so that meaning became transparent. When a shot of ocean waves appears in the film *Stories of the Southern Island* (*Nandao fengyun*, 1955), Qian Zhengzhuan and his team would insert a comment that said: "In the surging tide one wave chases another; like the tide, our army is winning one victory after another!"[73]

Compared to interpreting films, what was trickier was to make connections between diegetic events on screen and political campaigns, policies, and important party affairs. Selecting appropriate films to facilitate campaigns was already a common practice in the early 1950s. By 1954, the Jiangsu Provincial Cultural Bureau was well acquainted with the challenges of politicizing lecturing. In a work report, they specify two problems:

> One is only paying attention to the promotion of the films without using films to facilitate various "central tasks" in the countryside today. As a result, a few projection teams became indifferent to important events in the world, showing films in isolation. Another problem is neglecting the content of films. They forget that the propagation of central tasks should be built on the explanation of films; instead, they make forced connections between policies and films that are not relevant at all, doing great harms to the themes and artistic qualities of the films.[74]

In other words, it was considered problematic to either ignore the task of propagating "central tasks" or distorting the interpretation of a film to suit propaganda. The ideal situation was when a film and politics could be integrated seamlessly.

A good example was provided by the Fourth Projection Team of Hai'an County, which was tasked with showing *Li Shuanghuang* in December 1962. County officials had suggested that the current focus of work was to cultivate a collectivist spirit among peasants so that they could participate actively in building the economy of communes. The film, as projection workers saw it, showed the conflict between the more selfless and socialist-minded Li Shuanghuang and other peasants, including her husband Xiwang, who were more concerned with personal gains than collective interest. Therefore, when commenting on the film during screenings, the projectionists put emphasis on praising the good deeds of Li Shuanghuang and criticizing others' selfish thoughts and behaviors. When Li finds out that her husband and two other characters, Sun You and Jin Qiao, have tried to make economic gains for themselves, she goes to the village party secretary to report them. At this point, the projectionist would say, "disregarding Xiwang's objection, the selfless Li Shuangshuang is determined to let the party secretary know that Sun You and Jin Qiao have earned work points in an opportunistic way."[75]

The projectionist's lecturing thus shifted the locus of meaning from film to verbal discourse. Visual signs, such as the image of ocean tides, were inherently polysemic and open to interpretation. By helping audiences understand films, the projectionist effectually eliminated alternative interpretive possibilities and sought to ensure the production of socialist subjectivity. The attempt to control reception is heightened in the case of *Tunnel Warfare* (*Didao zhan*, 1965), a fictional film showing how peasants in Northern China fought Japanese armies with underground tunnels under the leadership of the CCP. The film itself already features an authoritative voice-over that situates events in relation to historical context and political discourse, but projection teams wrote scripts to supply even more lecturing during screening. In a transitional sequence in the film that is almost one minute long, the voice-over narration poses the question of how to continue guerrilla warfare in the aftermath of Japanese occupation. According to a lecturing script published in *Film Projection*, the projectionist is supposed to follow the narration with more reiteration of the importance of persistence in the war against Japan, referencing Mao's *On Protracted War* (*Lun chijiuzhan*) a work that is seen being read by multiple characters in the film.[76] In this case, the lecturing doubles down on the didacticism already embedded in the film, seeking to ensure that no audience would miss the message that is made increasingly blatant through the combination of the diegetic story, the voice-over narration, and the projectionist's lecturing.

A paradox thus emerges once we expand our focus from the exhibition of film to film exhibition as a multimedia institution of audiovisual education. While cinema enjoyed the privilege as "the most important of all arts," in practice, the ways in which film exhibition was organized in the socialist system indicated something else, that cinema was not enough, at least not for the purpose of political communication. The deployment of slide projection, folk performance, and lecturing each hinted at an inadequacy of cinema—its inability to respond to local events, its foreignness for rural audiences, and its density and uncertainty as a semiotic system. These limitations were openly acknowledged when exhibition literature repeatedly called for supplementation and provided abundant details elaborating the extra-cinematic techniques of exhibition. There seemed to be a subconscious unease for the projectionists to just be projectionists. At least on paper, both administrators and the projectionists themselves insisted on expanding the complexity of their labor, their visibility, and thus their vital role as the lynchpin of a system of multimedia interfaces.

In retrospect, however, audiences' memories tend to tell different stories. Neither my interviews nor publicly available testimonies indicate much impression of projectionists speaking during screenings beyond making announcements at the beginning. Could it be that projectionists decided to make their jobs easier by not lecturing? Perhaps the audiences had trouble hearing their speech due to poor sound amplification? Is it possible that the lecturing blended into the films so well or that it became so routine that it did not attract attention? The answer probably varied case by case. Nevertheless, the retrospective silencing of the projectionist may be read as an indication that despite efforts to control the moviegoing process, audiences might well have experienced films, and retained selective memory of their experiences, on their own terms. I myself know this firsthand: I watched *Tunnel Warfare* multiple times on TV as a kid, but when I re-watched the film again for research several years ago, I was utterly surprised to hear the voice-over narration and the narrator's didactic tone. In my memory, *Tunnel Warfare* was a fun film in which characters jumped out of kitchen stoves. If my childhood self naturally gravitated toward elements of play in a highly didactic film, it seems entirely possible that projectionists' teaching would fall on inattentive ears.

CHAPTER 4

Atmosphere

To commemorate the sixtieth anniversary of the Cannes Film Festival in 2007, renowned film directors from around the world contributed three-minute short films to an anthology film called *To Each His Own Cinema* (*Chacun son cinema: Une déclaration d'amour au grand écran*, 2007). Among the thirty-six contributors, two were from China: Zhang Yimou and Chen Kaige. Both filmmakers initially made their names in the global film festival circuits in the 1980s and continue to be two of the most famous and commercially successful Chinese directors working today. The anthology was supposed to pay tribute to the motion picture theater—"that magical venue of communication par excellence of film lovers the world over."[1] But neither Zhang nor Chen set their shorts in a movie theater; instead, both depict scenes that fall outside the original premise of the collective project but would be familiar to many Chinese moviegoers, namely, open-air cinema (*lutian dianying*).

Likely mirroring their own experiences watching films in their youths (Zhang was born in 1950, Chen 1952), both directors adopt a child's perspective. Zhang's film "Movie Night" follows a young boy from the moment when he enthusiastically welcomes the arrival of a film projection team to him falling asleep in a chair while the film continues to play on the portable screen. In about three minutes, the film presents many elements that are frequently seen in nostalgic discourses of open-cinema, such as the excitement that permeates the village when a mobile projection team arrives, the outdoor setting, the practice of arriving much in advance to "save seat" (*zhanzuo*), the fascination with technological artifacts (Zhang lavishes close-ups on the projector mimicking children's curious gaze), the projection of hand shadows before the film starts, and the overall joyous, festival atmosphere that puts a big smile on everyone's face.

Painting such a warm, rosy picture, Zhang joins many others in the commemoration of open-air cinema. In two popular films directed by Jiang Wen, *In the Heat of the Sun* (*Yangguang canlan de rizi*, 1994) and *The Sun Also Rises* (*Taiyang zhaochang shengqi*, 2007), open-air cinema is shown as an important part of collective culture during the Cultural Revolution. In a 1995 folk song titled "Open-Air Cinema" (*Lutian dianyingyuan*), singer-songwriter Yu Dong laments that "there are no longer open-air cinemas in the city. . . . When watching movies, one can no longer see stars." "Open-Air Cinema" (*Lutian dianying*) is also the title of a personal essay written by famous novelist Su Tong, known for novels like *Wives and Concubines* (*Qiqie chengqun*) and *Rice* (*Mi*), in which he remembers what it was like attending screenings at a threshing floor two hours' walk from his home. Television shows like *Childhood Flashback* try to cement open-air cinema in the collective memory of several generations of viewers. One can also find numerous articles and blog posts commemorating open-air cinema as "the memory of an era."

If Zhang Yimou offers a typical memory of open-air cinema, Chen Kaige's contribution "Zhuxin Village" comes closer to revealing its secret charm. In comparison, Chen's setting looks decidedly artificial, which largely removes local surroundings to foreground the screening situation itself—consisting of a screen, several rows of wooden benches, and the projecting equipment. Set in 1977, the film shows a group of young boys projecting Charlie Chaplin's *The Circus* (1928) for themselves. Soon after the film begins, the power generator fails, upon which the boys decide to power the projector by connecting it to their bicycles. As they pedal, the film continues. The convergence of rapid motions on and off screen makes the young projectionists/spectators burst into laughter until a grownup comes over scolding the kids for turning on the projector on their own. Everybody immediately runs away except for one boy, who has been seen as the only one sitting on a bench while others pedal their bicycles. The grownup comes over, waves his hands in front of the boy's face. Only then a realization would dawn on the less perceptive viewer that this boy is, in fact, blind. "May I finish watching the film?" he asks.

What exactly is he "watching"? Even though the silent film appears to be accompanied by a score, he cannot possibly *see* what makes others laugh—Chaplin's famous slapstick performance. But the reason that viewers can be fooled for a couple of minutes to not suspect this boy's blindness is because he displays a semblance of perception. Prior to the moment of revelation, the boy has his face angled up toward the direction of the screen with a look of rapt attention. He smiles when the other boys laugh. Through the prothesis of blindness, Chen thus confronts viewers with a powerful paradox: we know that the boy is blind, but how come he appears to be "seeing"?

What needs to be rethought, Chen's film thus implies, is what it means to "watch a film" in the first place. If we bracket the usual object of attention—that is, the film on screen—there are, in fact, many things we may reasonably expect the blind boy to perceive and feel during the screening: the cold evening air touching his face (the boys wear thick winter clothes), the hard surface of the bench, the hustle and bustle of the other friends, noises of the celluloid film running through the projector, and the heat emanating from machines and other bodies. While such interactions with the surroundings and other viewers are always present in collective viewing situations, they are rarely discussed as integral to cinematic experience proper. This case, where a blind boy enjoys a silent film in an open-air screening, urges us to reexamine our assumptions and directs attention to other ways viewers interface with cinema beyond the visual.

One dimension of cinematic experience, which open-air cinema particularly foregrounds, is the "air," or the overall atmosphere of an exhibition space that engages viewers through multiple senses. To make sense of nostalgic memories of socialist open-air screenings in post-socialist China, it is necessary to investigate what I will call "atmospheric spectatorship," a mode of cinematic experience that does not necessarily privilege the film as an object of attention but is characterized by presence in an experiential milieu that surrounds the viewer. In the movie theater, which has defined cinematic experience in much of film studies, the atmospheric is often downplayed or carefully controlled to enable concentrated viewing. By contrast, characterized by proximity to everyday space and porous boundaries, open-air screenings in socialist China tended to disrupt attention toward the films on screen and encourage a more holistic experience of environment, nature, community, crowds, and rituals, in addition to the cinematic. Out of the commingling of all these elements, a unique atmosphere of open-air cinema then emerged and became an object of nostalgia against the postsocialist environment of commercial entertainment epitomized by the multiplex. While socialist film exhibition was intentionally shaped into a system of multimedia interfaces that interpellated socialist subjects, as I turn to audiences' testimonies in the second half of the book, it will become clear that audiences always engaged with recalcitrant material interfaces like weather, the screen (as a physical object), and their own bodies that resisted or escaped ideological control. Even though audiences themselves were rarely subversive, their experiences and memories call for analytical categories beyond the familiar terms of propaganda, education, and subject formation.

OPEN-AIR CINEMA: A FORGOTTEN HISTORY

Although open-air cinema was made widely popular in socialist China, its history goes back to the very first years of motion pictures. Outside of China, open-air cinema began with the earliest display of cinema in traveling shows in the 1890s, which took place in both indoor and outdoor venues (parks, fair grounds, and street carnivals). As cinema moved into fixed exhibition sites, the open-air theater provided one destination alongside single-purpose movie theaters such as the nickelodeon and later the movie palace.[2] As a fixed screening venue, an open-air theater was similar to a movie theater in many ways except for being outdoor and often seasonal. Opened in 1916, Sun Pictures, an open-air cinema in Western Australia, is recorded as the world's oldest operating open-air cinema.[3] In America, the drive-in theater, which first emerged in the 1930s and enjoyed its heyday after World War II, constituted a unique kind of open-air cinema, which, by confining moviegoers to the inside of their cars, created its own distinct viewing situation. In Europe, a famous example of fixed-location open-air cinemas is the summer outdoor screenings in Athens, Greece. Located on rooftops, terraces, enclosed courtyards, and gardens, these so-called "cinemas under the stars" were already popular before World War II. In the 1960s, they numbered more than six hundred. With still more than ninety operating on a regular summer night in 2015, these Athenian open-air cinemas are now packaged as tourist attractions.[4] Moreover, open-air screenings were deployed together with mobile film projection to serve the goals of state propaganda and mass mobilization, which was the case during both world wars and in former socialist countries.[5] In the former British Empire, the British Film Unit (1939–1955) held mobile, open-air screenings as a way to instruct colonial citizens and legitimize the work of the colonial government.[6] In these arrangements, the mobility of film projection was more sought after than the open-air setting, which was frequently a necessary accommodation to allow cinema to enter new territories.

Similar configurations of fixed and mobile open-air screenings, including both commercial and political uses of cinema, can be found in China. As Chinese researchers document, the earliest instances of film exhibition in China were often open-air screenings, which took place in ad hoc spaces such as parks, temples, churches, train stations, and markets. The first film screenings in several provinces, including Sichuan, Yunnan, Jilin, Anhui, and Guizhou, took place outdoors.[7] In Shanghai, rooftop amusement gardens on top of department stores were among the first venues to exhibit films alongside a variety of indigenous and exotic entertainment options.[8] At least fifteen outdoor cinemas operated in Shanghai between 1908 and 1949.[9] In the early 1940s, a ban on air-conditioning is said to have made outdoor screening especially popular in the hot summer months.[10] Parallel to commercial operations, mobile open-air cinema was welcomed by both educators and state actors as a pedagogical tool. As discussed in previous chapters, many institutions such as Jinling University, the Zhenjiang Mass Education Center, and the Political Department of GMD's Military Committee had organized mobile open-air screenings prior to and during World War II.

Yet it was not until after 1949 that open-air screenings truly became everyday occurrences throughout China. While the PRC state's effort to rapidly cinefy the country led to an unprecedented deployment of cinema's mobility, open-air cinema presented a quick solution to the insufficiency of cinematic infrastructure nationwide. Since open-air screenings were usually free or of little cost to attendees, they also embodied the pursuit of a socialist mass culture that emphasized access. It is hard to trace the precise evolution of open-air screenings in the PRC as official statistics only keep exhibition records by types of projection units: theater, mobile projection team, or film club. But based on available documents and audience recollection, it is reasonable to estimate that open-air screenings made up the largest portion of all film screenings in China from the 1950s to at least the early '80s, when there was a push to improve viewing conditions in the countryside by building township cinemas. From the mid-1980s onward, overall film attendance in China entered a period of decline, exacerbated by market forces, the spreading of television and VHS tapes. A short film called *Open-Air Cinema*

(*Lutian dianying*, 2016, dir. Jiang Chao) captures these changes. When the film begins in 1986, an open-air screening is shown attracting a full crowd. As it cuts to the year 1997, we see that only a few people show up to a screening, and yet the projectionist insists on finishing showing the film until the last audience member leaves. In 1998, the State Administration for Radio, Film, and Television and the Ministry of Culture initiated a new program to deliver film to the countryside, known as "Project 2131." Today open-air screenings continue to be held with state subsidies and logistical support through this program, but their cultural influence is marginal in an overwhelmingly commercial film industry which derives most of its box office from urban multiplexes.[11]

In a nutshell, rather than an isolated phenomenon under Chinese socialism, open-air cinema is nothing short of a global paradigm that can be found in many places over time. However, although there have been some historical and theoretical discussions of open-air cinema in Chinese scholarship, there has been no in-depth study in English that examines how cinematic experience is shaped by outdoor film exhibition.[12] This neglect is not accidental, but due to what I will refer to as the theater bias in film studies. To appreciate the divergence of open-air cinema from what is usually taken as the norm, it is important to first recognize how ideas of spectatorship and cinematic experience have been dominated by the movie theater.

"THAT MAGICAL VENUE"

A recent example of the theater bias can be found in Julian Hanich's 2018 book *The Audience Effect: On the Collective Cinema Experience*, in which he expounds on the impact of collective viewing on individual experience. At the outset of his argument, Hanich locates an encounter with cinema in the movie theater: "When we go to the cinema we always arrive with a bag filled with expectations. Not only do we expect to follow an uninterrupted projection of a film in a dark space; we also expect to cross a threshold into a public auditorium separated from the outside world, a space with specific behavioral rules in which we encounter other people."[13] Aware of his potential bias, Hanich adds a footnote explaining that this description represents an "ahistorical prototype from which historically and culturally specific instances deviate."[14] Though the footnote relativizes the singular certainty of the main text to a certain degree, it nonetheless perpetuates an undeniable hierarchy: whereas the theater/cinema is considered ahistorical or transhistorical, prototypical, classic, and standard, characterized by uninterrupted projection, dark space, and separation from the outside world, other exhibition situations become "deviations." This division perfectly captures the problematic way in which film exhibition has been conceived in film studies.

As it has been widely criticized, psychoanalytical and apparatus theories, which ushered in film studies as an academic discipline in the 1970s, were blind to historical specificity as they strived for ontologies of cinema. But it is not that the spatiality, physicality, and sociality of the moviegoing experiences are denied in the accounts of Jean-Louis Baudry or Christian Metz, as Robert C Allen suggests.[15] Baudry, for instance, describes the theater space in great detail:

> No doubt the darkened room and the screen bordered with black like a letter of condolences already present privileged conditions of effectiveness—no exchange, no circulation, no communication with any outside. Projection and reflection take place in a closed space and those who remain there, whether they know it or not (but they do not), find themselves chained, captured, or captivated. . . . The arrangement of the different elements—projector, darkened hall, screen—in addition to reproducing in a striking way the mise-en-scène of Plato's cave (prototypical set for all transcendence and the topological model of idealism), reconstructs the situation necessary to the release of the 'mirror stage' discovered by Lacan.[16]

The two classic metaphors of cinema—theater as Plato's cave, screen as mirror—are in fact derived from careful empirical observation of the *dispositif* of the movie theater. What goes wrong from here is that a particular historical configuration of cinema is treated as cinema itself, foreclosing other possible exhibition arrangements and spectatorial positions. This need for singular ontology becomes especially pronounced when scholars compare film to other communication media. Sandy Flitterman-Lewis, for example, describes film and television in unambiguously opposing terms assuming that film belongs to the theater and television to the home (table 2). Published in 1987, Flitterman-Lewis's comparison betrays a certainty that is simply no longer possible in our current days of online streaming when both film and television are consumed in more ways than ever before.[17]

But cinema's "deviation" from the movie theater did not begin recently. Following the "historical turn," film scholars have directed attention to many "deviations" that go back to the earliest years of cinema. It has been shown that film was exhibited in a wide variety of venues before it found home in the movie theater. Most of these venues—such

TABLE 2 SANDY FLITTERMAN-LEWIS'S COMPARISON BETWEEN FILM
AND TELEVISION

	Film	Television
Space	Large, silent, darkened theater; cocoon-like enveloping situation	At home, familiar space, casual
Distance	Beyond our reach ("we go to the cinema")	Nearby, intimate
Temporality	There and then	Here and now
Attention	Sustained and concentrated gaze	Glance, intermittent attention
Spectatorship	Hypnotic fascination	Partial, dispersed identification

SOURCE: Flitterman-Lewis, "Psychoanalysis, Film, and Television."

as vaudeville theaters, penny arcades, fairgrounds, amusement parks, dime museums, and tea houses—were preexisting entertainment venues into which the showing of film needed to be integrated.[18] The ways in which early cinema addressed viewers and organized screenings were also distinct: rather than favoring quiet, concentrated viewing in a dark space, what Tom Gunning and André Gaudreault call "cinema of attractions" presented viewers with disjointed, self-conscious spectacles.[19] During the era of classical cinema (circa 1917–1960), the movie theater was consolidated as the primary exhibition site in America and Europe, but as recent scholarship demonstrates, films continued to be shown at "alternative" venues, such as drive-in theaters, museums, schools, factories, community centers, and domestic spaces.[20]

What historical research also shows is that the concept of the movie theater needs to be further differentiated. The luxurious downtown cinema palace is not the same as the nickelodeon that provided cheap, neighborhood entertainment, nor does its evocation of dream and exoticism continue to be relevant to the now standard multiplex that sells films like goods in a store.[21] The Indian cinema hall, with its culture of active audience participation and rowdy atmosphere, presents yet another variation.[22] Hanich's "ahistorical prototype" thus describes an imagined space. When we try to apply such a description to specific types of theaters, we are bound to run into difficulties. For example, Hanich speaks of a threshold that separates a public auditorium from the outside world. Where exactly is this threshold in a movie palace, where visitors are transported to exotic places by the heavily ornamented façade, foyer, and lobby even before entering the auditorium? What about the concession stand as well as the surrounding shopping mall of the mall multiplex, which integrates, rather than separates, moviegoing from a larger commercial milieu? There are no clear-cut answers.

However, despite "the historical turn" and the diversity of exhibition practices scholars have discovered, I agree with Charles Acland that "theatrical celluloid projections tenaciously reside in the scholarly imagination as part of a foundational definition of cinema, making extra-theatrical screens always appear to be second-best options or curiosity venues."[23] A consequence of this hierarchical thinking is that while "deviations" are sometimes acknowledged, they tend to disappear when a general understanding of cinema, or a discussion of medium specificity, is attempted. In other words, while non-theatrical venues can be studied specifically, the movie theater occupies the theoretical space of cinema itself.

The extent that the theater is taken as the model may be illustrated by Francesco Casetti's imagination of the cinema to come. Casetti identifies two paths of relocation for cinema. In the first path, what makes an experience cinematic is an environment analogous to the movie theater. Such is the case of the home theater, wherein the wide screen, the isolation from the outside, and the dim lighting all evoke a visit to the theater. In the second path, what is being relocated is the film itself which can be transferred from the big theater screen to other delivery systems from DVDs and online streaming sites to in-flight entertainment systems. Casetti claims that cinema, in this case, is a matter of "what to see, independently of how to see." However, his description of a hypothetical train passenger watching a movie on their DVD player betrays the lingering influence of the theatrical model:

I must modify the environment, in order to be able to watch a film. The acts I can perform are minimal, but useful: I stretch out on my seat, I draw closer to the screen so that it takes up a large part of my visual field, I raise the sound on my headphones so it is louder than the background noise, I minimise what is going on around me. The effect is the creation of a space all my own, in which there is only room for the film I am watching, and in which the flow of the external world seems suspended. It is an imaginary space, however, an *existential bubble* in which I take refuge because I want to, not a ready-made physical place in which I can take my seat, as the theatre is. . . . Naturally, this personal construct proves to be fragile and temporary: all that is needed is for the conductor to ask me for my ticket, or the people next to me to raise their voices, or for the train to simply arrive at my station for my bubble to dissolve. The experience, dependent on the film object and no longer supported by the environment, all of a sudden pales: I am no longer able to feel I am a spectator; I am once again just a traveler.[24]

What this passage offers is a step-by-step account of how the passenger tries to mimic the conditions of a movie theater. Whether by making the screen larger or turning up the volume, what this passenger hopes to achieve is a similar isolation from the outside world so that they can concentrate on watching the film. The choice of "bubble" as a spatial metaphor is telling: the bubble has an inside and an outside. There cannot be a middle ground, a blurring of the threshold, as the separation is its very raison d'être. Casetti's conceptualization of the space of personal screens as an "existential bubble" thus presupposes enclosure as a precondition of cinema. But why can't I be a spectator and a traveler at the same time, sharing attention between my screen and people around me?

In order to move beyond the theater bias, we must stop looking at instances that do not conform to mainstream practices in America and Western Europe as "deviations." "Deviations" can be left out of film ontologies. They are footnotes added for comprehensiveness. But these different variations of cinema have equal rights to participate in the definition of cinema just as the more dominant model. Indeed, they are more valuable precisely because they stretch our imagination of what cinema can be.

CINEMA AS ATMOSPHERE

Among the modes of exhibition that have been neglected due to the theater bias, open-air cinema is one of the most prominent. Not only because it has a long history and has attracted billions of audiences, but also because it highlights possibilities of cinema that are usually suppressed in a theatrical setting. Open-air cinema encourages a mode of experience that is best described as atmospheric. The meaning of the English word *atmosphere*, as Paul Roquet points out, originally referred to the layer of air surrounding the earth; it has only been expanded since the eighteenth century to mean "subjectively felt feeling and tone of a place."[25] The most common Chinese word for atmosphere, *qifen*, was used as early as the Western Han dynasty (206 BC–9 AD) to refer to clouds that could divine fortune.[26] By the early twentieth-century, its meaning had become aligned with the European notion of atmosphere. By atmospheric spectatorship, I refer to a mode of cinematic experience in which what is prominent is not the film being watched, but viewers' interaction with the overall exhibition environment.

Environment has emerged as a key word in recent media studies: studies of media infrastructure have highlighted the material, environmental consequences of media; there is a growing interest in environmental mediums such as light and fog; philosophically, scholars like John Durham Peters challenge us to rethink media as environment, and environment as media.[27] In film studies, Casetti has called for a rethinking of cinema as environmental medium to replace older approaches to cinema that emphasize the visual.[28] Weihong Bao also applies an environmental model of medium to her analysis of Chinese cinema in the early twentieth century. She coins the term *affective medium* to foreground the ability of media technologies to generate mediating environments in which affect connects the media product and the perceptual subject. As an affective medium, cinema literally touches and moves the spectator, engendering social space of shared affect (emotions, desires, physiological responses, sensations, etc.) in both commercial and political contexts.[29] Bao's analysis, however, is largely limited to the affective power of film texts, leaving open the question of how the spectator's body is also "touched" by the surrounding environment of exhibition. This environment not only conditions audience reception of films but always conjures up an atmosphere that is a consequence of, but more than, the totality of its discrete parts.

In a basic sense, since encounters with cinema must take place in some kind of environment, an atmospheric component is inherent in film spectatorship. The movie palace, with its elaborate décor, exotic design, and plush interiors, encouraged moviegoers to notice and take pleasure in the atmosphere of luxury and fantasy. Even if it was only for a brief moment before the light dimmed to draw audiences' attention to the screen, there is no denying that the experience of atmosphere was anticipated in the design of the movie palace. The multiplex appears to focus moviegoers' attention on the films by eliminating "distracting" architectural details, but there is still an atmosphere conjured up by the concession stand, the smell of popcorn, the pre-show commercials, and the sound of neighbors sipping soda. It is a casual and relaxing atmosphere that is expected to be pleasurable for moviegoers regardless of what movies are shown. In fact, movies may be defined by their compatibility with such an atmosphere. Such is the case of so-called "popcorn movies." In the popular parlance of film criticism, popcorn movies are characterized more by how they can enhance the atmosphere of fun and relaxing leisure consumption than by narrative conventions whereby genres are traditionally defined.[30]

Incidentally, the rise of the multiplex in America and Western Europe since the 1960s coincided with the popularization of ambient media in post-industrial societies. As Roquet argues, since the pioneering work of British musician Brian Eno, ambient media have been employed as "tools of atmospheric self-mediation."[31] Personal use of ambient music or videos, he argues, constitutes a form of mood regulation and self-care in the face of neoliberalism's impossible demands of self-determination.[32] Cinema is not immune to ambience. Not only has ambience found its way into film aesthetics (an example Roquet examines is Ichikawa Jun's 2004 film *Tony Takitani*), one can also find instances where cinema is intentionally employed to set the atmosphere of a public place. For example, the cinematic atmosphere is a main attraction of the San Francisco restaurant Foreign Cinema, which occupies the former site of a movie theater. Since 1999, Foreign Cinema has been projecting films onto a backwall in its courtyard at dinnertime. Its unique atmospheric usage of cinema can be observed in the somewhat contradictory logic of its exhibition. The restaurant appears to put much care into curating its films: the program changes about once a month; upcoming films are listed on the restaurant website with basic production details and short synopses.[33] But the films are projected with no sound, serving as quiet background to dinner conversations, shying away from attention. Another example where cinema is used as background to other activities is SLEEPINCINEMAHOTEL, an experimental project designed by the renowned Thai director Apichatpong Weerasethakul for the Forty-Seventh International Film Festival Rotterdam in early 2018. Weerasethakul created a pop-up hotel where guests could fall asleep while hypnogogic images play nonstop on a large screen. Whereas falling asleep during screenings is a common and yet usually undesirable incident (it means either the film fails to engage us or our own "missing out"), here the moving images serve the need to sleep so that they might enable what Weerasethakul hoped to be a kind of unconscious collective cinema of the mind.[34]

POROUS BOUNDARIES AND CINEMA OPENED UP

In this wider context of film exhibition, open-air cinema is not alone in its capacity to create atmospheric experience. But distinguished from both the movie theater, where conditions encourage attention to the screen, and ambient uses of cinema that completely relegate the moving images to the backdrop, open-air cinema occupies a middle ground. At open-air screenings, audiences come to watch films (rather than to dine or to fall asleep), but often end up experiencing the atmosphere more than the films. This is a result of the particular exhibition environment of open-air cinema characterized by openness and contingency.

As cinema ridded itself of the confines of an enclosed, theatrical space, one of the first changes was that it could be brought into the proximity of everyday space. A trip to the movie theater or the multiplex means leaving behind the everyday life world and entering a specialized, seg-regated, commercial space that some describe in terms of the Foucaul-dian heterotopia.[35] Socially, as Miriam Ross notes, the stadium seating, large screens, and the state of darkness at movie theaters encourage an individualistic and stationary experience.[36] Community exhibition, by contrast, lends itself to more interaction among audience members who are already coworkers, classmates, relatives, neighbors, and acquain-tances. Spatially, since open-air cinema does not occupy a segregated space carefully designed for a single purpose, it is opened up to the surrounding area and to the flow of everyday life. As Larkin observes, "open-air showings prevent the isolation of the cinema from the sur-rounding area and indeed the surrounding area has to be understood as part of the cinematic space itself."[37] Airscreen, a Germany-based com-pany that sells inflatable movie screens for outdoor screenings, actively promotes their products by emphasizing the ability of open-air cinema to be part of a larger environment, which is seen as its unique attraction. A press release of the company states that "the world can provide the perfect backdrop to your film. . . . There are no limits to the backdrops to an open-air cinema."[38] The spectator's sensory field is thus enlarged at open-air screenings. In addition to the screen, the spectator might see stars, trees, the moon, shapes of houses (figure 9). They might hear the chirping of birds and cicadas, and feel the temperature drop as the screening goes on into the night.

Another way to appreciate the openness of open-air cinema is to look at its porous boundaries. For Casetti, whenever a spectator pays attention to a screen, an existential bubble forms around them, creating an enclo-sure. Once one stops paying attention to the screen, the bubble bursts and one is no longer a spectator. Open-air cinema challenges this "either-or" scenario and defies enclosure. One viewer from Sichuan Province, Mrs. Cai (b. 1949), used to attend open-air screenings organized by her production brigade in the early 1960s. She recalls that screenings drew large crowds. As a result, "there were so many people I couldn't even see the screen. I also could not read. So, all I saw was people flickering across the screen."[39] Another viewer from Beijing (b. 1955) was sent down to a rural suburb of the city to be reeducated as a *zhiqing* in the early 1970s.

FIGURE 9. A scene of open-air cinema. He Shiyao, "Fangying dianying fengshou zhihou" [Showing the film *After the Harvest*], photograph, *Renmin huabao* [China pictorial] 11 (1965): 20.

There were film screenings in the village, but her memory is limited: "With so many peasants it was chaotic. I couldn't hear anything. Therefore, I don't have any impression of what movies were shown when I was in the countryside."[40] Were these two viewers, unable to see or hear the films clearly, inside or outside the bubble? Both of them lacked a meaningful engagement with the films. But can we say that they were not spectators? Even if they did not experience the films, what is undeniable is that they experienced cinema in a specific configuration. Not being able to see or hear clearly was precisely what constituted their experience of open-air cinema, which was also marked by the presence of crowds and noises. Because open-air screenings often extended in space without clearly defined borders, what these two viewers describe was not uncommon. And depending on one's eyesight, hearing range, and height, the same distance to the screen could also entail very different experiences for the viewer, making it impossible to draw a line separating the exhibition space from its surroundings.

The fluidity of boundaries was also embodied in the ease with which audiences could come and go. Since most open-air screenings in China after 1949 did not sell tickets to individuals but were paid for in advance with a fixed rental fee, the outer edge of a screening area could become quite busy. Mr. Zou (b. 1942) was an overseas returnee that came back to China in 1955 at the age of thirteen. After he became a high school teacher at an "overseas Chinese farm" (*huaqiao nongchang*) in Guangdong Province in 1961, he would attend open-air screenings with peasants from nearby areas. He noticed that while many would come with their own camping stools, there were also people who would arrive mid-screening on their bicycles, stop for a moment to check out the film, and then peddle away.[41] Viewers could chat while paying only occasional attention to the screen. Mrs. Zhou (b. 1949), a self-proclaimed film enthusiast from Beijing, was sent to the countryside as a *zhiqing* in the early 1970s. In her new habitat, she found most of the films shown at open-air screenings to be old, familiar ones that she had already watched:

We usually felt, "What boring movies are these?" But if you didn't watch them, there wasn't anything to do. So we would still watch. I would stand in the back. If I got tired, I would find a place to rest. Sometimes we ended up chatting in the back, quite casually, and we weren't necessarily looking at the movies. If there were too many people in the front [of the screen], we would go to the back to watch in reverse. It was very casual. . . . We watched whatever was available. Anyways they always showed those old and cheesy ones, whether or not you watched them. Would you rather sleep instead? Film screenings were not that common, perhaps only two or three times a year. Would you give up the opportunity when there was finally a screening? I don't think so.[42]

As her description "casual" (*suiyi*) indicates, the peripheries of open-air screenings offered attendees a great degree of freedom. While there could be viewers trying hard to see what was unfolding on screen, next to them, others could be crossing back and forth between watching the film and chatting with friends with little effort. One can of course try their best to concentrate attention on the film in open-air screenings, mimicking the theatrical conditions through subjective efforts—there were indeed reports that audiences were so engrossed that they would not leave even when it started to rain.[43] But it is the co-presence of the "outside" world in the spectator's sensory field and their activities that makes open-air cinema a unique paradigm.

Along with the porous exhibition space, open-air cinema introduces a variety of contingent factors that might interrupt viewing. It should be noted that in post-49 China, open-air screenings were commonly conducted with single 16 mm film projectors. For a feature-length film, the projectionist had to change film reels multiple times during a screening, which resulted in short intermissions that projectionists were supposed to fill with commentary. Interruption was therefore built into the premise of 16 mm film projection. In addition, the outdoor setting of open-air cinema presents many natural elements—wind, humidity, rain, heat, bugs—that may affect the performance of the projection apparatus. Mobile projection teams had to deal with more potential harms to the equipment as they traveled in remote places, their only measure of protection being their bodies (chapter 2). Consequently, technical malfunction was common. Incidents such as those involving power generator failures and "mute" or unclear images were reported and lamented in trade journals and government documents. Audiences, too, became vulnerable to contingencies. If the movie theater offered a comfortable, safe space where audiences were protected from nature, open-air cinema exposed them to nature's unpredictable "dark" forces. As a result, bodily discomfort became a shared experience (see chapter 5). Audiences could also be forced to leave in the middle of a screening due to terrible weather conditions. As Ma Weidu (b. 1955), a famous art connoisseur, recalls:

> There were two things that we feared about open-air cinema: one was wind and the other was rain. If it was just a breeze in the summer or autumn, it was still pleasant. But a strong gust of wind of level four or five could turn the screen into a monster that kept sticking out and sucking in its belly. The heroes on screen would look like they were limping, laughing and then immediately crying. Whatever the film was, it became a comedy. If it drizzled, everybody would endure through it. Those who brought raincoats would put them on; others would run back home to get them—home was only a few steps away. If you held an umbrella you had to stand in the back, otherwise you would be scolded for blocking the view.

Everyone who has attended open-air screenings has come across summer thunderstorms. When a new film got to an interesting place and then a thunderstorm unexpectedly arrived, the projectionist would definitely stay till the last minute. Only when raindrops became so dense that a sheet of water appeared in the light beam shooting out of the projector would everyone rush to leave.[44]

In this description, the wind and the rain, which are examples of what John Durham Peters calls elemental media, become part of the mediating environment of open-air cinema. Blowing on the screen, the wind not only threatens to damage the screen as a material object but also transforms the film on screen. In his essay on open-air cinema, Su Tong describes the effect of strong wind as a prank, which could make every character's mouth askew, regardless of whether they were men, women, heroes, or villains.[45] The comical effect caused by a flailing screen reveals that the seemingly immaterial illusion of the cinematic image is in fact deeply indebted to its infrastructural support. Whereas the wind reorients audiences' perception of the filmic text, the rain is described as having the power to reorganize audiences' behaviors, making them perform various actions and eventually terminating the screening. Peters has advocated for an expanded conception of media that not only describes cultural and technological formations but also includes nature. For Peters, natural elements such as sea, air, and fire are media in the sense that they constitute enabling environments that make our existence possible and give it form. He calls media as such "infrastructure of being."[46] What Ma Weidu demonstrates in this passage is that open-air cinema allows for the merging of cultural and natural media. Together, they form a mediating environment that shapes into being a memorable experience in which the filmic object, which is usually the center of attention, is subsumed by the environment.

In short, due to the open, porous, and unpredictable environment, concentrated, uninterrupted viewing is simply difficult to achieve in an outdoor setting. Movie theaters minimize distractions so that the spectator's sensorium can be cleansed and then be filled by the film. By contrast, open-air cinema magnifies sensory inputs beyond the film. Nature, the exposed screening apparatus, and the community audience all produce sights, sounds, smells, and sensations that amount to an immersive atmosphere that surrounds the spectator. The mode of experience in such an environment can be described as *presence*. Presence is different from what Casetti calls attendance. In attendance, the experience of a place (the movie theater) and the social situation of collective viewing converge to activate a gaze (including a capacity to listen). What is important, Casetti emphasizes, is that "one exposes oneself to film, that one concentrates upon it and follows its unfolding."[47] Presence should also be distinguished from distracted or diverted viewing, which still privileges the film as the central object from which the spectator's attention is distracted. Rather, being present in an environment is to have an all-around sensory and affective experience of an atmosphere. Presence does not take objects, let alone privilege one object (the film) among others out of the enveloping surroundings. When we think about moviegoing as presence, we zoom out from the screen to consider viewers' embodied interaction with the entire surroundings of which the film may constitute a big or small part.

The following paragraph describing Athenian open-air cinemas offers an excellent illustration of presence:

> Athenian summer cinemas bring back unforgettable memories of summer nights surrounded by potted plants and their aromas, gravel under the feet of the audience, limelights and water fountains. Occasionally a cat strolls in front of the movie screen and chases her shadow in the dark. Songs from loud speakers fill the gaps during the intermission while the canteen owner serves his customers and sometimes tries to sell his ware to the seated spectators by shouting "lemonádes" (lemonades). The ultimate freedom of outdoor smoking, the waning moon, the illuminated windows of the surrounding houses and apartments, the youngsters who watch free of charge from their balconies, a chance for them to watch "restricted" films without parental control. This unbelievable atmosphere became a song and escorted our happiest days.[48]

Films are a part of this overall picture, but there is so much more. The discrete elements listed by the author include sights, sounds, scents, and sensations; both the natural and the human; both the constant and the unpredictable, the near and the far. It is the intermingling of all these elements and the ways they speak to each other that make up an immersive atmosphere, an overall feeling that is beyond its constituent parts. In such a context, cinematic experience is most prominently defined by presence in the "unbelievable atmosphere" rather than by any individual films. Here, the Athenian open-air cinemas are further distinguished from the movie theater, particularly the multiplex, in two respects. If the movie theater represents a space that is artificially and commercially demarcated, carefully manipulated, and constantly disciplined, what is revealed in this passage is a space of transgression where the backdrop to the screenings expands to as far as the moon, and where animals and humans alike step outside their usual bounds (strolling around, smoking, watching "restricted" films from unauthorized spaces). Moreover, since open-air cinema has to be integrated into the local milieu, interacting with its climate, ecosystem, landscape, architecture, and social practices, it replaces the uniformity of the multiplex chains with unique local character. Hence, the uniqueness of Athenian open-air cinemas can be compellingly packaged as a commodity: you may watch a film anywhere, but you can only experience the "unbelievable atmosphere" of the "cinema under the stars" here in Athens.

KAN RENAO

In contrast to the Athenian case, the prevalence of open-air screenings in China after 1949 was primarily driven by the state mobilization of cinema as a tool of socialist propaganda and mass entertainment. For Li Daoxin, the close association between open-air cinema as a general paradigm and the state ideological apparatus is evidenced by the fact that open-air cinema became most prominent during war times (World Wars I and II) or in countries of high propaganda need.[49] But how would a mode of spectatorship that was predominantly atmospheric suit political purposes? How did open-air cinema subsequently become an object of nostalgia in China since the 1990s? In audiences' testimonies, one Chinese term that offers clues to these questions is *kan renao*, which alludes to how viewers themselves intuitively understood their spectatorship as atmospheric.

Renao and *kan renao* are common everyday expressions that are nonetheless difficult to translate. Literally meaning "hot and noisy," *renao* has been translated into English as "lively," "bustling," "exciting." But not only is the original meaning lost in such translations, the negative connotation of "hot and noisy" can also lead to misinterpretations of *renao* as "chaotic" and "problematic" when *renao* is in fact highly valued in Chinese culture.[50] Early usages of *renao* can be found in vernacular fictions dating back to the Yuan Dynasty (1271–1368) with two overlapping meanings: one described a state of interaction between people that was lively, loud, and probably filled with laughter; the other usage, which remains the most common today, concerned public places or events that bustled with noise, activity, and excitement due to the gathering of large crowds. Events, crowds, and noises are three elements considered necessary for a situation to be felt as *renao*.[51] Examples of typical *renao* scenes include temple fairs, festival celebrations, busy shopping districts, and parties. The Taiwanese night market has been studied as a site for the consumption of *renao*.[52] In a word, *renao* is about atmospheres. There is no equivalent of *renao* in English. Whereas English can describe discreet elements (noises, level of activity, etc.) that contribute to *renao*, it lacks a vocabulary for the atmosphere as a whole.

Kan means "to watch." If one stops to pay attention to a fight, an accident, or some sort of spectacle in the streets, one becomes a *renao* watcher. *Kan renao* is driven by curiosity but the term also implies a degree of nonchalance. The lack of empathy and care for the people being watched has led modern Chinese intellectuals, most notably Lu Xun (1881–1936), to criticize the onlooker mentality as a national flaw. By extension, *kan renao* is used to refer to the act of viewing without comprehending beyond what is immediately obvious as in the saying "*waihang kan renao* (the layman sees the *renao*—what is on the surface and the inessential), *neihang kan mendao* (the expert discerns the underlying principles)."

In my interviews with audience members, *renao* and *kan renao* are among the most repeated terms used to describe attitudes toward attending film screenings, especially open-air screenings. In one usage, *kan renao* indicates a desire to participate in *renao* occasions that were rare in everyday life. A Mr. Guo I interviewed at a village in the outskirts of Beijing was once a projectionist for his village (likely in the late '60s and '70s but he was not sure about the exact time period). When I asked whether he liked old revolutionary films, he gave a representative response: "Back then it was so boring in the countryside. There weren't many activities. You wouldn't go dancing or anything like people do nowadays. Watching movies was the entertainment. It was *renao* to watch. We also didn't have television. There was one television set that belonged to the collective. . . . When the production brigade announced that there would be movies today, we just would go. That was it."[53]

Because film screenings were relatively rare in the countryside, they often attracted large crowds, and thus became, first and foremost, occasions of *renao*. In this sense, the frame of *renao* could allow a new form of entertainment to be embedded in a much longer history of atmospheres. For a rural viewer, although the cinematic technology was novel, the atmosphere of *renao* was not. One important precedent to open-air cinema was village ritual operas. Staging opera performances to accompany religious festivals or the birthday celebrations of local patron deities has long been a tradition across rural China from the provinces of Shanxi in the north to Guangdong in the south.[54] On special days, opera troupes would be invited by prominent local families and stages would be set in or near temples. Spectacle was central to this ritual complex. According to Barbara Ward, who did fieldwork in a fishing village in Hong Kong, opera performance is supposed to bring "*wang*":

> The character *wang* . . . can be translated "busy, bustling, noisy, crowded" (all in a good sense); the same word used of business, or a fishing season, can mean "successful, prosperous." Theatrical performances draw crowds, and very lively colourful, holiday crowds they are too. The locality thus becomes *wang*—bustling—and everybody enjoys this as a value in itself; but (and this is the point) it also has a magical significance, for there is a hope that this kind of "*wang*-ness" will induce the other kind of "*wang*-ness" too, and so ensure good crops and fishing catches, prosperous business, financial gain, and so on.[55]

As an atmosphere, wang is very similar to *renao*.[56] Although the word *atmosphere* is missing in Ward's observation, what the *wang/renao* of the crowds generates is exactly an overall atmosphere of prosperity that envelopes and mediates all endeavors within that locality. After 1949, a large portion of rural ritual performances was suspended due to the party's official understanding of religion as superstition.[57] Cinema partly filled the void. Though not religious in itself, cinema could draw crowds and generate similar *renao/wang* as opera performances. The association between open-air cinema and ritual practices became full-blown in the 1980s. During this period, film screenings in front of temples were reportedly used by villagers in Guangdong as a less than ideal substitute for opera performances.[58] In Hubei Province, villagers invited projectionists to show films at a variety of special occasions, including birthdays, weddings, and funerals, a practice that gradually disappeared in the 1990s as ritual film screenings were replaced by music performances.[59]

Reminiscent of earlier ritual gatherings, the *renao* atmosphere of open-air cinema in socialist China, unsurprisingly, is also described in ritualistic terms. In audience testimonies, attending open-air cinema is repeatedly likened to celebrating a festival (*guojie*):

> At that time, watching movies was like a festival, a ritual to us. When you heard that there would be movies on Saturday, you'd feel excited the entire day. You'd feel every step was lighter when you walked to school in the morning. It was true! In the afternoon, you would bring your stool to save a spot. No matter how hot or cold it was, you'd go as early as you could. In the winter, I often sat there with thick cotton shoes, cotton hats, and a big cotton coat. When the film ended, I would go home shivering. It was a very special feeling. Before the film started, everyone played around, chasing

each other. When the projectionist tested equipment, as soon as light hit the screen, everybody would stick out their hands to make all kinds of shapes in the projection. You could say it was a goat or a dog. There were many kinds. This was an important activity too. We then watched films. A festival was complete.[60]

In this testimony by Jia Ding (b. 1960), a playwright who grew up in a military residential compound, open-air cinema is remembered as a ritualistic process, beginning with eager anticipation and complete with the film screening itself. In between, interactions among audience members, as well as between audiences and the apparatus, are described as integral components of the moviegoing ritual, contributing to a *renao* atmosphere that is lively and exciting.

In addition to expressing interest in *renao* atmospheres, *kan renao* also describes how viewers related to the films they watched:

At our age we didn't know much. It appeared no more than *kan renao*. It was fun. (Mr. Liao, b. 1939)

At that time, I was basically illiterate with no education, so I couldn't understand much. Besides, I was just a kid. So, I just went to *kan renao*. (Mr. Zhou, b. 1940)

I think I saw *Taking Hua Mountain by Strategy* (*Zhiqu huashan*, 1953). I remember a scene that shows soldiers climb on a very steep cliff. It looked so incredible at the time! But what would a kid know. It's enough to *kan renao*. (Mr. Chen, b. 1937)[61]

As these three interviewees try to recall experiences of attending open-air screenings as kids, their evocations of the term *kan renao* carry a clearly self-deprecating tone, which distinguishes them from viewers who can speak more enthusiastically and confidently about their love for cinema. Yet in their modesty, a distinct spectatorial orientation emerges, which was not determined by how films addressed viewers. Rather than seeing spectatorship as something predicated by the filmic text, Janet Staiger has argued for an approach that decouples the mode of reception from both the mode of exhibition and the mode of address. Every period of history, she emphasizes, may witness several different modes of reception, and a viewer may even engage in several modes of reception during the same moviegoing experience.[62] Although Chinese cinema after 1949 has been described as a classical cinema largely following the Hollywood model of storytelling with occasional didactic moments, audiences did not necessarily find themselves absorbed in narratives.[63] Rather, *kan renao* implies a lack of understanding of, or a lack of interest in, the narrative. By evoking this term, the three viewers thus position themselves as *"waihang"*—outsiders to cinema, although rather than seeing this as a "failure" on their part, they seem content with what they got out of the experience.

Kan renao further relieves the viewer of the burden of aesthetic evaluation. In the case of Mr. Chen, while he finds the cliff shot from *Taking Mount Hua by Strategy* so impressive that it is retained in his memory for more than half a century, he nonetheless tries to temper his enthusiasm by pointing out his limited frame of reference as a child. Through the vernacular language of *kan renao*, his self-representation in fact converges with a common observation made by film exhibition workers in the 1950s and '60s, that rural audiences preferred war films and opera films, genres that displayed more *renao* elements on screen.[64] Taking into consideration the environment of open-air screenings, it is reasonable to speculate that the appeal of these genres was not only a matter of taste, but also because they were more suitable for a *renao* atmosphere in which interruptions by nature, noise, and technical conditions were frequent. Under such circumstances, it would be unrealistic to expect audiences to sustain their attention throughout a feature film. Yet even if one had been distracted earlier or had trouble hearing dialogue, a spectacular fight scene could still be appreciated on its own, independent of narrative context. In the end, whether due to inability or unwillingness, the moviegoer as *renao* watcher is best described as an outsider who nonetheless enjoyed their presence at open-air screenings.

THE IDEOLOGICAL AMBIVALENCE OF *KAN RENAO*

Socialism, however, does not allow outsiders. In other forms of mass gatherings employed by the CCP, notably struggle meetings and speaking-bitterness sessions, cadres would deliberately arouse the crowd's emotions, encouraging and carefully orchestrating public expressions of indignation toward class enemies and counterrevolutionaries.[65] To distance oneself from collective sentiments or to appear unmoved when emotions soared was to risk being ostracized and become aligned with the enemy. Film screenings were not like these other political meetings as they fell in the category of state benefits and recreation. But in the overall structure of Maoist politics that acknowledged no middle ground between friends and foes, what did it mean to be an "outsider"—even just temporarily—at film screenings?

Kan renao cannot be easily placed in conceptual frameworks that distinguish different modes of spectatorship along the lines of passivity/activity, uniformity/heterogeneity, and conformity/subversion. A dominant view in film studies, as Hanich points out, assumes that unruly, expressive, active audiences are sites of resistance, whereas silence and immobility are signs of bourgeois oppression and discipline. In other words, by sitting quietly in a movie theater, the spectator relinquishes power to the film industry that controls and standardizes consumption. Hanich challenges this view by pointing out the false equivalence between outward audience activity and political potential: in quiet attentive viewing, he argues, audiences are still active and can engage in joint action; being expressive and diverted, on the other hand, can be a rule in some contexts to which audiences have to conform.[66] Hanich's schema, however, still has problem accounting for a mode of experience like *kan renao*, which may be quiet without being attentive, diverted without being expressive.

It is more productive if we compare the *renao* viewer with the ideal socialist film viewer—a figure that was concretized in Chinese media through personal accounts of moviegoing. In Tina Mai Chen's words, the ideal viewer was supposed to engage in a "mimetic model of spectatorship" in which identification with film characters would lead to a reformulation of identity.[67] In other words, the ideal viewer was someone who could be effectively positioned by the film text as a socialist subject. More than understanding films in a way that aligned with the dominant ideology, the ideal viewer was supposed to integrate lessons learned from films into daily activities. In a short article in *Mass Cinema*, for instance, the author, a worker named Sun Shungen, talked about how *Zhao Yiman*—a 1950 film about its eponymous heroine, a resistance fighter that was executed by the Japanese in 1935—changed him. The article is neatly divided into two paragraphs. In the first paragraph, the author describes his individualism prior to watching the film. Thinking only about his personal interest, he sometimes made up excuses to avoid doing work for the workers' union and easily got into arguments with coworkers. Even after being admonished by other workers, he could not discontinue his self-centered ways. Yet, as the second paragraph begins, the author says that he finally realized the problems with his previous thinking after watching *Zhao Yiman*. The sacrifice Zhao Yiman made for the Chinese people inspired him to be courageous and determined in the struggle against his own thought. Now he wants to emulate her revolutionary spirit and dedication to the people and become a good worker.[68] This short article situates film at a critical moment in the personal development of the viewer. It gives readers a sense of his personality and behaviors before the viewing and describes his thoughts regarding the film. What is not mentioned is the circumstances in which viewing happened: where and when it took place, what the physical space of the venue looked like, with whom, etc. The article inserts film text directly into the viewer's life through a two-paragraph structure that neatly depicts a "before" and an "after." The rich atmospheric experience of cinema disappears, as what matters is simply that moviegoing becomes a useful stop in a longer narrative of ideological growth. Active viewer participation is thus highly desired, but not during screenings. Emphasis was instead put on everyday political action in the aftermath of a filmic experience. The ideal viewer was supposed to internalize moral lessons and act in small ways that could nonetheless benefit the country.

In comparison, *kan renao* was definitely not ideal, but it also was not subversive. In one sense, being a *renao* viewer implied a degree of nonchalance—not an outright rejection of ideology, but mere disinterest or inability to comprehend, which made the viewer somewhat impenetrable. For this kind of audience member, films evoked neither desires to emulate heroic characters nor skepticism (both cases can be found among my interviewees). What happened was that films left little impact on them. A retired factory worker I interviewed claims that he used to go to the factory auditorium to watch films whenever films were shown (at least several times a week). But he added, "I did not save anything in my brain. When a movie was over, it was over."[69] Another interviewee, a college-educated geology researcher, had a similar attitude: "It was *renao* to watch *Guerrilla on the Railway* (*Tiedao youji dui*, 1956), since it was a war movie. Afterwards I just forgot about it."[70] Interestingly, since arts and literature were supposed to serve the people, such audience nonchalance was seldom the target of criticism. Rather, it was observed as symptomatic of failures of the film industry to appeal to audiences and engage their attention. Film exhibition circles put great emphasis on how to help audiences, especially rural audiences, understand films. As I show in chapter 3, film projectionists were supposed to perform the role of film lecturers, explaining film plots and morals to audiences. Whenever a problem of nonrecognition or incomprehension occurred—whether it was peasants complaining that images moved too fast or children applauded for the wrong side in a war film—it was the projectionist that was called on to play a more active role rather than the audience.[71]

Meanwhile, it was also possible that audiences attended screenings merely looking for *renao* but ended up learning from the films. As one retired middle school teacher comments, "Watching movies was for *kan renao*. Objectively, would you learn something as a result? Sometimes you felt inspired. But you wouldn't say that you went there for education on purpose. You watched movies to be entertained."[72] A Chinese phrase that captures this "unintended" consequence of moviegoing is *qianyi mohua*—exerting influence in subtle and imperceptible ways. That film can transform spectators unbeknown to them is not a new idea. In a 1924 article, for instance, Shen Enfu (1864–1944), an influential educator and advocate of film education, recognizes that the pedagogical function of cinema is first predicated upon it being a form of entertainment that can attract the masses.[73] Hence *kan renao* does not necessarily foreclose the possibility of a more meaningful engagement with the film text. Viewers might have been penetrated by socialist ideology, internalizing its terms while not paying active attention to "being educated." They might have been influenced by films to a greater degree than they themselves realize. *Kan renao* was thus an ambivalent gesture. It was not politically motivated but remained ideologically open. The fact that such an outlook was common among moviegoers indicates that film screenings, though explicitly serving the party's purpose for propaganda, could not close the room for experiences (not just alternative interpretations of films) that exceeded the expectations of the authorities.

"WE CAN NO LONGER SEE STARS"

Another implication of *kan renao* is that contemporary nostalgia toward socialist open-air cinema is frequently directed toward its atmosphere, rather than the films that were shown. This tendency partly explains why the beginning of economic reforms in the late 1970s does not register as a break in memory discourses of open-air cinema. As Chinese society opened up for more liberal policies and cultural practices, the 1980s saw the emergence of new film genres that were not permitted in the past, including "entertainment films" (*yule pian*), which was officially recognized as a genre in 1987.[74] Even in the early '80s, there were already widely popular films like the martial arts classic *Shaolin Temple* (*Shaolin si,* 1982), starring a fresh-faced Jet Li, which broke free of earlier constraints put on socialist cultural production. The availability of new film genres, however, did not necessarily alter the dynamics of open-air screenings, which, in retrospect, became associated with highly romanticized narratives of the socialist past. This past is imagined to be one devoid of political campaigns and propaganda, where human beings existed in harmony with nature and with each other in close-knit local communities.

As this audience member fondly recalls in an article:

> I remember in the countryside back then, people would run around letting everyone know that "the film projectionists are here! Let's all go tonight!" We would finish eating dinner early, and then went on the country lanes with grownups, holding flashlights under the stars. The children would be ecstatic; the parents chatted and laughed. The stars in the sky were especially bright. In summer, there were fireflies in the paddy field. Frogs and cicadas chirped on and off. This kind of *renao* not only provided us with hope and positive energy, but also let children experience an uplifting spirit. It let us feel not only neighborly love among friends and families, but also a greater, harmonious attachment to the native place.[75]

What is being remembered is the lyrical atmosphere that preceded the actual showing of films. Images of childhood, native place, starry night skies, and muddy country roads, as Liu Jian observes, have marked contemporary discourses of open-air cinema.[76] These elements are also evoked here, weaving a lovely picture in which the lights and sounds of nature blend in with laughter. There is, in fact, nothing in the passage that sounds particularly "socialist" if we understand socialism as a political ideology. For Dai Jinhua, postsocialist nostalgia can be considered a singular phenomenon regardless of its particular objects. Whether one is nostalgic for life under socialism, old Shanghai under semi-colonial rule, or a mythical, idyllic rural world, what is in common is that imagined past moments are constructed to soothe the pains of the present.[77] Market reforms have initiated profound changes in China. Amid overall progress, economic development and large-scale urbanization have caused social and spiritual problems from the disintegration of communities and the polarization of society, to widespread environmental and moral crises. Against this backdrop, open-air cinema provides a surprisingly potent image, allowing people, especially those who came of age in an age of drastic transitions, to articulate an imagined homeland characterized by harmony with nature, community, and festivity. Meanwhile, what is being erased in collective memory is the entire chapter of the rural township cinema. Eagerly promoted throughout most of the 1980s as an upgrade from open-air cinema, the township cinema was supposed to improve viewing conditions by allowing viewers to watch films indoor while seated. Ironically, what was seen as inferior is later remembered with nostalgia whereas township cinemas not only closed doors due to poor box office performance but were also erased from popular memory.

Nostalgic discourses of open-air cinema not only speak to the present consumer society in general but can be seen as reactions to a specific development—the rise of the multiplex. In the early 2000s, the state phased out its dysfunctional old film exhibition network with the new "theater circuit system," allowing commercial theater chains to acquire and distribute films according to market demands. This reform coincided with a real estate boom and the popularization of shopping malls, resulting in the rapid growth of multiplexes, which Yi Lu describes as "a state-led nationalized project of 'controlled commodification.'"[78] The impact of this development has increasingly been felt by the global film market. In 2017, China reportedly surpassed the United States to become the country with most film screens in the world. By the end of 2018, official statistics recorded a total number of 60,079 screens in the country, which was 3.6 times higher than in 2012.[79] As of 2020, the country is well on its way to become the world's largest film market.[80]

As news media and scholars take notice of these developments, a linear narrative is often adopted to describe the history of the Chinese film industry. The state-run Xinhua News Agency claims that "China's cultural industry has posted rapid growth since the founding of the People's Republic of China in 1949 with the number of film screens ranking first in the world."[81] The increasing theater attendance in China is enlisted by scholars to prove the continuing relevance of cinemagoing. Casetti writes: "Yet the cinema has certainly not died. Movie theaters, for example, not only continue to exist, but also are increasing in number. In 2012, theater screens multiplied by 5 percent worldwide, due to the double-digit *growth in the Asia Pacific market*, raising the total number to just under 130,000. In the same year, box office grosses rose by 6 percent, reaching $34.7 billion *with the help of increasing attendance in countries such as China, Brazil, and Russia*. Going to the cinema seems to be a firmly entrenched habit."[82] Casetti treats the fate of movie theaters across the globe as one, but the countries named as contributing most significantly to the increases in statistics—China, Brazil, and Russia—are all countries where cinema used to function primarily as a propaganda tool when the commercial movie sector was growing in the West. Casetti thus constructs a universal narrative by grafting divergent regional histories onto each other. What is ignored in the process is the particular historical trajectories in which the emergence of new theaters occurs. In China, the building of new theaters does not mean a previously existing cinema-going culture did not die. Although people did visit movie theaters, moviegoing took place in such different environments that it is safe to say that for older moviegoers, "going to the movies" in a mall multiplex nowadays entails a whole new set of practices that need to be learned. Moreover, what is disavowed by the circulating myth of continuing development is the astonishing records of moviegoing to be found before the wholesale marketization of cinema. In 2019, 1.727 billion movie tickets were sold in China, which was the highest in the world (1.239 billion were sold in North America in the same year).[83] What is less known is that, although attendance was in steady decline throughout the 1980s, between 1978 and 1987, national film admissions in China exceeded 20 billion every year, with 1979 holding the highest record of 29.3 billion.[84] While limited access to television and home videos partly explained the immense popularity of cinema during this period, what played a bigger role in producing such jaw-dropping numbers was the continuing expansion of the old socialist film exhibition system, in which open-air screenings organized by film projection teams attracted large crowds. This system, however, soon lost its appeal. Many regional distribution offices, theaters, and projection teams were shut down in the '90s due to financial difficulties. When the new theater circuit system was introduced, it took place at the end of a declining system that once had its glorious days. To portray the Chinese film market as one of linear growth was thus deeply misleading.

It is Chinese moviegoers that better register the sense of rupture. For older generations, the difference between "then" and "now" is acutely felt. They find going to the movies to be too expensive now and many new movies too alienating for their taste. In memory, open-air cinema easily codifies what is lacking in the new multiplex: the latter offers isolated viewing experience in a standardized, enclosed, commercial environment; open-air cinema returns viewers to a holistic state not yet disturbed by capitalist modernity. In the words of one film projectionist named Yang Shiming: "Although today's movie theaters are extravagant, they do not have the human flavor of open-air cinema. When everyone sits around and watches movies together, it is more enjoyable; the atmosphere is better."[85] The lyrics of Yu Dong's sentimental song "Open-air Cinema" also describe the present in terms of loss:

> There are no longer open-air cinemas in the city,
> I can no longer see the back side of the screen;
> Are you still playing the games from back then?
> When you watch films, you can no longer see stars . . .

With the disappearance of open-air cinema, the unique pleasures of watching films outdoors also vanished. Here Yu Dong mentions three distinguishing components of open-air screenings: watching from the back side of the screen, playing games, and seeing stars. While games are also tied up with childhood, the other two features were rooted in the *dispositif* of open-air cinema. As I will further discuss in chapter 6, watching from behind the film screen was a common practice that allowed viewers to get closer to the screen. And it was the openness of open-air cinema that afforded viewers sights of stars. The movie theater, by contrast, is seen as closing off these possibilities, thus causing melancholy and lament. In other words, Yu Dong's sentiment belongs to what Svetlana Boym calls reflective nostalgia, a longing for the past that fully recognizes that one can no longer return to the past.[86]

It was not coincidental, therefore, that both Zhang Yimou and Chen Kaige chose not to set their short film in a movie theater in *To Each His Own Cinema*; rather, it reflects the prevalence of open-air cinema in China over a period of more than forty years. Chen Kaige, in particular, draws our attention to the heart of the open-air cinematic experience. In his film, a blind boy attends the screening of a silent film. "What is he watching?" was the question I posed at the beginning of the chapter. We can now answer this question: he is not watching a film; he is experiencing the atmosphere of cinema. If there can be a love for cinema that does not necessarily involve particular films, it is to be found at open-air screenings. In a way, Chen Kaige presents the blind boy not as an actual spectator, but as a spectatorial position anticipated by open-air cinema. From this position, the viewer's *attendance* to film is impaired, but they are compensated by multisensory stimuli from all around them, which constitute their *presence* in an environment of *renao*.

Of course, neither concentrated viewing in a darkened theater or atmospheric spectatorship at open-air screenings is inherently superior to the other. They represent two possibilities of cinema. It is problematic, as I have critiqued, to privilege the theatrical model as what defines cinema. But we should also contextualize the nostalgia of Chinese audiences and avoid taking their praises of open-air cinema at face value. After all, not everyone would find the conditions of outdoor screenings appealing, especially if they are looking for uninterrupted viewing in predictable comfort.

It is also important to recognize where nostalgia is silent. Collective memory of open-air cinema by no means offers a complete picture of what life was like under socialism. While it romanticizes aspects of the past to assuage the present, what it eschews is the sacrifices and traumas of everyday life, which were frequently justified through the very propagandist institution of cinema. Meanwhile, the forgetting of politics in nostalgic discourses is not only a symptom of the postsocialist nostalgia industry, which gears toward "light" subjects for easy consumption, but also has to do with the multiple interfaces of cinema, which can potentially generate divergent or conflicting meanings, pleasures, and experiences. Audiences can reminisce about the lyrical atmosphere of open-air cinema regardless of the content of the films they watched. By the same token, if this chapter magnifies the relatively apolitical side of atmosphere, as the next two chapters will show, it does not mean that narratives of revolution and class struggle did not become mediating factors in other ways.

CHAPTER 5

Discomfort

As idyllic as open-air cinema might be remembered, the physical challenges it presented cannot be ignored. Born in 1960, Ren Ming was
forced to relocate with his parents at age seven to a May Seventh Cadre
School (*wuqi ganxiao*) in rural Liaoning Province, a labor farm where
party cadres and intellectuals were reeducated through hard manual
labor. As he remembers, while there were no other entertainment options,
open-air screenings were held at the farm several times a month. In the
winter, it was so cold that when he and his friends arrived at the screening area with their campstools, they had to keep running to stay warm.
"There was no fire or even a hot water bag during the screenings. We
were freezing. It was so cold that we couldn't even smile. Nothing but
the eyes could move." In the summer things were not necessarily better,
because of the mosquito bites. "I wore socks, but I could feel one bite
after another on my feet. Mosquitos hid there. When you took off the
socks, you would see lots of holes on them. They looked like fishing
nets."[1] Despite all this, Ren Ming declares, he still felt extremely happy
when he could watch films.

Moviegoing is not typically associated with unpleasant bodily feelings or nuisances such as freezing weather and mosquito bites. Quite
the contrary, since cinema's early days, exhibitors have mostly presented
moviegoing as an activity of comfort and strived to shield audiences
from disruptive natural forces. In the United States, attention was paid
to maintain a pleasant viewing environment as early as the nickelodeon

era as exhibitors tried to ensure cleanliness and good ventilation.[2] With the rise of movie palaces, exhibitors went above and beyond in wooing patrons with opulent architecture, lush interiors, comfortable seating, and comprehensive customer services. In her study of women's moviegoing in 1940s and 1950s Britain, Jackie Stacey points out that the sensuous, material pleasure of the cinema was a main attraction for women during the war. As opposed to the shortage of fuel, clothes, and other basic supplies in everyday life, cinemas provided warmth, luxury, fancy lighting, and "the feel of the plush seats."[3] In Republican China, luxurious cinemas modeled after movie palaces in Europe and America once set the standards for moviegoing in major cities, priding themselves on providing visitors with comfortable sofa chairs and air-conditioning. Since the 1990s, China has embraced the multiplex like the rest of the world. Doing away with the ornate details of the movie palace, multiplexes can put more emphasis in comfort as a main attraction for moviegoers. This pursuit of comfort has reached a new height in the United States with the recent adoption of reclining seats by theater chains like AMC and Cinemark. AMC's website is unabashed about promoting its signature recliners: "Seat warmers make it cozy, AMC makes comfort easy! Take your movie experience to the max when you tilt back and sink into the comfort now reclining near you!"[4]

Against this broad picture of cinemagoing, the harsh material conditions and physical discomfort that Chinese moviegoers were willing to endure appear, at least at first glance, quite puzzling. Why did audiences continue to go to the movies and remember the experience as enjoyable if the conditions were so harsh? How was the cinematic experience redefined when the well-being of the viewer's body was rendered precarious? References to extreme cold, heat, mosquito bites, and sore feet and buttocks in audiences' testimonies challenge us to recognize a commonly ignored dimension of cinematic experience, namely, the interfacing between the spectatorial body and the viewing environment. If a comfortable theatrical setting predisposes viewers to forget about their corporeal existence, discomfort "fleshes out" the body by calling attention to it. This chapter examines the uncomfortable spectatorial body and how it shaped memories of socialist moviegoing. Discomfort, I will show, not only draws attention to conditions of scarcity but also has the potential for sublimating the activity of moviegoing via a revolutionary structure of feelings that celebrates struggle. An investigation of discomfort also has implications for film studies in general as it foregrounds the diverse ways in which the spectator is embodied in moviegoing.

THE EMERGENCE OF DISCOMFORT

How did moviegoing become an activity marred with discomfort in the first place? A comparison between pre- and-post-49 rhetoric regarding moviegoing as a form of consumption will show how comfort became downplayed, if not ideologically suspect, as demands were put on cinema to be productive.

Similar to their Western counterparts, commercial film exhibitors in Republican China subscribed to the thinking that movie viewing required an enclosed, comfortable, and carefully moderated environment that would facilitate viewers' complete immersion in the films. In her analysis of an ad for the Peking Theater (opened in Shanghai in 1926), Zhen Zhang observes that the ad mentions many specific features of the viewing environment, such as seating, aisle lighting, and hygiene. With comfortable seats, unobstructed sight of the screen, convenient but non-distracting lights, and adjustable temperature, the theater strived to constitute its own artificial environment separate from the outside world.[5] Commentaries on movie theaters in the 1930s and 1940s repeated the same theme. A 1932 review of Shanghai's Cathay Theater (*guotai dianyingyuan*) humorously commended its extremely roomy and comfortable seating by saying that "no matter how tall you are or how large your buttocks are, you will sit comfortably."[6] When the Roxy Theater, which had a seating capacity of fifteen hundred, opened in Shanghai in December 1939, it was touted as the "best-equipped movie palace in the East."[7] In a special booklet commemorating its opening, one article remarks in detail on the seating, projection, and sound quality of the theater, three elements that the author considers the theater's "heart" (as opposed to architecture and decor, which made up its "outer clothing"). To this author, since watching a movie requires moviegoers to sit still for two hours, one cannot overemphasize the importance of seating. The sofa chairs at the Roxy Theater feature wide surface, low installation, and extra springs, which all serve to enhance patrons' comfort. As a result, the article claims, the seating "provided unparalleled pleasure to both the body and the heart, while preventing any back pain resulting from long periods of sitting."[8]

The last quote is a revealing one. On one hand, in understanding the pleasures provided by a comfortable seat, the author moves beyond the purely physical and locates pleasure in the heart. This idea evokes a famous description of cinema by the film critic Huang Jiamo (1916–2004), a major advocate of "soft film" in the "hard film (*yingxing dianying*) vs. soft film (*ruanxing dianying*)" debate in the mid-1930s. "Cinema is ice-cream for the eyes and sofa for the heart and the mind," Huang famously writes.[9] Through striking synesthesia and a fusion of the physical and the mental, Huang advances a vision of cinema that emphasizes its ability to provide audiences with sensual enjoyment. What has been overlooked is that "sofa" was not a random metaphor; the choice of phrase was inherently connected with the way cinema was experienced in the modern metropolis of Shanghai where Huang lived. In other words, cinema as sofa is grounded in the *dispositif* of cinema being experienced from sofa—it is the latter that makes possible an ontology of cinema as pleasure, relaxation, a "treat." On the other hand, the description of seating at the Roxy Theater clarifies the purpose of comfortable seating as the prevention of negative bodily sensations. In the pursuit of an absence of distracting pain or soreness, what is being sought after is a body that does not call attention to itself, a body that is a blank slate waiting to be activated by the films on screen. In this sense, comfort, more than a pleasure in itself, is a cleansing mechanism that separates the everyday body from the viewing body.

By contrast, building on the "hard film" conception of cinema as an instrument for raising consciousness, the post-49 reorientation of cinema toward the "worker-peasant-soldier" masses was accompanied by the downplaying of comfort. The mandate of "serving workers, peasants, and soldiers" was a double-edged sword. In urban areas, the building of new movie theaters was touted as achievements of socialism, and improvements in viewing conditions could be seen as progress. In 1954, for instance, *Guangming Daily* reported on the opening of Peace Movie Theater (*heping dianyingyuan*) in the worker concentrated Tiexi district in Shenyang, Liaoning Province. In addition to noting how workers welcomed this new movie theater, the report briefly describes the interior of the auditorium as "spacious and bright" with brand new leather folding chairs.[10] A year later, the opening of People's Theater (*renmin dianyingyuan*) in Urumqi also received coverage in *Guangming Daily*, which devotes slightly more space to praising the seating at the theater: "The theater has three parts—stalls, balcony, and a lounge. In the stalls and the balcony, there are more than a thousand fixed, single seats that have leather-top cushions and iron legs. The width and distance of these seats were designed according to common standards. Audiences not only can watch movies comfortably in these seats but can also walk in and out conveniently."[11] Such detailed descriptions of theater seating and affirmation of comfort, however, were rare at the time and only appeared in reports of high-profile new movie theaters that opened in major cities. In the countryside, the demand to increase mass access to cinema entailed the quick expansion of rural film exhibition networks in the absence of basic infrastructure. When access to cinema depended on mobile projection teams, who were encouraged to set aside their own physical well-being, concerns for the comfort of audiences were out of the question. It was not until the 1980s that comfort began to be acknowledged as a legitimate need of rural audiences, giving rise to the short-lived movement of township cinemas.

More than a practical necessity, the disregard of comfort was also an ideological by-product of the socialist reevaluation of consumption. As Karl Gerth notes, CCP internal literature and mass media in the early 1950s displayed "an almost monomaniacal obsession with production wherein production seemed to be an end in itself."[12] At the same time, those that had fallen into a consumerist lifestyle were described as bourgeois, pleasure-seeking, morally corrupt, and degenerate. The anti-consumerist, pro-production rhetoric had a tangible effect on how the activity of moviegoing was construed. In the early '50s, two opposing arguments were made. One perspective downright rejected moviegoing as a wasteful consumer activity. During the Three-Anti Campaign (*san-fan yundong*) launched in 1951, which targeted the problems of corruption, waste, and bureaucratism within the party, so-called "patriotic pacts" (*aiguo gongyue*) were drafted with pledges to "never watch films again in the future."[13] In the countryside, local cadres were sometimes reluctant to facilitate projection teams with screenings, which they saw as detracting from production. In a 1953 document from the Shanghai Municipal Archive, a cadre was quoted saying that if peasants spent time watching films at night, they would not rest well, and their productive labor would be affected the next day.[14] For moviegoing to have a proper place in the revolutionary teleology, it must not be a distraction, but become a source of productivity. The argument in support of moviegoing, therefore, emphasized that watching films, rather than being detrimental to the building of socialism, could actually transform viewers into more dedicated producers. In one 1950 article from *Mass Cinema*, a Shanghai high school student explains her reasons for denouncing American films and embracing Soviet films: the former used to encourage her to waste time on Hollywood stars whereas the latter inspire her to devote her life to the construction of a new China.[15] In some cases, a direct causal link was established between watching films and economic production. It was reported that after watching a newsreel documentary called *Make Steel Like Mad* (*Dagao gangtie*), eight thousand mine workers in the Nantong area of Jiangsu Province immediately increased the daily output of iron ore by 20 percent.[16] A 1963 film named *The Fight for Power* (*Duo yin*) was described as having a similar effect. While the film focuses on the struggle against counterrevolutionaries in a village, *Film Projection* reported that it raised peasants' class consciousness as well as their enthusiasm for production: after watching the film, members of a commune were able to make four more trips every day transporting fertilizers.[17]

As the emphasis was put on the aftermath of moviegoing, audiences' experiences during the moviegoing process were rarely articulated in archival sources. Retrospective accounts, however, reveal the diverse ways moviegoing was uncomfortable. In provincial cities and small towns, the material conditions of movie theaters were likely to be much worse than those that would make the pages of national newspapers. Zhai Junjie (b. 1941), a film director, offers this description of the conditions of movie theaters in Kaifeng, a medium-sized historic city in Henan Province, in the 1950s: "At that time, movie theaters in Kaifeng were simple and crude (*jianlou*). Judging by today's criteria they were pretty bad. People's Auditorium, Workers' Theater, and Liberation Theater were some of the more famous movie theaters in Kaifeng. They were bigger than others. Audience seating was rows of long wooden benches. Around the auditorium there was red cloth although some light would peek through. Of course, at the time there was no air-conditioning. There weren't even electric fans."[18]

Although wooden benches and the lack of temperature control were well below today's standards, the movie theater as an enclosed, built environment provided a level of protection that was simply unavailable at open-air screenings. By taking place outside, the latter immediately rendered the well-being of the participant's body precarious. If nature could enhance the lyrical atmosphere of open-air screenings, it could also be threatening by unleashing onto viewers cold, heat, wind, rain, snow, and mosquitos. In the case of Ren Ming, both winter and summer presented challenges. Even in China's southernmost Guangdong Province where winter is supposed to be mild, viewers had to wrap themselves in thick cotton quilts to sit through outdoor screenings in the winter.[19] Meanwhile, even sitting could be a luxury at open-air screenings. While many brought their own campstools to screenings, especially children who would arrive early to save precious spots (*zhanzuo*), it was also common to stand through screenings. After screenings, many still had to walk long distances to return to their homes. Su Tong writes that several times during his long walks home by himself, he had to pass by a large cemetery. Scared, he would run very fast as the wind bellowed across his face.[20] Film director Gao Xixi (b. 1962) recalls that when he was about seven or eight, he had to walk four to five kilometers (about two to three miles) to attend screenings. On his return trip, he would be so exhausted that he would fall asleep while walking.[21] In other words, there was a physical aspect of rural open-air screenings that was far removed from "soft film" ideals of moviegoing as relaxation from the sofa chair.

Furthermore, audience testimonies also reveal what Jie Li recently describes as "guerilla tactics" of moviegoing, such as sneaking into screenings, which often involved putting oneself in physically strenuous positions.[22] Liu Jin (b. 1963), an actor who later became famous for playing the prime minister Zhou Enlai in films and on TV, once snuck into a theater and crouched for hours above the rafters so that he could watch a film.[23] Yi Xiangdong's short story "Film Oh Film," which I discussed in chapter 2, discloses the hidden danger of such practices. Desperately wanting to watch the popular North Korean film *The Flower Girl* (*Kkot Pa-neun Cheo-nyeo/Maihua guniang*, 1972), the story's child narrator and his friend Xizi decide to climb onto a tree outside of the school courtyard where the screening takes place. The narrator describes what he observes from the tree:

> *The Flower Girl* was indeed a good film. It was quiet in the courtyard except for the sound of people sobbing. The snow also fell silently onto the crowd in front of the screen, covering them with a layer of white. Although it was freezing, no one in the yard was rubbing their hands or stomping. But clinging to the tree, we had to move constantly. When our hands and feet turned numb in the cold, we slipped downward. Then we had to hurry to hold onto the trunk, trying to drag our bodies up a little.[24]

Snowy weather, the precarious physical position, bodily discomfort, and the extraordinary effort young viewers exert to attend a screening culminate in this moment. What comes after is heartbreaking: no longer able to hold onto the tree, Xizi falls from the tree and dies.

It would require additional archival work to determine to what extent fatalities associated with open-air screenings have occurred.[25] But Xizi's tragic ending does dramatize a common situation—that is, open-air cinema not only normalized discomfort as a regular component of the cinematic experience, but it also exposed the viewer's body to potentially dangerous harms. How then can we reconcile the seemingly negative experience of discomfort with audiences' enthusiasm for moviegoing? What is revealed of Chinese socialist moviegoing by the remembrance of discomfort?

SCARCITY AND THE PLEASURES OF MOVIEGOING

After spending his childhood and adolescence in rural Sichuan, where he was impressed by the cliff shot in *Taking Hua Mountain by Strategy*, Mr. Chen (b. 1937) joined the PLA in 1960. During the four years he was in the military, he attended many film screenings where, as he remembered, soldiers were trained to be highly disciplined: "In the training field, each company would occupy a square. There was no campstool, and we all sat on the ground. We would sit down in unison, following orders to put on clothes or take off clothes. Back then we all wore white shirts. Everybody would roll up their sleeves to the same place. It looked really good."[26] Despite the strict regimentation imposed on the body, Mr. Chen said that he welcomed screenings eagerly as much-needed breaks from the rigorous physical training he had to undergo on a daily basis. As a PLA soldier, Mr. Chen's experience may be unique, but it illustrates a shared sentiment: when moviegoing was seen as a rare opportunity to experience something out of the ordinary, discomfort may be tolerable in comparison to the pleasures of moviegoing.

Duanfang Lu has observed that the pro-production, anti-consumerist rhetoric of the CCP had tangible consequences. To the CCP state, the disparity between a reality of underdevelopment and the advanced system of socialism intensified a perception of scarcity. In order to accelerate development and modernization, the state concentrated resources on industrial production and capital accumulation which, in turn, caused more scarcity in social provisions.[27] With additional reference to the growing abundance of consumer goods and entertainment options since the 1990s, postsocialist discourses frequently confirm the socialist past as one of scarcity. In this context, audience members often mention that the reason why moviegoing used to be so popular was because they did not have other things to do. Mrs. Song (b. 1951), who grew up in a work-unit compound in Beijing, once had the luck of living in an apartment building right next to an area used for open-air screenings. Even so, she felt the need to attend every screening: "Was there more cultural life at the time? No. There wasn't much culture or entertainment. I was already luckier than most people since I could watch films. Others had to go to movie theaters and pay. We didn't need to spend money. Whenever we heard about a screening, we went."[28] When asked about why they liked watching films, Mrs. Li (b. 1948) from Shanghai and Mr. Chen (b. 1926) from Suzhou offered similar answers:

> I can't tell why I like watching films. Because there weren't many fun things to do at the time, if I could watch a film, I'd be really happy. There wasn't much to do at home except for doing homework, you know. A lot of families had little money. If you had a radio, that was really nice. People didn't have many things.[29]

> There were few leisure activities. Unless you organized some cultural activities yourself, it was just watching films. Ordinary Chinese people only had films in their lives.[30]

The memory that cinema was the only entertainment in the 1950s and '60s was not factually accurate, especially in major cities, where one could also find theatrical performances such as ballets, plays, and traditional operas. Although tickets to these performances were more expensive than film tickets, they were still relatively affordable. What prevented live theater from reaching more audiences appeared to have less to do with cost than with its limited reach, whereas cinema was more widely available, contributing to the impression that there was little to do beyond watching films.

In rural areas, there were decidedly fewer entertainment options beyond film screenings and drama troupe performances, and even with the state's tremendous effort to expand the exhibition network, film exhibition was uneven. Some remember relatively regular screenings every month, while for others, screenings were rare and unpredictable. In the early 1950s, the novelty of the cinematic technology and the unpredictability of its arrival almost guaranteed the curiosity of the rural audience. Explaining why they liked to watch films, interviewees used expressions such as "novel and fresh (*xinxian*)," "exciting (*xingfen*)," and "rare (*xihan*)." Before television started to tear viewers away from the film screen in the mid-to-late 1980s, open-air screenings continued to draw large crowds. One interviewee recalls that in her home village in Sichuan, "as soon as it was announced that there would be a film screening, young people would start running."[31] How the enthusiasm of rural audiences led them to disregard physical discomfort is best illustrated in a story told by Lu Shukun, a former projectionist who was a member of Shaanxi Province's first all-female projection team from 1953 to 1954:

> There was an incident in Puyang village when we showed *Fighting North and South* (*Nanzheng beizhan*, 1952). We had to paste posters in nearby

villages, and I had made announcements about it. Many people came that night, because common people liked films that had the word "battle" (*zhan*) in the title. . . . When we showed *Fighting North and South*, each projection team was given a large oil-cloth umbrella in case it rained in the middle of screenings. Then it really started to rain right after we started the second reel. . . . At first, we didn't pay attention, and then the rain got heavier and we opened the umbrella. The audiences did not move. There were four reels and we finished showing the rest of the two reels. When we played the third reel, it was almost pouring. I shouted to the peasants: "We should stop tonight, you can go back, and we'll come back tomorrow night to show the film." But all I heard was people saying, "We'll watch," "Go on," and "We don't mind." So, we held the umbrella over the equipment. Everyone else was in the rain and stayed to the very end. After the audience left, the school field [where the film was shown] was overflowing with water. The power cord of the engine was all muddy, so were we the projectionists. That was how enthusiastic people were.[32]

The anecdote not only offers a vivid demonstration of the contingent nature of open-air cinema (chapter 4) and projectionists' care for the screening apparatus (chapter 2), but also captures the extent to which a desire for watching films could prompt audiences to ignore something as unpleasant as pouring rain.

THE HAPPINESS OF STRUGGLE

For some viewers, discomfort was more than a negativity to be overcome so they could enjoy the pleasures of moviegoing; the body's endurance of unpleasant feelings could paradoxically become a source of pleasure in itself. In Ren Ming's case, open-air screenings became more memorable not despite the coldness and the mosquito bites, but because of them. Zhai Junjie, after commenting on the crude conditions of movie theaters in Kaifeng, immediately adds: "When we watched films there, we relished the experience. I think compared to upscale movie theaters nowadays, it was much more satisfying, much more fun, and much more enjoyable. Because there was a [special] feeling there."[33]

Once discomfort is associated with enjoyment, it is tempting to resort to psychoanalysis to explain spectators' "masochistic" tendencies. Gaylyn Studlar, for example, famously recognizes the pleasures of cinema as masochistic. Countering Laura Mulvey's emphasis on the controlling male gaze as the dominant spectatorial position of narrative cinema, Studlar argues that cinematic pleasure is much closer to masochistic scopic pleasure that is associated with desires and identities of the pre-Oedipal phase. The spectator, according to Studlar, regresses to a narcissistic, infantile state that also defines the masochist. As a "passive receiving object," the spectator must comprehend, but cannot control, the cinematic image.[34] Writing about the problem of torture in the contemporary world, Hilary Neroni also relies on psychoanalysis to articulate a complex relationship between the subject and bodily pain. According to Neroni, the dominant view of the body in today's neoliberal societies is a biopolitical body, which seeks its own survival above all else, and thus can be "made visible, known, characterized, catalogued, and completely controlled." Torture, which purports to be an act of extracting information by threatening the body, thrives under biopower, which sees the body as "the sole political battleground." To combat torture, Neroni argues, one must begin with a psychoanalytic conception of the body. In psychoanalysis, there is no pure body. The body is always mediated through unconscious desires and drives, which can make the subject undermine their own self-interest. Neroni links *jouissance*, which is the imperative to enjoy to a painful degree, to both humanity's historical tendency for destruction, violence, and self-destruction and to individuals' "inexplicable proclivity" to "hurt the ones they love, and to offend those they desire" on a personal level. Torture therefore ultimately does not work, because the subject, rather than giving up the truth for the sake of the body's survival, would in fact derive "a shameful enjoyment" out of torture just as torture provides sadistic pleasure for the torturer.[35]

However, I agree with Carl Plantinga that one major flaw of psychoanalysis is that it lacks a theoretical mechanism to deal with historical specificity.[36] Psychoanalytic theory as a whole is too general to explain why some moviegoers can tolerate negative bodily feelings more than others. In addition, I find Neroni's attempt to describe the psychology of victims of torture to be quite reductive. By attributing the endurance of torture to an irrational "pleasure in pain," Neroni juxtaposes people who would actively withstand torture—jihadists, "terrorists," soldiers, and revolutionaries—with people who unfortunately succumb to drug addiction and substance abuse, explaining the actions of all these groups by referring to humanity's uncontrollable desire for self-sabotage. This shows to me a failure to understand how torture can be endured as an active and rational choice made to achieve an end.

Rather, if audiences' memory of discomfort is counterintuitively positive, it has to do with the unique structure of feelings of Chinese socialism. Raymond Williams uses the notion of "structure of feeling" to capture "the particular quality of social experience and relationship" that comes to define a period or a generation.[37] A structure of feeling is not just ideology or worldview but refers to emergent thoughts and feelings as they are lived and experienced. It is within specific structures of feeling that thoughts and feelings acquire meaning. What is important in our case is a structure of feelings in which active struggle, including the struggle of the body to overcome pain and discomfort, were seen as revolutionary, transcendent, and desirable.

The dominant Maoist values and ethical norms have often been described as ascetic.[38] Ironically, while comfort was denounced by the party as bourgeois and corrupting, Maoist values, as Maurice Meisner points out, actually shared many similarities with the original bourgeois virtues—what Max Weber describes as "Protestant ethics"—including emphases on self-denial, sacrifice, diligence, hard work, and frugality.[39] These values were imparted through Mao's writings, such as the famous "three constantly read articles" (lao san pian), which were memorized and quoted religiously during the Cultural Revolution.[40] They could also easily be found in newspapers, magazines, literature, and films of the time. For example, one of the most influential Soviet novels in China— How the Steel Was Tempered (Gangtie shi zenyang liancheng de) by Nikolai Ostrovsky (1904–1936) offered a powerful articulation of the meaning of life through its protagonist Pavel Korchagin.[41] Many young people learned to recite a line from the book that says: "One only lives once, and he must live it so as to feel no tortured regrets about wasted years and never know the burning shame of a mean and petty past; to live so that in dying he might say: "all my life, all my strength, were given to the finest cause in all the world—the fight for the Liberation of Mankind."[42] Conveyed in this well-known quote is an ideal for how one should live their life. In Meisner's words, "not only was material waste sinful but waste of time even more so."[43] Time was in severe shortage in the race to create the socioeconomic prerequisites for socialism. At a macro level, development required the drafting of goals and quotas, and the conversion of time into productivity through Soviet style "five-year plans" that emphasized urban industrialization and a rationalized, prioritized use of time. At a personal level, the realization of national goals depended on the ordering of the individual's personal time to gear toward work and production. Ascetic values thus served a teleological purpose. Ideals like hard work and diligence, Meisner emphasizes, were not propagated for their own sakes, but as means to achieve a utopian, communist future. It was the latter that made revolutionary struggle meaningful.[44]

Moreover, struggle was seen as the true source of joy and happiness in the Maoist ethical system. A well-known quote from Mao is that "to struggle against Heaven, what boundless joy; to struggle against Earth, what boundless joy; to struggle against people, what boundless joy!" Although this is in fact a misquote, which mistakes "*fendou*" in the original as "*dou*" thus altering the meaning from "struggle with" to "struggle against," what is unmistakable is the euphoria Mao associates with the act of struggle itself.[45] A passage Meisner quotes from the magazine *China Youth* (*Zhongguo qingnian*) further illustrates this point: "One has the greatest pleasure and happiness when one wages a heroic struggle for a noble goal, a great ideal, and a political direction, particularly when one sees that such goals, ideals and political directions are finally realized after many sacrifices have been made by revolutionary martyrs. One's pleasure and happiness is the greatest when one devotes oneself to a definite cause by means of which to transform society and promote the wellbeing of mankind, especially when one sees that one's work is achieving brilliant success."[46]

The description of Maoist values as ascetic or puritanical has been criticized for ignoring how the Maoist revolutionary culture was imbued with emotion. In his analysis of revolutionary cinema, Ban Wang makes a compelling argument for how films like *Song of Youth* (*Qingchun zhi ge*, 1959) and *Nie Er* (1959), rather than repressing individuals' psychic and emotional energy, redirect and sublimate such energy toward revolutionary goals, thus affording the audiences with "libidinal satisfaction and emotional fulfillment."[47] What the *China Youth* quote shows, however, is that seemingly negative, self-denying, ascetic practices did not necessarily imply a repression of emotions. Although the revolutionary subject was required to give up certain indulgences of life, hard work and devotion could in fact generate profound emotions. Emotion, as Martha Nussbaum has shown, is not merely libidinal energy or bodily affect, but has a cognitive component. Unlike affect which can describe amorphous bodily sensations or intensities, emotion, by definition, involves appraisals of external objects and their significance to our well-being.[48] In the case of Maoist culture, the struggle to achieve communist goals became a source of happiness because it was deemed as fundamental to the meaning of life. This essentially was the emotional structure of many religions: by forsaking worldly pleasures, the revolutionary opened up the possibility of obtaining a more profound spiritual fulfillment on a higher plane.

In the age of postsocialism, the revolutionary structure of feelings may be especially alluring for people fed up with consumerism and its incessant demands on instant gratification. The abundance of consumer goods and the ease with which culture can be accessed contrast with conditions of scarcity and the "struggle" one undertook to attend screenings—traveling for hours, sneaking into theaters, sitting or standing in the rain to watch a movie. For the generations that have experienced both, the latter can fill the spiritual void that feels increasingly enlarged; these struggles are also more memorable and meaningful because they involved the kind of active participation that is conducive to long-term memory. Although socialist-era sources put more focus on the aftermath of a viewing experience and paid little attention to the process of moviegoing, the significance of "struggle" in retrospect is manifested in the details audiences include in their narrations of the actions and feelings leading up to screenings. As an example, we can look at the following story shared by a Mr. Zhou (b. 1946) from Suzhou:

> At that time, I needed to take the bus for a few stops to go home from school. I needed to take the number 4 bus from Changmen to Jiejiaqiao, which cost 3 cents. But my parents would give me five cents every day, not three cents. So [one day] I decided not to take the bus but walk instead. There was a Taowu Theater at Jiejiaqiao. The afternoon ticket happened to be five cents. So I saved it for the films. The theater was quite empty at the time. I bought row 8, seat number 10.[49]

Although Mr. Zhou claimed to have a clear memory of one of the short, animated films he saw that day (*Princess Frog/Qingwa gongzhu*, 1954), he did not say anything about the actual viewing of the film, which makes the preciseness of the seat he purchased even more striking. It is reasonable to speculate that Mr. Zhou remembers "row 8, seat number 10" so distinctly because buying the ticket marked the culmination of his active physical effort, a moment of heightened joy and anticipation. The shape of his narrative suggests that this, rather than the film, constituted the emotional high point of the entire moviegoing experience. What is left implicit in this viewer's testimony is articulated by actress Liang Danni (b. 1954). In Liang's case, the "struggle" to watch films consisted of passing one ticket back and forth between friends so they could all attend screenings. As she reflects on this experience, she says: "Thinking of so many tricks just to watch a film, the joy of this process already surpassed watching the film itself."[50]

MOVIEGOING AS "TORTURE"

What further endowed discomfort with meaning, I will speculate, were narratives of torture in revolutionary cinema and literature, which molded both the socialist structure of feelings and the collective horizon of reception. Set in pre-49 China, revolutionary cinema and literature portray the arduous struggle of communist heroes and heroines, many of whom share the common fate of being captured and tortured by enemies. For those who can withstand the torment, torture serves as a narrative turning point after which their resolve would be further strengthened, their commitment deepened. Chris Berry has observed three common characteristics in Chinese representations of torture on screen in the Mao era: torture only takes place in "the old society"; display of physical suffering is foregrounded to move the spectators somatically and emotionally; the moral and political right and wrong are absolutely clear.[51] In some cases, such as classic films *The Red Detachment of Women* (*Hongse niangzi jun*, 1961) and *Two Stage Sisters* (*Wutai jiemei*, 1964), the torment of the protagonist (often female) is publicly displayed to mark her class belongings and a beginning of her revolutionary journey. In other cases, the enemy's torture chamber is where the heroic battles occur. Torture, which is the only method the ideologically impotent enemy has to extract information, is shown as a test that one must pass to become a true revolutionary. The influential novel *Red Crag* (*Hongyan*, 1961) by Luo Guangbin and Yang Yiyan, for instance, centers on a group of Communist revolutionaries imprisoned in Guomindang's notorious Refuse Pit (*zhazi dong*) near the end of the Chinese Civil War. It uses graphic details of torture to shore up the revolutionaries' extraordinary wills, which allow them to disregard and transcend bodily pain.

Torture narratives have left profound impact on several generations of Chinese youths, who had to negotiate a romantic revolutionary ideal revolving around torture with the fact that movie-like revolution was more of a fantasy than something that could come true in their own lives. Feminist historian Wang Zheng, who grew up in Shanghai in the 1950s and '60s, is frank about her obsession with underground work:

> I wanted to be like many heroes and heroines in the movies and novels. The most dangerous work for the revolution was underground work. Underground Communists were often arrested, and horrible torture was a common procedure to force them to talk. I fantasized about becoming a Communist underground worker. Taiwan was not yet liberated, and two-thirds of the

people in the world were still living in the darkness. It was very likely that I would be sent to do some underground work when I grew up, I figured. But could I endure the torture if I was arrested? I wasn't sure. I was afraid of many things, besides pain. My mother used to raise chicken in our backyard. Once when a rooster suddenly charged at me, I was so frightened that I climbed through a window to escape. . . . How could I pass the torture test?[52]

While the mission of liberating oppressed people around the world allowed Wang to project her fantasy onto the future, the components of her fantasy—underground work and torture—came straight from imaginary representations of the past. In her unintentionally comical juxtaposition of torture with the mundane situation of being chased by a rooster, what is revealed is how distant from reality the possibility of torture actually is. Wang soon gave up the dream of being an underground worker, realizing that her generation had missed out on the romance and adventures of the past and that she needed to rechannel her heroic aspirations into the construction of socialism.[53]

Other young viewers, by contrast, found an outlet for their revolutionary fantasies in playful reenactments of scenes of torture. A screenwriter named Li Qiang (b. 1968) tells the following story:

> When I was in primary school, our class monitor was a girl. At that time, we all watched *Sparking Red Star* (*Shanshan de hongxing*, 1974). In the film there is a scene where Pan Dongzi's mother is burnt to death. The class monitor loved this scene. Since she had the authority, every day after school she would make a few male classmates stay behind to act out this scene with her. We would move all the desks to form a circle and let her stand in the center. "Will you confess?" we'd ask. "No, not even if you kill me!" she'd answer. She got off on the thrill of being tragic and heroic. I think she just loved that. She was fascinated with that kind of heroism. We "burnt" her every day for about a year.[54]

What stands out in this story is not only the length of repetitions ("a year" has to be an exaggeration) but also the confusing of narrative events. In *Sparking Red Star*, Japanese troops have the mother surrounded in a building, which they then set on fire, but she is never interrogated or tortured. On the other hand, the familiar line of "Will you confess?!" (*ni shuo bu shuo*) appeared in interrogation scenes from many other films such as *Undying Wave* (*Yong bu xiaoshi de dianbo*, 1958) and *Living Forever in Burning Flames* (*Liehuo zhong yongsheng*), a 1965 film adaptation of *Red Crag*. Between the young viewers acting out an interrogation scene and the later recollection, somewhere there has been a mix-up. But as Alessandro Portelli reminds us, "The importance of oral testimony may often lie not in its adherence to facts but rather in its divergence from them, where imagination, symbolism, desire break in." What people say about the past is not just about what people did, but "what they wanted to do, what they believed they were doing, what they now think they did."[55] In its very exaggeration and confusion, Li Qiang's testimony is revealing: first, the "year-long" repetition bespeaks a deep desire that cannot be satisfied by a substitute for the real thing; second, the mash-up of narrative details points to the existence of a cultural intertext of revolution in viewers' minds, which consists of common tropes that go beyond any one particular text.

Rae Yang's memoir *Spider Eaters* provides another example where the cultural intertext of torture is central to the revolutionary fantasy. In a chapter titled "The Hero in My Dreams," Yang contrasts her disenchanted life in the 101 Middle School with a vibrant fantasy world revolving around an imagined hero. "Each time I read a book, saw a movie, or heard a story from someone, a few new episodes would appear in my story," writes Yang. Not surprisingly, her story is an encapsulation of the shared revolutionary intertext full of references to other well-known revolutionary works (in more disparaging terms, it was full of familiar clichés). The hero, for example, can fire with one pistol in each hand and never misses the mark—a trait that calls to mind the guerrilla war fighter Li Xiangyang from the film *Guerrilla on the Plain* (*Pingyuan youjidui*, 1955). Yang fantasizes in great length about the horrible torture that the hero endures before his death. The hero has his fingertips pierced by sharp bamboo sticks, is tortured on the "tiger bench," hit by electric current, and branded with a white-hot iron—all of these methods were familiar to Chinese audiences through works like *Red Crag*. Even though no human being of flesh and blood is believed to be able to go through such torture without confessing the truth, the hero remains convicted and loyal, and at last enters martyrdom with a smile on his face.[56]

The three examples—Wang Zheng's worry about passing the torture test, Li Qiang's interrogation play, and Rae Yang's elaborate fantasy—show the different ways torture narratives entered the consciousness of Chinese youths. Although I have not found a testimony that makes a direct link between torture on screen and audiences' discomfort off screen, it does not seem too farfetched to suggest that narratives of torture could have mediated attitudes and feelings toward discomfort. It may even be argued that cinematic spectatorship shared a similar structure with torture and could serve as an easy, everyday substitute or rehearsal for the fantasized object that belonged solely in an imaginary, sublime past.

Despite their vast differences, both torture and cinema seek "passive," immobile bodies. Spectatorship is an inherent element of torture. For Elaine Scarry, torture converts the infliction of pain into a "wholly illusory" spectacle of power, and what assists this process is "an obsessive self-conscious display of agency."[57] In Chinese revolutionary cinema, this power dynamic is translated into the visual pattern where the torturer often anxiously jumps up and down demanding information while the revolutionary, bound, incapacitated, and refusing to confess, becomes a most scornful spectator of the torturers' desperate spectacle. In *Living Forever in Burning Flames*, for example, shots and reverse shots contrast a screaming, hand-waving GMD torturer with a tethered Sister Jiang, whose brightly lit face exudes unwavering determination against the dark background surrounding her. Against the torturers' wishes, the revolutionary thus reclaims the theater of torture as a spectacle of consciousness for the audience, wherein the spiritual conquers the physical. In film exhibition, when viewers are encouraged to restrict bodily movements so they can be "tethered" to the screen (like how Plato's prisoners are chained to the wall of the cave), they are put in a similar position vis-à-vis the cinematic spectacle as how the tortured revolutionary is positioned against the display of power. Like the latter, they are expected to suppress their material existence in order that their mental activities become heightened.

Furthermore, similar to how pain could give rise to joy, discomfort could be interpreted as precisely that which elevated moviegoing from entertainment to a higher plane. The joy of pain inflicted by torture is not the irrational self-destructive *jouissance* suggested by psychoanalysis. Rather, it is the joy of entering the otherworldly, akin to the religious experience of pain. Torture, Scarry suggests, annihilates the victim's world; however, in religion, the denial of the world is precisely what is sought after. As she explains, "The self-flagellation of the religious ascetic, for example, is not (as is often asserted) an act of denying the body, eliminating its claims from attention, but a way of so emphasizing the body that the contents of the world are cancelled and the path is clear for the entry of an unworldly, contentless force. It is in part this world-ridding, path-clearing logic that explains the obsessive presence of pain in the rituals of large, widely shared religions."[58] Torture can be "path-clearing" as it sharpens a single-minded focus on the revolutionary, which in turn generates profound joy. As one Chinese critic Wu

Xiangyu describes, "the pain of torture is displaced. The torment of the body is converted into a price that must be paid for the ideals of a better tomorrow, which then gives rise to a kind of religious passion."[59] In the moments before execution, such revolutionary passion is often heightened through ritualistic practices, such as combing one's hair or smoothing out one's clothes—gestures that bespeak the sacredness of sacrifice and the revolutionary's calm acceptance of their fate. In *Red Crag*, Sister Jiang faces her execution as if "she is preparing to go to a joyful gathering, or attend a solemn ceremony."[60] In Rae Yang's story, the hero "dies with a smile on his face."[61] While the torturer mistakenly believes that threatening the body would make the revolutionary confess the truth, the true revolutionary desires martyrdom as the ultimate sublimation of their subjectivity. For the viewer that had internalized this script, discomfort could sublimate the cinematic experience and may appear especially so in retrospect. In comparison to the present era dominated by commercial moviegoing, the past can thus be seen as pure, meaningful, enchanted, and spiritually enriched, whereas the present is deprived of meaning precisely because of its abundance. This explains why Zhai Junjie finds the uncomfortable theaters in Kaifeng more "enjoyable" than modern-day luxury cinemas: the latter, by removing discomfort, also eliminates the room for sublimation.

Xiaobing Tang has characterized modernity as the dialectic movement between the utopian, the heroic, and the sublime, to be found in grand projects of anti-imperialism, revolution and nation building, and elements of the everyday, the routine, and the banal.[62] "One choice always seems to reveal an unbearable lack in the other," he writes.[63] Perhaps the allure of discomfort comes precisely from a temporary balance between the two. On one hand, the physical sensation of discomfort drew the spectator closer to the revolution on screen, making it easier for audiences to imagine what it would be like to be part of a revolutionary community and to partake in its heroism. On the other hand, the revolutionary discourse made mundane, everyday feelings meaningful. Discomfort thus stopped being a condition imposed by the environment and became evidence of active struggle.

OF THE MOVIES, OR AT THE MOVIES?

To conclude this chapter, I will discuss how a study of Chinese moviegoers' physical discomfort has broader implications for film studies. After both "the historical turn" and "the phenomenological turn" in the last decades, film studies, in my view, still have not grasped the multiple dimensions of the spectatorial body as lived in history. With emphasis on the social-historical, historians of exhibition and moviegoing have not paid particular attention to the body in past experiences. This is not surprising considering that reconstructing the latter in a detailed manner is likely to be an extremely difficult task. In comparison, film phenomenology, which aims to study embodied experiences, lacks a method for engaging with the historical. Relying on thick, first-person descriptions, the phenomenological method generates rich experiential details, but it also limits the observer to experiences that can be directly observed from their own perspective. As this method has so far been employed by mostly Western critics, film phenomenology has been prevented from venturing into historical or non-Western experiences of cinema.

Moreover, despite professed interest in studying the multisensory, lived-body access to the world *at* the movies, phenomenological inquiries have continued to focus on viewers' experience *of* moving images. Vivian Sobchack, who is critical of the psychoanalytical focus on vision and on the spectator as an abstract "eye" or point of view, has specified the multiple senses that inform an experience of cinema: "At the movies our vision and hearing are informed and given meaning by our other modes of sensory access to the world: our capacity not only to see and to hear but also to touch, to smell, to taste, and always to proprioceptively feel our weight, dimension, gravity, and movement in the world."[64] In this description, spectatorship is treated as an all-around experience of being present in a screening situation. Even "the tactile contact of my posterior with the theater seat," as Sobchack writes elsewhere, is considered part of the package.[65] However, the weight in her analysis easily shifts from how vision is grounded in the body to the interfacing between the body and the film.

Sobchack argues that it is not just the viewer that is situated in a lived body. The film also has a body that sees (through camera) and shows us its act of seeing (through projection). In a cinematic encounter, the viewer's body and the film's body interact in a way that blurs the boundary between subject and object through the mutual act of touching.[66] Other phenomenologists share a similar focus. Both Laura Marks and Jennifer Barker center their discussions on the "touch" between the viewer and the film. Marks conceptualizes the film as a skin, capable of evoking memories of the senses through tactile vision.[67] Barker suggests that film's penetration of embodied viewers goes deeper than the skin to reach the level of musculature and viscera.[68] She writes that "the forms of tactility filmgoers experience at the movies are shared—in complex, not always comfortable ways—by both spectator and film."[69] In one sentence, she goes from talking about the experience of a *dispositif* ("at the movies") to a bilateral interfacing relationship ("both spectator and film"). In her book on contemporary body mutilation films, Laura Wilson aims to "complicate the notion of a body that pre-exists the text" by "drawing attention to how the viewer's sense of embodiment is constituted by cinematic representations of mutilation."[70] While films can certainly activate the body or draw attention to parts of the body in different ways, if an analysis of cinematic experience does not take into full consideration "the body that pre-exists the text," would it not risk a new kind of textual determinism where, rather than an ideal visual position, it is a particular sense of embodiment/physicality that is considered to be textually constructed?

This focus on the viewer's relation to the film may not be surprising given how spectatorship theory traditionally focuses on the reception of films, but it also has to do with the theater bias as the movie theater is often taken as the default space for phenomenological inquiries. In his study of the experiences of horror films, Julian Hanich makes explicit that his analysis is situated in the multiplex. What the multiplex provides, he elaborates, is an environment of individualized immersion, where the film is foregrounded as the center of the experience through a combination of factors such as stadium seating arrangements, airconditioning, tidiness, and the minimization of noise.[71] In other words, if the classical narrative system strives to conceal the cut to construct a seamless viewing experience, the multiplex exerts systemic efforts to prevent the preexisting spectatorial body from being felt during screenings. In this context, a theoretical focus on viewers' relation to the film may be justifiable. But what is problematic is when the multiplex dominates phenomenological approaches to cinematic experience. After all, phenomenology supposedly aims to describe "invariant structures of the film viewer's lived experience when watching moving images in a cinema or elsewhere."[72] If that is the case, then it cannot limit itself to first-person narratives derived from contemporary, Euro-American, theatrical exhibition. If it is possible to distill some common structure of cinematic experience despite the constant transformation cinema has undergone over time and across the world, a wider range of possibilities must be considered.

In the context of Chinese socialist film exhibition, a similar focus on the film as what defined the cinematic experience cannot be justified because unpleasant bodily feelings caused by the viewing environment were in fact not negligible. It is in the absence of many of the usual efforts to direct audiences' attention away from their own bodies that the body truly becomes an independent term that shapes experience and memory. Embodied spectatorship, therefore, should not just be about how the spectatorial body is activated by the film text, but should very much concern the interfacing between the body and its viewing environment.

CHAPTER 6

Screen

The last exhibition interface of the book may be a familiar one, that is, the film screen. But if film studies have treated the screen mostly as the boundary between the theater space and the filmic space shown on screen, it is the materiality of the screen to which open-air cinema in socialist China drew attention. It is worth returning to Zhang Yimou's short film "Movie Night" in *To Each His Own Cinema*, first mentioned in chapter 3. In addition to offering a typical scene of open-air cinema, "Movie Night" is prominent for both highlighting and displacing the film screen. The film's first shot of a film screen is an extreme low-angle shot showing a group of kids cheering and jumping with their hands up in the air, touching and brushing against a horizontally spread screen that seemingly flies over them from left to right (figure 10). Already there is defamiliarization. While the screen is immediately recognizable due to its black frame, its positioning above the children's heads, our viewpoint from under it, and the tactility evoked by the excited little hands visualize a very different relationship to the screen than what theatergoers may be used to. For the latter, the screen is a distant blank space waiting to be filled by images. In Zhang's shot, however, the screen appears as something to be played with, a device that enables the delight of multisensory experience. Next, we see the screen being pulled up by strings in the more conventional frontal position. In front of the screen, children continue to jump and cheer. Some touch the screen; some play

FIGURE 10. Screenshot from Zhang Yimou's "Movie Night" showing kids touching a screen. Zhang Yimou, "Movie Night," in *To Each His Own Cinema* (2007).

FIGURE 11. Screenshot from Zhang Yimou's "Movie Night" showing kids playing in front of the screen. Zhang Yimou, "Movie Night," in *To Each His Own Cinema* (2007).

among themselves as the young protagonist of the film picks a spot to set down his bench (figure 11).

Later, with a loud click and a close-up of the light beam coming out of the film projector, Zhang appears to announce the beginning of the film screening. But what follows is not a film being shown; rather, it is a series of shots and reverse shots between the screen and the audience. In one shot, the diegetic film screen almost fills the frame. It flickers and blurs as the projected area slowly comes into focus. Giuliana Bruno describes the screen as the surface that clothes filmic matters, "the fabrication and the fabric of film."[1] Here it is as if the fabric is being smoothed out to get ready for the film. (Is it merely a prelude to cinema?) But the film does not start. Instead, accompanied by the rambunctious soundscape of a crowd gathering, Zhang shows how the audience casts shadows on the screen with their hands, arms, and objects, including a fan and a chicken. There is a cadence of laughter and cheers. A hand shadow imitating a dog elicits amusement; a chicken, thrown in the air by the mischievous protagonist, shrieking and flapping, causes an eruption of laughter. The joyous faces of audience members are captured by three consecutive shots.

The film still does not start. All of a sudden the projector is off. Following the curious gaze of our protagonist, we realize that the projectionist is having dinner with an older man (perhaps a local cadre?) in a small area enclosed by white curtains behind the audiences. Unbeknownst to the two diners, the curtain, back lit by a lamp on the dining table, reveals their silhouettes to the entire audience, which has turned around to look at them. The curtain has become a screen. In three pairs of shots/reverse shots, we see the protagonist gazing intently upon the actions unfolding in an accidental shadow theater until he begins to yawn. At last, the film starts. Zhang gives us one final look at the film screen. From a side angle, the camera seems as if it is perching on a tree, offering a panoramic view of the screening area. The diegetic screen now appears near the left edge of the frame in a profile view. The image on screen is visible but unclear; what is clear in the duration of the shot is that the screen does not stay still. Gently heaving back and forth, the screen distorts the filmic matters, making its own unstable presence felt. Next the camera cuts back to our protagonist. In the last shot of the film, he appears sound asleep in his chair.

By ending his short film at this point, Zhang seems to suggest that the rest of the screening need not be told; rather, it is more interesting to question when an experience of cinema begins. Does it begin when the projection team arrives? Does it begin when everyone is seated and ready? Does it begin when the first light beam shoots out of the projector? When the film actually begins in the diegesis, it feels like the cinematic experience, punctuated by the protagonist's yawn, is beginning to come to an end. Throughout this process, the screen maintains its presence, as an object to be touched, a backdrop to collective play, a surface for shadows and laughter, and a projection medium subjecting the image to destabilizing natural elements. Bruno has urged that visual studies should go beyond the image to investigate "what is tangible, material, spatial, and environmental."[2] The screen in Zhang's film illustrates this need perfectly. To understand cinematic experience, we cannot merely treat the screen as the location of the image but must consider the various ways a screen calls attention to itself as an architectonic and material form, exerting its own interface effect on the audience.

Like Zhang's film, memories of socialist open-air cinema contain many references to physical and tactile interactions between audiences and the screen. In this chapter, I question the common interpretation of spectators who touch the screen as naive, credulous spectators. Instead, in instances where audiences touched, marked, or physically engaged with the screen, the screen is best conceptualized as an object that invites attention and play. Although this was true for all viewers, it was in children's often undisciplined and unrestrained behaviors that the play potential of moviegoing was most fully realized. The public projection screen thus does not necessarily need to be excluded from what may be called a ludic media tradition that links nineteenth-century optical toys with contemporary touchscreens and interactive game media.

SCREEN ENGAGEMENTS

If Zhang Yimou leaves open the question of when an experience of cinema begins, Cui Yongyuan, whom I quote in the introduction, offers a definitive answer: "When the screen is hung, that's when a film screening began."[3] In a movie theater, the screen is already there; it is a given and thus self-effacing. But in an exhibition context where the screen first appeared as an object to be handled, it easily became part of the *narrative* of moviegoing. There are four ways in which audience members physically interacted with the screen that stand out from their retrospective accounts.

The first kind of interactions occurred between the spectator and the screening apparatus, including the screen itself. As mentioned in previous chapters, open-air cinema has an effect of exposure. While the projection booth separates both the projectionist and the projection apparatus from the audience, open-air cinema reconnects audiences to the apparatus. This newly established relationship is first and foremost a visual one. In Zhang Yimou's film, the protagonist's gaze follows the projectionists as they set up the projector, take out the film reels, plug in electric cords, and rewind the reels manually. The close proximity and sense of amazement are conveyed by a series of medium and close-up shots. The body is involved in physical movement as the protagonist comes close to various equipment. Meanwhile, touch becomes a real possibility. Writing about community film exhibition in contemporary New Zealand and Latin America, Miriam Ross notes that community exhibition presents a higher possibility for audiences to help with apparatus malfunction and participate actively during prescreening processes.[4] Similarly, Chinese viewers at open-air screenings did more than watch the projectionists work from the sideline. Some of the youngest viewers were also the most eager helpers. Ma Changchun (b. 1952), a successful businessman who grew up in the suburbs of Changchun, recalls helping the projectionist with various tasks at open-air screenings held at his elementary school. The tasks ranged from hanging the screen to plugging in the amplifier and collecting entry tickets.[5] To hang a screen, its four corners needed to be tied to erected poles with strings. As it was not an easy task, it often involved collective effort, making this act an even more apt beginning for the collective experience of movie-going. In an incident Cui Yongyuan remembers, a teenage boy saved the day by being the person who eventually succeeded in hanging the screen after the projectionist's several failed attempts. Cui recalls that when he accomplished the task, a crowd watching him burst into cheers, treating him like a hero.[6]

The pleasure of being in close proximity to the screening apparatus went hand in hand with the ability to physically lay one's hands on the apparatus, which could be considered by young viewers as a privilege. After Ma Changchun recalls how he used to help the projectionists on *Childhood Flashback*, the host of the show immediately responds: "It must be honorable to be able to do some work related to cinema. Initially it seemed so mysterious. Now I could also touch the screen and hug the machine. It felt like an honor."[7] For Cui Yongyuan, one highlight of his experience attending open-air screenings as a child is that he could sit on the wooden boxes for storing film reels during the screenings. His father was a political commissioner in the military. In order to flaunt his status as the son of someone in power, Cui insisted on sitting on the boxes. Although the boxes were not actually comfortable to sit on, Cui felt that it was such a privilege that when other envious children came to ask for some time on the boxes, he would only let them sit in the corner, for a brief moment.[8] In this story, the boxes, due to their proximity to the matter of cinema—the film reels, are transformed into surprisingly auratic objects, while tactility becomes the ultimate way to express and demonstrate intimacy with cinema.

Before the film began, audiences might engage in a second kind of physical interaction with the screen by projecting hand shadows onto it. This was possible because the projectionists at open-air screenings had to adjust the focal length of the projector on the spot by turning on the projector without film, thus shooting light onto an empty screen. In this case, the hand did not literally touch the screen, but by engaging with light, another essential medium of cinema, it was able to mark the screen, transforming it into theater. Zhang Yimou's short film, which spends a significant portion of its three minutes on this part of the screening, does not exaggerate audiences' behaviors much. Attendees of open-air screenings describe projecting hand shadows as an essential element of the prescreening rituals. As Jia Ding remembers, "When the projectionist tested equipment and the light was projected on the screen, everybody would stick out their hands and project all kinds of shapes—a goat or a dog. There were many kinds. This was an important activity too."[9] Wang Zhong (b. 1963), an artist based in Beijing, also recalls hand shadows being projected in the middle of screenings while projectionists loaded reels.[10] The extent to which the projection of hand shadows was routinized is indicated by the fact that these recollections are characterized by what Annette Kuhn calls "repetitive memory discourse"—narration in the habitual mode with first-person plural narrators ("we" or "everyone").[11]

The third kind of interaction involved audiences watching films from the back side of the screen. In his nostalgic song "Open-Air Cinema," Yu Dong particularly mentions the back side as the token of an irretrievable past as he sings, "There are no longer open-air cinemas in the city; I can no longer see the back side of the screen." Such a longing for the back side of the screen may be peculiar to moviegoers and observers elsewhere. In most theatrical settings, watching a film from the other side of the screen is simply impossible. Situated on a stage or the front of an auditorium, the screen is supposed to be a threshold connecting the theater space and the diegetic world. The inaccessibility of its back side is very much integral to the *dispositif*: to maintain the cinematic illusion, the screen itself must not be seen; by hiding its back side, it also hides its materiality. In other cases, the back side of the screen may be marked as a location of inferiority. According to Andrea Kelley, this was the case in the segregated American South where the screen literally functioned as a segregation device, separating white and black viewers.[12] By contrast, Chinese attendees of open-air screenings remember the back side of the screen in very different terms. Watching from behind the screen was normalized as a common practice.[13] Because of the large crowds that screenings often attracted, the reverse side not only was not seen as an inferior location but became a shortcut that allowed viewers to get closer to the screen. It was so common to watch from the back side that viewers sometimes did not even realize that they sat on the back side until later.

Consider this anecdote shared by Bi Fujian (b. 1959), a television show host:

> The Legend of the Red Lantern (Hong deng ji, 1971) was the most memorable film for me. There is a story here. At the time we always went to open-air screenings. We would sit behind the screen if we arrived late. After I watched The Legend of the Red Lantern, I got into an argument with people. In the film there is one point where the character Li Yuhe looks around holding a red light. They all said that Li Yuhe held the light with his right hand. I said bullshit. I saw him using his left hand the day before. . . . A month later the film was shown somewhere else. I trekked through mountains to watch it. Afterward I admitted I was wrong. I saw the right hand, no doubt. I couldn't figure out how come it was first the left hand and then the right hand. I thought Li Yuhe was a lefty and he couldn't suddenly switch to his right hand. I went back to watch the film one more time before I finally figured it out: when I saw it for the first time I was on the back side, and during the second time I was on the front side. From the front Li Yuhe uses his right hand; from the back, he is a lefty.[14]

Several observations can be made about this anecdote. First, the film became memorable for this viewer not because of its content but the moviegoing experience associated with it. Second, moviegoing was a social experience that continued beyond the screening. It was only through the exchange with fellow viewers that Bi Fujian realized his different relationality toward the screen. Third, compared to other conversations that could happen around a film, the "left hand or right hand" debate at the center of the story appeared to be a trivial one at first sight. Interest in seemingly marginal details in cinema was not unheard of. In post–World War II French cinephilic culture, Christian Keathley has noticed an intense preoccupation with what he calls "cinephiliac moments"—fragments of films and often unintentional details that could not be reduced to or tamed by interpretation but rather reveal the essence of the filmic medium.[15] It may be argued that a similar concern with the working of the cinematic apparatus underlined Bi Fujian's confusion too: what confused him was really the nature of cinematic projection and how the same film could result in such differences in perception. The answer, as he eventually realized after multiple viewings, was that the cinematic image was not inherent in the apparatus but was a matter of relations.

Access to the back side of the screen not only drew attention to the act of projection itself, but also transformed spectatorship by encouraging viewers to activate a more mobile form of screen engagement. In Bi Fujian's case, he was motivated by his confusion to travel to several screening sites. Movement could also occur during the screening as viewers were free to circle around the screen. Xiang Hong (b. 1949), a doctor born in Henan Province, recalls how she and her friends would deliberately run to the back side of the screen to see who could recognize the most Chinese characters in reverse.[16] When asked about which film was most memorable, Jia Ding, like Bi Fujian, shares an anecdote involving the screen:

> One detail that was really memorable was the last scene in the Albanian film *Victory over Death* (*Ngadhnjim mbi vdekjen/Ningsi buqu*, 1967). Two female guerrilla war fighters walk toward the camera, and then walk away from the camera into the distance. We immediately ran from the front of the screen to the back side of the screen, hoping to see their faces. But when we got to the other side, we still saw their backs. Somebody said: "they turned around!" We all rushed back to the front again. It felt very serious: we ran between the front and the back just so we could see their faces clearly.[17]

What may immediately stand out to some observers is the young viewers' seemingly "naive" belief that by getting to the other side of the screen, they should be able to acquire a reverse perspective in the diegetic world.

If the child spectator's supposed "naivety," which I will discuss later, manifested as a desire to circle around the screen for Jia Ding, the temptation for other young viewers was to touch the screen. While touching the technical apparatus before screenings could be a way to demonstrate intimacy with cinema, touch could also be motivated by diegetic actions on screen. Two groups of spectators have been described as particularly susceptible to this kind of touching. The first group is peasants. Anecdotes about how first-time rural audiences mistook the cinematic image to be real circulated among film projectionists. Viewers allegedly ran away from cars on the screen, threw rocks at evil landlords, and prepared meals for actors who they thought were present.[18] On *Childhood Flashback*, a film projectionist named Wang Zhong'an (b. 1950) shared the following stories:

Shen Li (host): In your memory was there anything that was particularly interesting?

Wang Zhong'an: Yes. For example, after watching war films, the ones with machine guns, airplanes, and canons, the next day I saw a few old men probing the ground with sticks while carrying a big basket on their backs. I asked them what they were looking for. They said that war was over, but where were the bullet shells? They were looking for bullet shells. They also asked where all the planes, canons, and tanks went. I said I put them in a box.

Shen: What about when they saw villains? How would they react?

Wang: When we showed *The White-Haired Girl*, for example, the character Huang Shiren was evil. When he forced Yang Bailao to pay his debt, kids would hit him with slingshots. In films like *Tunnel Warfare* or *Mine Warfare* (*Dilei zhan*, 1963) there were scenes showing Japanese devils entering villages. Sometimes an old lady would suddenly stand up to hit the Japanese devils on screens with bamboo sticks, or to hit the bearded officers. This indicates that film has a strong infectious power.

Shen: It penetrated deeply into people's hearts. As they watched on, it became real.

Wang: The audience was so engrossed that they sometimes forgot that they were watching films.[19]

Narratives like this fit into a larger discourse about rural audiences as naive, unsophisticated, and thus in need of guidance. As discussed in chapter 3, unfamiliarity with the medium, lack of historical or cultural knowledge, linguistic difficulties, and other barriers to comprehension were factors used to justify the need for lecturing, through which the projectionist could guide audiences to understand films correctly.[20]

Another group of "handsy" spectators was children, who would grow up and remember their own innocent selves (innocence being the predominant lens through which "inappropriate" childhood viewing behaviors are viewed). One story that captures many typical sentiments happens to also involve *The White-Haired Girl*. Zheng Zhenhuan (1942–2013), who was the head of the state-owned August First Film Studio from 1998 to 2001, grew up in a village in the outskirts of Beijing. He recalls that a projection team once traveled from village to village showing *The White-Haired Girl*. After watching the film in his own village, he followed the projection team to another village the next day. To his surprise, the film did not pick up from where it left off previously, namely, the execution of Huang Shiren; instead, it started from the beginning again when Huang Shiren was still alive. Bewildered, Zheng and his friends came up with a plan: the next day they would follow the projection team to another village and would mark Huang Shiren's face so that when the film was shown again, they could tell whether it was the same Huang Shiren that was alive and bullying Xi'er, Yang Bailao's daughter. The next day, holding mud in their hands, they climbed onto trees near the screen, waiting for close-ups of Huang Shiren so they could throw mud onto his face. As soon as they did it, Huang disappeared from the screen and other characters appeared. But now the screen was dirty, and everyone had black spots on their faces! The film was ruined. The kids were caught and punished. Their punishment, aptly, was to wash the screen, a job that fell on their unfortunate mothers, who had to wash the screen, dry, iron, and fold it before their children could take it back.[21]

The lesson Zheng himself draws from the experience is one of childhood innocence: "What this shows is that a child's heart is really like a sheet of white paper. It's very clean. They have a distinct sense of good and evil."[22] What he does not seem to find out of the ordinary is how in the aftermath of being marked with mud, the screen was not only touched, but returned to a state of pure materiality as sheet. If the child's heart was so innocent that it mistook a character on screen as real, when the material stuff of the screen was laid bare, was that when credulity turned into disillusionment?

A NAIVE AUDIENCE?

One conclusion that one can certainly draw from these audience accounts is that spectatorship in socialist China was not like how Western observers often take it to be—coercive, oppressive, and uniform. Jason McGrath quotes one such account written by a Western journalist in 1967 about the audience at a revolutionary skit performance: "I have never seen in China an audience as totally engrossed as this one. They did not applaud much, but it seemed as if they thought they shouldn't interrupt. They stared fixedly at the stage with faces completely rapt; each new scene creased their brows, wiped them smooth, furrowed them again more deeply, all in unison. Heads stretched forward so that not a single detail would escape their eyes." McGrath critiques that this account provides a "stereotypical representation of the Maoist masses as brainwashed automatons," a depiction of "almost unprecedentedly successful propaganda."[23] However, this stereotype was not created by Western media alone, as domestic accounts of moviegoing depicted audiences in a similar manner. In a 1951 report about a screening of *The White-Haired Girl* in the rural outskirts of Shanghai published in *Mass Cinema*, a paragraph reads:

> When the film first began, one could still hear the sounds of people talking. Gradually as the plot developed, the conversation died down and the screening area became quiet. More than five thousand pairs of eyes stared at the screen. When Huang Shiren's servant comes to grab Xi'er, Xi'er falls over her father's dead body and screams, "uncles and aunts save me. I'd rather die than go to the Huang's!" Characters on screen were wiping tears; rural women in the audience were doing the same. . . . In front of this film, the love and hate of peasants were as intense as fire.[24]

Here, too, the audience is described in terms of rapt attention and unified, synced emotion, with no less indication of "a seamless transmission of political ideology."[25] The Western imagination of the Maoist masses thus converges with the communist one (one that was publicly sanctioned). Moreover, one may even argue that the socialist ideology has nothing to do with this mode of attention at all. The deep absorption such as what the audience displays here is not only the goal of classical Hollywood cinema, but also what some theorists believed to be inherent in cinematic spectatorship. Tom Gunning describes this vision of film audiences as "submitting passively to an all-dominating apparatus, hypnotized and transfixed by its illusionist power," which may be applied to this situation as well.[26]

Yet, as shown by the anecdotes above, audience members of "propaganda" films like *The White-Haired Girls* did not necessarily fit into this model as they interacted with the screen and the screening apparatus. Instead, it may be tempting to compare them to early film audiences from the time of cinema's invention. The descriptions of rural and child audiences as innocent and naive echo what has been said about spectators who supposedly panicked at the sight of a train coming at them during Lumière brothers' presentation of *The Arrival of a Train* (*L'arrivée d'un train à La Ciotat*, 1896). The act of touching the screen reminds one of classic rube films like *Uncle Josh at the Moving Picture Show* (1902), in which the spectators on screen are supposedly fooled by cinematic realism to such a degree that they cannot help but touch the screen, mistaking the imaginary images to be real. Such interpretations of naivety in the Western context has been the object of much criticism. Gunning points out that claims of audiences' credulity ignore the historical context of visual entertainments that had long explored the uncanny effect of realism before moving images came along. If the first film audiences were astonished, Gunning suggests, it was not because of their credulity but because they were acutely aware of the illusion-istic power of the cinematic apparatus.[27] Calling the supposed panic of Lumière brothers' audiences cinema's founding myth, Martin Loi-perdinger finds no contemporary report that confirms the existence of such panic reactions and calls for relegating the myth to "the realm of film historical fantasy."[28] Situating the country rube films at the transi-tion from the cinema of attractions to one of narrative integration, both Miriam Hansen and Thomas Elsaesser recognize the disciplinary func-tion of these films achieved through comedy.[29] Rather than interpreting the urge to touch as naivety, Hansen emphasizes the excess of pleasure that the country rube trope came to embody. These films, in her eyes, articulate a need to integrate such excess into a more "mature" mode of viewing. Wanda Strauven proposes yet another way to look at the country rube genre, which she suggests could be nostalgic rather than didactic. She situates the rube's impulse to touch in a longer tradition of hands-on media practices that involved precinematic devices such as optical toys and hand-cranked viewing machines. Touching, therefore, is not a sign of naivety but a different mode of engagement, an alterna-tive cultural and historical practice.[30]

In the Chinese context, a similar myth of naive first-time spectators has not yet been interrogated. But despite eyewitness accounts, there are many reasons to question to what extent spectators could mistake cinematic images as reality. The open-air setting, where most anec-dotes of this nature were reported, exposed the screening apparatus. In *Uncle Josh at the Moving Picture Show*, the downstage location of the screen completely conceals the rear projection until it is torn down at the end of the film, revealing the mechanism producing the illusion. By contrast, Chinese audiences would have had ample opportunities to interact with the screening apparatus before the screening even began. As I have shown, while projectionists set up their equipment, both the projector and the screen could become objects of spectators' gaze and touch. The screen would have had a tangible material presence as a sheet to be unfolded, raised, and secured, and as an installation that divided and transformed space. For Gunning, the fact that in the ear-liest Lumière screenings, films were initially shown as frozen images undermined any naive belief in realism.[31] Similarly, it is hard to imagine

Chinese audiences who had prolonged exposure to the screening apparatus would still mistake projected images as real. Perhaps confusion could arise for people who arrived late and those who only caught a glimpse of the images or heard the faint sound of what happened on screen. But considering the close-knit local communities in which rural film screenings took place, it is also doubtful that one would not have learned a few basics about cinema from someone they knew.

Access to the back side of the screen further challenged illusionism. Writing about the traditional Chinese painted screen, Wu Hung argues: "An awareness that a screen painting has a reverse side destroys any sense of pictorial illusion but reestablishes the materiality of the medium and redefines the concept of the surface. In other words, instead of erasing the surface, the image confirms its existence."[32] It is reasonable to expect a similar effect from the film screen that was watched from both sides. Compared to the typical theatrical screen that appears to be a portal into the film world, access to the back side of the screen should reveal the cinematic illusion as illusion and confirm the materiality of the screen.

Even if viewers could be so affected by the film that they would throw rocks at the evil landlords on screen, it was not necessarily a testament to the realism of cinema per se. Similar incidents of audience overreaction were also widely reported in the world of theater. Shakespeare's *Othello* is famously known for inspiring strong reactions from the audience. Among the anecdotes that have been circulated, a soldier allegedly fired a weapon at the actor playing Othello and broke his arm at a performance in Baltimore in 1822.[33] In another nineteenth-century staging of the play, an actor who played Iago was supposedly shot dead by an appalled audience member. According to legend, his tombstone reads: "Here lies the greatest actor."[34] *The White-Haired Girl* left a trail of similar stories of overidentification. A projectionist from Jiangsu told me that once a PLA soldier was so angry that he tried to shoot the landlord Huang Shiren.[35] Initially under the impression that this happened at a film screening, I later found out that this legendary incident was in fact at a production of the opera *The White-Haired Girl* several years before it was adapted into a film. In 1946, the art troupe of North China United University (*Huabei lianda*) performed the opera for soldiers at the battlefront of the Civil War in Hebei. During one performance, when Huang Shiren forces Yang Bailao to sell his daughter to him as a concubine and drives him to suicide, it was reported that the audience was so infuriated that many threw rocks and dirt at the stage, bruising the left eye of Chen Qiang (1918–2012), the actor playing Huang Shiren, who later reprised this role in the film version. In another instance, a soldier reportedly drew his gun and aimed at Chen. Luckily, he was stopped from taking action. From then on, soldiers were no longer allowed to bring loaded guns to performances of *The White-Haired Girl*.[36] Similar incidents also happened with a performance of the play *Liu Hulan* by the Combat Dramatic Society in 1947. Depicting the real-life story of a peasant girl's execution by her village landlord and Guomindang soldiers, the performance allegedly provoked the enraged audience to throw rocks and fire guns at the stage.[37]

These anecdotes involving the suspension of disbelief are fundamentally different from a supposedly "naive" reaction to cinema that confuses projected images with the actual objects. In the train myth, what supposedly terrorized the audience was cinema's unique reproductive power. Put on display, its indexicality confronted viewers directly without being integrated into a narrative. By contrast, the emotional power of *The White-Haired Girl* and *Liu Hulan* was grounded in narratives designed to mobilize class sentiments and then magnified by actors' convincing performance. It was a transmedial power that could be claimed by both theater and cinema. Audience members of such narratives who could not restrain themselves, whose intense emotions manifested as aggression, were certainly undisciplined. But can we say they were naive? After all, contemporary audiences everywhere continue to cry for characters, mourn fictional deaths, yell at the screen, and in the case of some passionate sports fans, smash their television sets when their favorite teams lose. Rather than naivety, the overwhelming of disbelief may well be the willing choice of a seasoned consumer who has realized that they can derive more pleasures from losing themselves in a narrative than being reminded that "it's just a movie" all the time.

This knowing disavowal brings us into the realm of play, which presents a more productive lens to look at "unruly" audience behaviors than the linear categories of naivety or maturity. Scholars like Wanda Strauven have identified a ludic media tradition in which resonance can be found between nineteenth-century optical toys, arcade games, and early cinema and present-day home cinema, video games, and touchscreens. Home cinema is said to have brought cinema back to its "cradle" and the country rube is said to have returned in the digital age after a long middle period of classical cinema.[38] But the accounts of Chinese audiences suggest that even the screen of public celluloid projection could still be played with. Whether people were touching the screen, casting hand shadows, circling around the screen, or throwing rocks at evil characters, they were, consciously or unconsciously, playing with the screen.

PLAY, FILM STUDIES, MEDIA ARCHAEOLOGY

Play is not a new concept in film and media studies. The German notion of *spiel*, which has the meanings of "play," "performance," and "gamble," was seen by Hansen as a central notion in Walter Benjamin's thinking of technology, modernity, and cinema. For Benjamin, Hansen argues, cinema, as a "play form of the second nature," that is, of modern technology, has the potential to reverse the numbing of the human sensorium and other catastrophic consequences of technology through a utopian aesthetic of play that offered mimetic innervation, repetition, and second chances.[39] Play also features prominently in recent scholarship on nineteenth-century optical toys as scholars reorient from seeing them as precinematic visual devices to media objects that were supposed to be touched, handled, and played with in both prescribed and open-ended ways. Meredith Bak advocates play as an archival methodology. Defining play as not only an act but "an attitude, mind-set, or approach that facilitates productive encounters and discoveries within the archival context," Bak believes that being a player, experimenting and experiencing the objects firsthand would help the researcher imagine the original user's experience.[40] Strauven puts optical toys, including devices such as the thaumatrope, the phenakistoscope, the zoetrope, and the praxinoscope, in Roger Caillois's category of *ilinx*—a category of play based on the pursuit of vertigo. She makes an important contribution by contextualizing optical toys in a culture of hands-on practices that were also embodied in early museum practices, arcade games, and public entertainment, based on hand-cranked viewing machines. Although the adoption of optical devices for public viewing, which separated the viewer from the apparatus, and the later emergence of cinema shifted audiences into a more visual mode of engagement, the hands-on aspect, Strauven reminds us, would occasionally reemerge in the form of "interactive" cinema from sing-alongs to avant-garde practices as well as in films that may be said to invite viewers to "play" by staging acts of screen touching. She also connects contemporary home cinema back to optical toys in terms of its domestic setting, interactivity, and tactility.[41] Other scholars see the study of recent media technologies and accompanying viewing practices as an area that can benefit from play theories.

Karin Beeler, for instance, examines children's DVD screen culture as play and demonstrates how key ideas from play theories such as structured and unstructured play, repetition, control and spontaneity, and pretend play and identification, are helpful in understanding the ways in which children use DVDs. One conclusion that she draws is that as a child engages with bonus features and other extras in the DVD, the experience of viewing the film may no longer be at the center. She thus encourages film scholars to pay more attention to "the kinds of media content that have previously been called mere add-ons."[42]

All of these studies, however, focus on Western media practices, thus offering a limited horizon for drawing general conclusions about when screen touching has taken place and why it is generally discouraged. For instance, after mentioning a few examples of screen touching in films such as *Sherlock Jr.* (1924), *Les carabiniers* (1963), and *Minority Report* (2002), Strauven states that "it is only in avant-garde practices that (nondiegetic) film screens are actually touched."[43] She then adds:

> One could also object that the (nondiegetic) film screen has never been touchable in the restricted realm of (nonexpanded) cinema and that bodily interaction with the apparatus was possible only in the precinematic *dispositif* of domestic optical toys and public hand-cranked peepshows. . . . These precinematic *dispositifs* were screenless *dispositifs*. The cinematic *dispositif* (re-)introduced the screen. More rigorously than its predecessors, the film screen is a screen that protects the apparatus from the touching hand, creates a safe distance between the view and the viewer, and thus acts as "shield" (according to its uncertain etymology, presumably deriving from the Old High German *skirm, skerm*).[44]

One objection that can be brought to Strauven is that outside of the Western context, the observation that film screens are touched only in avant-garde practices simply is not true. As in the case of Chinese socialist open-air cinema, a different configuration of the cinematic *dispositif* could annihilate the distance between the viewer and the apparatus, making the screen much more touchable.

Another point that calls for scrutiny here is Strauven's appeal to the etymology of the word *screen* as an explanation for its untouchability, which distinguishes it from screenless media devices that more readily lend themselves to play. Etymology has been central to media archaeological approaches to the screen, or what Erkki Huhtamo names "screenology," which aims to study the screen by "relating different types of screens to each other and assessing their significance within changing cultural, social, and ideological frames of references."[45] The goal of media archaeology, as Huhtamo defines, is to find earlier patterns or schemata behind phenomena that may appear new and unprecedented.⁴⁶ Excavating the multiple meanings and semantic shifts of *screen* has allowed scholars to make sense of the ambivalent ways in which the screen has figured in changing media imaginations over time. Beginning with its origin in the thirteenth-century French word *escran*, which referred to a piece of furniture that shielded heat, Strauven examines six overlapping connotations of the word *screen* in another article and discusses how these connotations can be found in early cinema.⁴⁷ Dominique Chateau and José Moure, in their introduction to the edited volume *Screens*, also begin with an etymology of *screen*.⁴⁸ Contributors of the volume further look back at early tensions in the concept of screen, such as between showing and concealing, between monstration and protection, in order to understand the "current multifarious forms and practices of screening."⁴⁹

Given the predominance of media archaeology in studies of screen cultures, one may wonder if the "playability" of the open-air screens in socialist China can also be explained through some kind of etymology. There are two problems with this approach. First, media archaeology has been vague on exactly how earlier material or discursive forms impact the present. Beyond pointing out similarities or resonances between the past and the present, scholars have not explained whether such connections are a result of shared linguistic conditioning, cultural memory, social consensus, individual insight, or something else. In particular, one wonders how prior meanings factor into specific audience behaviors. In what ways did the notion of "shield" make the early film screen untouchable? Did it, consciously or subconsciously, influence how exhibitors set up the screen or the ways in which audiences approached the screen? To what extent were people aware of this older connotation? Merely recognizing resonance leaves many questions unanswered.

Second, an archaeology of the screen becomes even more complicated in transcultural contexts. What happened when Western screen practices traveled to China? To what extent did the prior etymology of *screen* in European languages influence conceptions of the screen in the new context? How did foreign concepts intersect with indigenous traditions to produce new, hybrid forms? While fully answering these questions is beyond the scope of the current study, it is worth pointing out how the most common Chinese term for the film screen, *yinmu* (a direct translation of the term *silver screen*), has etymological elements that are both similar to and divergent from the word *screen*. Although *yinmu* is now used to refer to any kind of film screen and functions as a synecdoche for cinema, its first usages emerged in the 1920s with the import of silver lenticular screens. In earliest Chinese accounts of lantern shows and film screenings from the 1880s to 1890s, many terms were used to refer to the screen, most of which either described the screen as a cloth curtain (*buwo, buman, bumu*) or a white sheet (*baibu*).[50] In some cases, commentators also pointed out that the white curtain was employed as a divider, evoking the traditional divider screen (*pingfeng*).[51] However, the latter connotations of division or shield, which are shared by the English word *screen*, later largely disappeared from the semantic field around the cinematic screen and reemerged in the term *pingmu*, which now refers to television and digital screens. *Mu*, at the same time, was adopted over alternative terms as the standard term for the cinematic screen. In the early second-century dictionary *Shuowen jiezi*, *mu* is described as either a canopy ("a curtain that is above") or a tablecloth, both sharing the idea of a piece of fabric covering something from above. *Mu* thus also came to denote curtains, tents, general's quarters, stage curtains, and theatrical acts. The association with stage drama was likely what distinguished *mu* from other terms that were temporarily evoked to refer to the projection screen. As Hongwei Thorn Chen suggests, the use of *mu* stabilized in the 1920s as cinema came to be seen as a theatrical art.[52] In contrast to Strauven's suggestion that the connotation of "shield" is behind the ability of the film screen to "protect the apparatus from the touching hand," it may be suggested that the pliability of curtains and sheets were behind Chinese audiences' tactile interactions with the screen. But such an archaeological approach lacks the ability to explain historical variations. It also neglects other more direct explanations of audience behaviors. Theatrical audiences are generally prevented from touching the screen due to the *dispositif* involving the frontal placement of the screen and fixed seating at a distance from the screen. For rural audiences in socialist China, the screen did not just have the connotation of being a curtain, it was *literally* carried around as a sheet (it was not unheard of for projectionists to use actual bedsheets as screens).[53] In a word, the archaeological method may reveal changing conceptions of the screen, but etymological underpinnings do not translate into moviegoing practices. To understand the play permitted at socialist open-air screenings, I will instead turn to anthropological approaches to play that emphasizes its nature as a framed, subjunctive activity.

PLAY, RITUAL, AND PRETEND

For Gregory Bateson, play presupposes a paradoxical frame. While play actions may imitate or denote the real things, they need to be understood with the simultaneous message "This is play" and therefore not to be taken seriously. He famously uses the example of two monkeys playing at the zoo to illustrate the play frame: the two monkeys exhibited signals as if they were engaged in combat; yet they were not actually at combat but were playing.[54] Adam Seligman, Robert Weller, Michael Puett, and Bennett Simon develop a similar idea through the notion of the subjunctive, which denotes "the creation of an order as if it were truly the case," a "could be" shared by participants.[55] In their view, play is similar to ritual, as both "construct a third space where we create, experience, and share alternative realities and orders" except that ritual lays claim to more permanent truth, and thus encourages greater predictability and repetition.[56] Based on this understanding of play, it would be reductive to equate play with hands-on interactions or touch, as play is not limited to specific actions but is first and foremost an attitude. As such, at least three levels of play can be identified in audiences' interaction with the screen.

On the first level, moviegoing itself can be seen as play. Not only does moviegoing fit John Huizinga's classic definition of play as free, disinterested, and separate from everyday life, it also constitutes a subjunctive with its own realities and rules.[57] The last point cannot be underestimated. If moviegoing is rule-bound, the implication is that it can abide by different sets of rules in different contexts. From this perspective, approaching moviegoing in socialist China as play means abandoning teleological (and ideological) tropes such as "early audience" or "naivety" and recognizing an order that is simply different. One unique aspect of this order, as this book consistently aims to show, is the foregrounding of non-filmic exhibition interfaces that resulted from both the state's need for propaganda and the unpredictable environment of open-air cinema. What also disrupted the usual teleology of cinema and made socialist moviegoing unique was the disjuncture between the cinematic mode of address and audiences' modes of engagement. Unlike audiences of early cinema in the late nineteenth and early twentieth centuries, first-time viewers in 1950s-China were not presented with short films of attractions, but feature-length films developed from classical narrative conventions. Comparing these viewers to early cinema audiences does not do justice to the demand of narrative comprehension put on them that actual early cinema audiences did not have to face. If viewers could refuse concentrated viewing and immersion, choosing to *kan renao* or engage with the screening apparatus in tactile manners, it was not because of their naivety, which I have shown to be a questionable assumption, but because open-air screenings permitted a set of rules that allowed for greater degrees of interaction and movement than what is usually permitted in commercial movie theaters in the West. A well-known Western example of interactive cinema that challenges mainstream norms is the midnight showing of *The Rocky Horror Picture Show* (1975), during which audiences would loudly talk back at the screen and throw objects at it.[58] If contemporary Western audiences attending these shows are not perceived as naïve but as activating an alternative mode of engagement, why cannot viewers with similar behaviors in China be seen in a similar way?

On a second level, many of the boundary-setting activities at film exhibition clearly acquired ritualistic qualities, thus resulting in the widespread perception of moviegoing as a ritual. Among others, tactile contact with the apparatus and the projection of hand shadows not only demarcated entry into the subjunctive space of play, but also foregrounded this space as one of communal participation. Zheng Zhenhuan's story in which a screen was defaced by children and then washed by their mothers illustrates the depth of such communal involvement. While touching the screen was not forbidden, the children clearly went too far and broke a rule. But it was not the rule of "do not touch" but the socialist rule of collectivism that mattered in this case. By throwing mud onto the screen, the children were being individualistic. They neglected to consider either the interest of the rest of the community or the civic duty of protecting public property. In contrast to rural projectionists who were praised for their efforts in protecting and maintaining the screening equipment, the irresponsible behavior of the kids needed to be punished. The punishment was also in line with the communal ethos, which forwent a rigid division between film professionals and audience members. As mothers were enlisted to rectify the mistake of their children by washing and caring for the screen, they ceased to be onlookers of film screenings while the screen was transformed from a surface for the projection of images to household fabric.

Communal participation thus had the effect of domesticating cinema, assimilating it into the space of everyday life. The projection of hand shadows had a similar effect by allowing participants to play a domestic game in a public setting. Although in Europe, hand shadows used to be both a private pastime and the basis of a kind of stage performance known as *ombromanie*, there is little evidence suggesting that hand shadows were widely performed in public in China, where it was shadow puppetry, which utilized flat cut-out figures, that has a long history and many regional variations.[59] For the most part, hand shadows remained a domestic children's game. Open-air screenings created the opportunity for hand shadows to exit the private sphere into the public. By marking the screen with their bodies, the crowd laid claims on an alien apparatus that literally entered their space from the outside, temporarily making it their own. They were empowered to explore the apparatus of projection in a playful way. As participants changed the shape of their hands or moved them closer or further away from the screen, they could observe the interaction among some of the basic components of projection such as light, shadow, and distance. They could experience the conjuring of illusions and practice staying in the state of "pleasurable vacillation between belief and doubt."[60] In Zhang Yimou's short film, the portrayal of this part of the open-air cinema is ended by a child throwing a rooster into the air, causing the crowd to erupt into laughter. This moment is funny precisely because it violates the premise of hand shadows, substituting the amusement of "I know it's not real but . . ." with the realization of "wait, that is actually real."

The "I know but . . ." frames the third level of play in the moviegoing experience in the same way as Bateson's "this is play." Instead of reading audiences' interaction with the screen "as is," it is possible to read it through the play frame. In other words, audiences could pretend that the images were true without truly believing that was the case. For child viewers, such a pretense gave permission for more playfulness. The temporary disavowal of the apparatus could be an active choice, an "excuse" to involve the body in the viewing process.

In Jia Ding's story, a group of friends ran to the other side of the screen when characters faced away from the camera. I have quoted Jia Ding several times in the book. In his self-description, he was an enthusiastic moviegoer that regularly attended open-air screenings. It is hard to imagine that someone like him would genuinely believe that the front and back side of the screen offered opposite views of diegetic characters. More likely, by pretending that it was the case, he and his friends invented a game of chase, in which the pleasure was sustained by never being able to catch up to the other side that was not on screen. In doing so, they playfully confronted the nature of projection and the transparency of the white sheet screen.

Zheng Zhenhuan and his friends pretended that they could cross the threshold into the diegesis as they threw mud onto the screen to mark Huang Shiren's face. The sincerity of their belief, however, is belied by their apparent awareness of the reproducibility of cinema—that is, a film can be shown again and again. Could the self-confessed desire to mark Huang Shiren so that multiple versions of him could be set apart be merely a pretext for the comical effect of seeing mud on serious faces? The cut from a close-up of Huang's face to elsewhere must have instantly brought awareness to the separation between the mudded surface and the diegetic world. But just as a child can enjoy a stuffed animal talking to them while fully knowing a parent is supplying the voice, the viewer does not have to drop the play frame even with rational knowledge of the cinematic medium. In fact, the innocence of childhood remembered by moviegoers may have little to do with naive credulity, but a lot to do with the play spirit, which, for many, would become much less available in their adult years.

In play, audiences improvised with fun, creative ways to insert themselves into the screening process. In the long term, as the political promise of socialist open-air cinema faded, it is not surprising that what is left in audiences' memories, and what they are encouraged to remember by the nostalgia industry, is the multifarious pleasures of open-air cinema. As the last three chapters have shown, these pleasures could come from the lyrical atmosphere, the physical struggle that nonetheless elevated moviegoing, as well as the playfulness permitted by the outdoor, communal setting. Both Zhang Yimou's short film and the *Child Flashback* interviews came out at a time when the touchscreen had not yet become a globally shared component of childhood. I cannot guess whether the older generations of moviegoers would see any similarities between themselves and kids playing on their iPads and tablets today. But what is certain is that if we make a generalization about cinema in the public setting as an institution that discourages physical interaction with the screen, then we are ignoring the ludic elements that may just be waiting for the right condition to reappear.

Postscript

Recognizing Cinema

A surprising reference to socialist open-air cinema appears in a review of Ang Lee's 2019 film *Gemini Man* by Chinese film scholar Li Daoxin.[1] Released in the United States on October 11, 2019, and a week later in China, *Gemini Man* tells a familiar story of a secret agent on the run: Henry, played by Will Smith, is hunted by an assassin sent by his former employer; he is then surprised to find out that the assassin is actually a cloned version of his younger self. A quick survey of reviews on Rotten Tomatoes and the Chinese review/social media platform *Douban* reveals an almost unanimous disappointment in the quality of the story (one American critic thinks the dialogue of the film sounds like it is "written by an AI").[2]

But what distinguishes *Gemini Man* from a failed action movie, and what makes it both controversial and interesting, is its use of cutting-edge technology. Ang Lee, who has been experimenting with 3D and high frame rate (HFR) since *Life of Pi* (2012) and *Billy Lynn's Long Halftime Walk* (2016), shot *Gemini Man* in 120 frames per second (fps), 4K resolution, and 3D, a format so advanced that there was not a single theater in the United States that could show the film as intended and only fourteen could show it in 120 fps, 2K and 3D. Meanwhile, in China, *Gemini Man* opened in its original format in twenty-seven movie theaters across seventeen cities that featured the new CINITY cinema system. Debuted in August 2019, less than two months before the film's premiere, CINITY is a product of the partnership between China-based

Huaxia Film Distribution, and US-based Christie Digital Systems and GDC Technology. According to Christie's press release, CINITY is "designed to combine and optimize a variety of high technologies, including 3D, 4K resolution, Wide Color Gamut (WCG), Extended dynamic range, High Frame Rate (HFR), Immersive Sound, to project better and more pixels onto the screen and create a superior immersive audio-visual experience."[3] Ang Lee himself describes the system as a "milestone advance in the film industry, and a trend for the future development of the film industry in China and around the world."[4]

It may be hard to imagine that China is now joining the United States as a leading force in the global development of cinematic technologies when only a few decades ago the country was still in the pursuit of an "alternative" socialist modernity. Yet it is precisely the hidden connection between socialist film exhibition and the emerging technology that Li Daoxin seeks to bring to light by evoking open-air cinema. Li observes that whenever the showing of new films, such as James Cameron's *Avatar* (2009) and Ang Lee's recent films, introduced cutting-edge cinematic technologies to China, a mechanism of shortage was activated as only a small number of venues were equipped to show these films. For him, this calls to mind the bygone era of open-air cinema. Why? Because the limited screenings of new films at select theaters and open-air screenings elicit a similar combination of confusion and anticipation among moviegoers. "When to go see it? Where to go? What will happen when we watch the film?" These are questions shared by audiences then and now. In other words, what allows Li to connect the current theatrical exhibition of *Gemini Man* with open-air cinema is the practice of moviegoing. Furthermore, Li emphasizes that the "movie" in "moviegoing" is not about any particular movie that the spectator chooses to watch; instead, the inner logic of moviegoing has more to do with the opportunity (*jiyu*), venue (*changsuo*), mechanism (*jizhi*), and atmosphere (*fenwei*) associated with it. Therefore, according to Li, years later when we remember *Gemini Man*, our personal memory will be less about the technology or the plot of the film and more about when we watched the film, in which city and which movie theater. Similarly, for several generations of Chinese people, it is not the films screened in the open air but open-air cinema itself that changed their fate.[5]

In the unexpected move of juxtaposing socialist open-air cinema and the theatrical experience of *Gemini Man*, what Li accomplishes, and what makes his review an apt ending for this book, is a demonstration of how film exhibition and moviegoing in socialist China can be brought into the ongoing definition of cinema. For Casetti, when we negotiate emerging moving image forms with the form of cinema with which we are already familiar, we perform two simultaneous operations that he calls "the paradoxes of recognition." On one hand, "we manipulate what we have in front of us to make it more compatible with what we know." We might ignore certain elements so that an older model of cinema continues to apply. On the other hand, we adjust our idea of cinema by projecting new characteristics back to the past so that we can claim that what appears new already has precedents.[6] The novel technologies employed in *Gemini Man* beg precisely the question "Can the film be recognized as cinema?" On this matter, critics in the United States and in China came up with opposing answers.

In the United States, the dismissal of the film began with exhibitors, who showed no interest in upgrading their projection systems to accommodate the advanced format of *Gemini Man*, believing that customers would be unwilling to pay an upcharge for the full experience.[7] Critics equally view HFR with suspicion. Alissa Wilkinson, worrying about how the ability to digitally create a twenty-three-year-old Will Smith will lead Hollywood to abandon real human actors, announces that the film "may be a harbinger of cinema's demise." In terms of the film's visual effects, Wilkinson writes: "I had to watch the action sequences by looking away, then glancing up every few seconds because I felt ill almost instantly . . . also bright flashes . . . and loud noises and, well, anything you would go to a theme park attraction to experience. Cinema, am I right?" The ability to keep actions on all planes of the image in sharp focus is a major innovation of HFR. But for this critic, "it looks terrible, like motion smoothing on a massive screen; with everything in focus in the frame, it's hard to tell what to look at."[8] Motion smoothing is the technology that digitally inserts frames into television broadcasting to minimize blurring, creating what is known among American critics as the soap opera effect. Film critic Chris Evangelista cites the same reason for concluding that "HFR just doesn't look right."[9] Keith Phipps goes further in trying to figure out exactly why HFR does not look right: "In Lee's hands, HFR's you-are-there effect can feel otherworldly, offering so much vivid realism that it can start to feel unreal. . . . The incredible clarity allows for, well, incredible clarity. But it also makes it hard to sink into the film. . . . Its nonaction scenes still have a distancing too-real feeling: The actors seem too present and the surroundings too tangible for it to seem like a movie, or at least a movie as we've come to know it over the last 100-plus years of filmmaking."[10]

In short, HFR might have brought something new to cinema, but it matters less than the jarring fact that it makes movies look uncinematic. One can sense the ghost of Susan Sontag haunting in the discomfort of these critics. At first sight, it may appear that what troubles them is simply a new mode of looking, but deep down, what makes HFR unwelcome is still a matter of location. For Sontag, it was the relocation of cinema to the living room that was degrading; for these critics, it was the overtaking of the big screen by what does not belong, namely television visuality (motion smoothing, soap opera effect), that is alienating. Both sets of attitudes are fundamentally conservative. For the cinema conservatives, it is simply jarring when cinema no longer is what it used to be.

Some of the observations made by American critics are shared by Chinese critics and fans, that HFR provides theme-park-like spectacles, that it looks different, and that its too-real realism is distancing. But not being familiar with either motion smoothing or the unique aesthetics of the American soap opera, Chinese viewers, as famous film critic Zhou Liming observes, display a much higher level of acceptance of advanced formats than American audiences. Zhou's own review of *Gemini Man* is ambivalent, not being able to make up his mind whether Ang Lee is a far-sighted pioneer or someone deluded by the false promise of technology.[11] Other commentators demonstrate a willingness to adopt a longer historical view and to question what is taken for granted. For example, a *Douban* user with the ID "Daqite (Grinch)" similarly notes how HFR makes the film lose some of the traditionally cinematic qualities. However, they also emphasize the following: "We should not evaluate new technology with traditional standards, because traditional standards have taken roots within us, but new technology has yet formed its new aesthetics. The situation was the same when cinema was first born. It was the same during the transition from film to digital, from 2D to 3D. And now it is the same from 24fps to 120fps. There is always a process."[12] This is a sharp contrast with the American critics. While perhaps not enthusiastic about the film's style personally, "Daqite" is reflexive enough to recognize how aesthetic preferences are historically conditioned by previous technology and thus refrains from rushing to judgment. Further down on the spectrum of acceptance, we can also find those who show palpable excitement for the film, hailing it as revolutionary and groundbreaking. Critic Xiulong refutes the idea that 120fps merely provides a brighter and clearer image. What HFR achieves, Xiulong suggests, is challenging the very foundation of what constitutes the visual aesthetics that we are accustomed to.[13] For another *Douban* user, "ripple," what the deep focus of HFR allows is no less than the opening up of what Gilles Deleuze calls microperception, a nonhuman-centered, all-perceiving capacity that has the potential to overcome the limitations of our habitual mode of seeing and politics. If, as Casetti suggests, cinema can be defined primarily as "a mode of seeing, feeling, reflecting, and reacting,"[14] in HFR's ability to further differentiate the camera vision from the human eye (no wonder it doesn't look right), what "ripple" sees is a deepening of the potential of 24fps, a "total cinematization."[15]

These Chinese reviews of *Gemini Man* are impressive for how they are able to articulate both discontinuity and continuity, recognizing the transformation brought by technology while confirming the identity of the emergent imagery as cinema. The "paradoxes of recognition" are central in the ways both "Daqite" and "ripple" came to accept the novelty of *Gemini Man* as cinematic: the former by underscoring technological update and disruption as an inherent part of cinema; the latter by recognizing microperception as an ontological tendency that is realized with increasing frame rates. Perhaps to their own surprise, in trying to make sense of *Gemini Man*, these viewers end up writing cinema history and defining cinema.

By evoking open-air cinema, Li Daoxin engages in a similar task—that is, to integrate something new and potentially revolutionary into a more familiar model of cinema. He does so by underscoring moviegoing, but not so much moviegoing as a social or spatial practice as the subjective feelings associated with it (anticipation, memory, etc.). Li is definitely nostalgic and yet his nostalgia is different from Cui Yongyuan's. As the book has shown, collective memory of open-air cinema in postsocialist China is more often mediated by a perception of difference. Against the standardized, de-individualized setting of contemporary movie theaters, the lyrical, communal atmosphere of open-air cinema, its playful spirit, and even its harsh conditions become reasons for nostalgic yearnings, underlying which was China's epochal transformation from socialism to postsocialism. Someone like Cui Yongyuan makes the difference absolute, privileging one mode of exhibition as more authentic than others. Li, instead, is interested in articulating a broader notion of cinema that encompasses both.

Meanwhile, by connecting *Gemini Man* to not just the general paradigm of open-air cinema but open-air cinema as it was experienced by several generations of Chinese viewers, Li also accomplishes something else beyond the scope of Casetti's original idea of "paradoxes of recognition." For Casetti, recognition relies on a negotiation between the past and present. It is also this temporal dimension that occupies most of the Western debate on cinema's identity crisis. But by referring to Chinese open-air screenings, Li foregrounds another dimension: the geographical dimension. When we speak of cinema's past, present, and future, what is the geographical scope we assume? Are we speaking about all of cinema, regardless of the country, region, culture, and polity that embeds it? The specific location of cinema clearly has an impact on how American critics view HFR as uncinematic. It is only in the American media environment wherein the soap opera is seen as a low, inferior media form that the "incredible clarity" of HFR would be stigmatized simply due to its visual likeness to soap operas. In this case, culture prevents "the paradoxes of recognition" from happening. But I have not seen cultural difference being discussed in the dialogue of medium specificity. In her recent analysis of the oral accounts of former and current cinema projectionists in Britain, Charlotte Brunsdon does not consider to what extent "the projectionist's tale" she constructs may be a uniquely British one. Instead, empirical details are used to draw attention to the labor and performance of cinema projection, which is seen as "the pivot that brings together film as a medium and cinema as an institution during cinema's twentieth century."[16]

Not surprisingly, this leap from what is geographically situated to a deterritorialized conclusion about "cinema's twentieth century" is easier done for the Euro-American critic examining Euro-American cinemas than for those studying the non-West. Chapters 2 and 3 of this book, in fact, perform similar work as Brunsdon's article by illuminating the labor and performance of the Chinese projectionist under the socialist film exhibition system. The rural mobile projection team, I demonstrate, was a crucial interface in the system, as it constituted a delivery infrastructure, an embodiment of socialist values, and a mediating agent of multimedia technologies. This is a historically and geographically bounded argument. Should I bypass this middle level and jump to the same conclusion as Brunsdon, thus jumping into the space of theory, how would my argument be perceived? Would the Europeanists and Americanists, as Paul Pickowicz predicts, not like it at all when "universal" theories are developed based on empirical studies of China? Would they object by saying that some of the phenomena are particular to China or socialist China and therefore cannot support a general conclusion about "cinema's twentieth century"? I would agree with part of this objection. Because of the unique combination of ideological and material factors, the pivotal role played by the rural projectionist in Chinese socialist film exhibition was almost unparalleled. This, I do not intend to generalize, but the observation that film exhibition is a system of interfaces does have broader applications beyond China. In a word, the question is not whether we can develop theory based on empirical studies (yes, we can); what is crucial is that in order to do that, we must work through the historical and cultural. Studies of non-Western cultures should not be confined to the space of the particular; scholars like Brunsdon might also want to think twice before making generalizations. The question to keep in mind is this one: When the work of British film projectionists is taken to represent "cinema's twentieth century," whose experience is privileged and whose is left out?

While open-air cinema has been largely left out of film scholarship, let alone the debate of cinema ontology, what Li Daoxin does in his article is recognize open-air cinema as cinema. If we introduce a geographical dimension into the "paradoxes of recognition," then the negotiation of identity that Casetti describes does not only occur between the past and the present, but also between the dominant and the "alternative," the familiar and the lesser known, the urban and the rural, the capitalist and the socialist, the Western and non-Western. It means that "the idea of cinema" against which we consider new situations needs to remain open not only to the ongoing transformation of cinema, but also to the past that continues to be unearthed and rediscovered. It is thus also possible to compose new historical trajectories, as Li does, by linking a disappearing mode of exhibition with what is so new that existing exhibition contexts are not yet ready to welcome it. The former was outside of the global mainstream of commercial, theatrical exhibition, whereas the latter is a product of the ever-expanding global film market, in which China's influence is increasingly felt (in addition to backing advanced projection technology like CINITY, Chinese investment was also behind *Gemini Man*). Juxtaposed, they not only offer a glimpse into the unbelievable transformation of China in the last several decades, but also allow Li to redefine a shared notion of cinema as an anticipated and remembered event.

If, as Casetti says, we recognize identity based on difference, this book aims to expand the ways in which we can identify cinema by introducing into global cinema history and film theory a different mode of exhibition and moviegoing, which happened to be socialist and Chinese. However, in contrast to Li Daoxin and other critics that try to give a singular identity to cinema, I agree with Gunning that "cinema has never been one thing" but a "braiding together of diverse strands."[17] Efforts to boil down cinema to any one "essence" is self-defeating at best, since one can always find examples that defy the boundaries drawn by the theorist. John Belton, for instance, proposes that "the cinema is the projection on a screen of life-size—or bigger than life size—images before an audience; everything else is movies."[18] For Belton, "watching *Jurassic Park* in 5.1 digital sound in DTS in a THX-certified theatre is a decidedly more immersive experience than seeing and hearing it on a laptop."[19] But what about watching a movie on a life-size screen in the open-air setting where you can barely hear the sound? Moreover, I have not yet seen any film theorists successfully swaying the public opinion on cinema. Industry, filmmakers, and audiences charge on in their intuitive ways. The Academy of Motion Picture Arts and Sciences puts Netflix original films in the same categories as films intended for the big screen without much resistance; at the same time, we do not need the help of film theory to understand that streaming movies in our living rooms is not the same experience as going out to the movie theater with a friend.

After all, the real paradox of Casetti's "paradoxes of recognition" is that what asks to be recognized is already recognized. When "cinema, affected by a series of changes, asks for confirmation,"[20] there is no question that it has already been identified as cinema either by common sense or by shared cultural practice. The work of recognition or confirmation, therefore, is really about justifying the collective intuition to call something cinema. Meanwhile, the initial recognition, to me, is less likely to be based on clearly articulated definitions of cinema than on a principle of family resemblance as discussed by philosopher Ludwig Wittgenstein (1889–1951). Wittgenstein uses the example of games to illustrate how we identify categories. We all have the concept of game, but if we examine different types of games (board games, ball games, Olympic games, etc.), we will not find something that is common to all games, but "a complicated network of similarities overlapping and crisscrossing: sometimes overall similarities, sometimes similarities in details." Board games may share with pretend play the assignment of roles, but the latter does not necessarily involve winning or losing, which is shared by some board games and sports. Sports require training and skill, which is not always needed to play board games. Therefore, games are not defined by a common essence, but by family resemblances, "for the various resemblances between members of a family: build, features, colour of eyes, gait, temperament, etc. etc. overlap and criss-cross in the same way."[21] If games form a family, is not cinema, with all its variations and potentials in the past, present, and future, a family too? If cinema is the intersection of many strands, should it not be the case that we only need some of them to recognize something as cinema? I believe so. Otherwise how come critics can think of so many different ways to confirm *Gemini Man* and HFR as cinema even when Ang Lee himself declares that with 120fps, "it's not a movie anymore"?[22]

This book, therefore, does not identify a definitive site of medium specificity, but names elements and interfaces that help us recognize some of cinema's lesser-known family members.

Interviewee Profiles

Surname	Year of Birth	Gender	Past Residences	Biographical Highlights	Interview Date
1. Anonymous	1926	Female	Rural Zhejiang	Spent most of her life in a village near Ningbo; mother of seven children; rarely watched films	September 26, 2013
2. Anonymous	1940s	Male	Rural suburbs of Beijing	First moviegoing experience was screenings organized by Japanese troops during the war	September 19, 2013
3. Anonymous	1938	Male	Beijing	Grew up near the Guang'anmen Theater in Beijing; attended many film weeks; claimed to have watched 95% of the films shown in the '50s; became a worker in 1956	May 17, 2014
4. Anonymous	1950s	Male	Shanghai	Favorite film genre during childhood was war films; became very patriotic under the influence of films	April 8, 2014

Surname	Year of Birth	Gender	Past Residences	Biographical Highlights	Interview Date
5. Mr. Bao	1949	Male	Shanghai	Used to be a cadre in charge of culture and propaganda; very knowledgeable and opinionated about Chinese film history; likes Soviet films because of their realism	September 25, 2013
6. Mrs. Cai*	1944	Female	Rural Sichuan, Xinjiang	Parents were poor peasants; married at age fourteen and later joined the Xinjiang Production and Construction Corps (XPCC) with husband; Envied film characters for their freedom	February 15, 2014
7. Mrs. Chen	1930	Female	Shanghai	Worked in hospital administration after leaving the military in the mid-1950s; particularly liked war films	September 28, 2013
8. Mr. Chen*	1938	Male	Rural Sichuan, Xinjiang	Originally from rural Sichuan; watched films at least once a week while in the military (1949–1964); then joined the XPCC	February 18, 2014
9. Mr. Chen	1936	Male	Beijing	Retired middle school math teacher (the school distributed film tickets every week); liked anti-espionage films; finds the character Xiwang from *Li Shuangshuang* particularly memorable	May 9, 2014

Surname	Year of Birth	Gender	Past Residences	Biographical Highlights	Interview Date
10. Mr. Chen	1926	Male	Suzhou	Retired party cadre that used to work for a trade union; liked Soviet films and Chinese comedies	April 19, 2014
11. Mr. Chen*	1937	Male	Rural Sichuan, Xinjiang	Former PLA soldier originally from rural Sichuan; proud of his identity as a CCP member	February 13, 2014
12. Mr. Cheng	1934	Male	Shanghai, Beijing, Nanchang	Influenced by Soviet films in high school; attended Tsinghua University (1953–1958) before becoming an engineer	March 27, 2014
13. Mrs. Dai	1934	Female	Suzhou	Retired film projectionist from a steel factory	April 3, 2014
14. Mrs. Feng	1926	Female	Shanghai, Suzhou	Retired textile worker; did not have time to watch films; Suzhou Mr. Chen's wife	April 19, 2014
15. Mr. Guo	1947	Male	Rural suburbs of Beijing	Became film projectionist for his brigade sometime after the beginning of the Cultural Revolution; emphasizes past moviegoing experience as *kan renao*	September 19, 2013
16. Mr. Guo	1929	Male	Shanghai	Retired factory security personnel; too busy to watch films	April 8, 2014
17. Mrs. Han	1934	Female	Harbin, Beijing	Originally from the Northeast region; relocated to suburban Beijing with husband in 1958 and worked at a factory; seldom watched films due to work and childcare	May 17, 2014

Surname	Year of Birth	Gender	Past Residences	Biographical Highlights	Interview Date
18. Mr. He*	1940	Male	Rural Sichuan, Xinjiang	Participated in the 1961 National Day celebration in Beijing as a PLA soldier; never watched films while he was in his home village in Sichuan; watched mainly war films in the military	February 15, 2014
19. Mr. Huang*	1935	Male	Rural Sichuan, Xinjiang	Former PLA soldier from rural Sichuan	February 16, 2014
20. Mrs. Ji	1937	Female	Beijing	Retired fitter from a locomotive factory; used to watch films every weekend	May 9, 2014
21. Mrs. Li	1941	Female	Beijing	Attended many open-air screenings in the suburbs of Beijing before becoming a factory worker in 1965	May 17, 2014
22. Mrs. Li	1948	Female	Shanghai	Grew up in Shanghai; began going to the movies by herself in primary school	September 24, 2013
23. Mrs. Li	1957	Female	Hebei Province	Retired rural film projectionist	June 12, 2014
24. Mrs. Liang	1946	Female	Tangshan (Hebei Province), Beijing	Retired high school chemistry teacher; grew up attending open-air screenings on the university campus where her parents worked	May 17, 2014
25. Mr. Liao*	1939	Male	Rural Sichuan, Xinjiang	Former PLA soldier who later joined the XPCC	February 16, 2014
26. Mr. Liu	1951	Male	Shanghai	Collector of old films and projectors	October 1, 2013

Surname	Year of Birth	Gender	Past Residences	Biographical Highlights	Interview Date
27. Mrs. Liu	1935	Female	Hohhot, Beijing	Studied Russian in college; worked at universities and other research institutes since 1958; went to the movies about once a month when teaching at the university; deeply moved by Pavel Korchagin; did not like war films	September 11, 2013
28. Mr. Lu	1946	Male	Shanghai	Enthusiastic about Western culture growing up in Shanghai; was struggled against in the Cultural Revolution for celebrating Christmas	April 8, 2014
29. Mr. Luo*	1940	Male	Rural Sichuan, Xinjiang	Former PLA soldier (1959–1964) who then joined the XPCC	February 18, 2014
30. Mr. Ma*	1942	Male	Rural Gansu, Xinjiang	Originally from rural Gansu; worked at a steel factory 1957–1960 before joining the XPCC; remembers being very excited when there were film screenings	January 23, 2014
31. Mrs. Ma	1940s	Female	Beijing	Began teaching math at a middle school in 1963 after graduating from college; valued the educational function of cinema; liked foreign films	September 12, 2013
32. Mr. Miao	1931	Male	Shanghai	Former police officer	September 27, 2013
33. Mrs. Nie	1955	Female	Beijing	Sent down to the countryside as a zhiqing in the Cultural Revolution	September 13, 2013

Surname	Year of Birth	Gender	Past Residences	Biographical Highlights	Interview Date
34. Mr. Qian	1948	Male	Shanghai	Son of a screenwriter who worked for the Shanghai Film Studio; attended many internal screenings as a child	September 29, 2013
35. Mr. Qin	1937	Male	Rural Hebei, Beijing	Retired geological researcher	May 9, 2014
36. Mrs. Shan	1939	Female	Wuhan, Beijing	Graduated from college in the early '50s and then worked at a research institute; remembered watching American films before 1949; liked Soviet films	September 17, 2013
37. Mrs. Song	1951	Female	Beijing	Grew up watching films at open-air screenings in her parents' work unit	September 13, 2013
38. Mrs. Sun	1937	Female	Rural Liaoning Province, Beijing	Retired locomotive factory worker; mother of four children; did not have time to watch films	May 17, 2014
39. Mr. Tang	1949	Male	Shanghai	Frequented open-air screenings in military residences as a child; later joined the military; believes that films taught him to be heroic; once broke up a street fight despite seeing that one person had a knife	September 26, 2013
40. Mr. Tang	1950s	Male	Rugao, Jiangsu Province	Worked at the Rugao Film Distribution and Exhibition Corporation from 1979 to 2002	August 24, 2013
41. Mrs. Xiao	1937	Female	Rural suburbs of Beijing	Influenced by film to combat traditional gender ideals in the countryside; left her village to become a worker in 1958	May 17, 2014

Surname	Year of Birth	Gender	Past Residences	Biographical Highlights	Interview Date
42. Mr. Wang	1928	Male	Rural Liaoning, Beijing	Former PLA soldier; worked at a factory in suburban Beijing till retirement; frequently went to the workers' club to watch films	May 17, 2014
43. Mrs. Wang	1944	Female	Xuzhou (Jiangsu Province)	Retired shop assistant; used to go to the movies on dates; liked foreign films because they opened up new worlds for her	September 29, 2013
44. Mr. Wang	1935	Male	Wuxi (Jiangsu Province), Beijing	Graduated from college in the '50s and then worked at a research institute; enthusiastic about film songs	September 12, 2013
45. Mr. Wang	1934	Male	Shanghai	Retired police officer; most memorable film is *Today Is My Day Off* (*Jintian wo xiuxi*, 1959), which is about a day in the life of a police officer	September 24, 2013
46. Mr. Wang	1930s	Male	Beijing	Retired science researcher; loved Soviet films	September 17, 2013
47. Mr. Wu	1928	Male	Tianjin and various port cities	Worked in port construction after graduating from Tsinghua University in the early '50s; watched films infrequently due to traveling for work	March 27, 2014
48. Mrs. Ye	1937	Female	Quanzhou (Fujian Province)	Retired university professor specializing in inorganic chemical industry; loved reading literature and Soviet films in high school	March 27, 2014
49. Mrs. Ying	1937	Female	Shanghai	Studied art in college; liked romantic stories	September 30, 2014

Surname	Year of Birth	Gender	Past Residences	Biographical Highlights	Interview Date
50. Mr. Zhang	1936	Male	Quanzhou	College graduate; taught at a university in Quan Zhou until retirement; Mrs. Ye's husband	March 27, 2014
51. Mr. Zhang	1946	Male	Shanghai	Retired worker; speaks highly of Chinese films from before 1949; passionate about *pingtan*, a traditional storytelling form from the Suzhou area	April 8, 2014
52 Mr. Zhao	1934	Male	Tianjin, Beijing	Retired engineer; preferred Peking opera to cinema	September 14, 2013
53. Mr. Zhou	1936	Male	Shanghai	Retired steel factory worker; routinely went to screenings at the workers' club	April 8, 2014
54. Mr. Zhou*	1940	Male	Rural Sichuan, Xinjiang	Parents were poor peasants from Sichuan; relocated to Xinjiang to join the XPCC in 1964	February 13, 2014
55. Mrs. Zhou*	1944	Female	Rural Sichuan, Xinjiang	Taught at a village school	February 15, 2014
56. Mrs. Zhou	1949	Female	Beijing	Grew up in downtown Beijing near several movie theaters; avid moviegoer	September 11, 2013
57. Mr. Zhou	1946	Male	Suzhou	Began going to movies by himself in primary school; became more interested in foreign films in middle school	April 15, 2014
58. Mr. Zhou	1953	Male	Shanghai	One of the most memorable moviegoing experience was watching *The Thief of Baghdad* (1940) as a child	September 19, 2013

Surname	Year of Birth	Gender	Past Residences	Biographical Highlights	Interview Date
59. Mr. Zhou	1957	Male	Suzhou	Remembers seeing *Zhang Ga the Soldier Boy* on a school trip in primary school	April 15, 2014
60. Mr. Zou	1932	Male	Guangdong Province	Born in a rich overseas Chinese family; came back to China in 1955 at age thirteen; applied for the Beijing Film Academy but was rejected due to his class background; later became a schoolteacher at an overseas Chinese farm	September 30, 2013

*Interviewed by Lu Yunnan

Character Glossary

PINYIN	CHINESE CHARACTERS
aiguo gongyue	爱国公约
aiji hupian	爱机护片
aodi'an	奥迪安
baibu	白布
baimaonü	白毛女
Baoding dianying jiaopian chang	保定电影胶片厂
Beijing huandeng zhipian chang	北京幻灯制片厂
Beiping pingjiao zonghui	北平平教总会
Bi Fujian	毕福剑
buwo	布幄
buman	布幔
bumu	布幕
Cai Chusheng	蔡楚生
changsuo	场所
Chen Kaige	陈凯歌
Chen Qiang	陈强
Cui Yongyuan	崔永元
da litang	大礼堂
dagao gangtie	大搞钢铁

daguangming yingxiyuan	大光明影戏院
danwei	单位
dazhong dianying	大众电影
dengzhou wenhui guan	登州文会馆
dianhua jiaoyu	电化教育
dianhua jiaoyu gongju zhizaosuo	电化教育工具制造所
dianhua jiaoyu yanjiu	电化教育研究
dianying chuanqi	电影传奇
dianying de luogu	电影的锣鼓
dianying fangying	电影放映
dianying fangying ziliao	电影放映资料
dianying fangying zongdui	电影放映总队
dianying jianchafa	电影检查法
dianying julebu	电影俱乐部
dianying o dianying	电影哦电影
dianying puji	电影普及
dianying xuexi jinjiang	电影学习金奖
dianying yu boyin	电影与播音
didao zhan	地道战
Dong Cunrui	董存瑞
douban	豆瓣
duoyin	夺印
e lang Li Laoyao	恶狼李老窑
enpaiya	恩派亚
fang dianying	放电影
fangzijing	放字镜
fendou	奋斗
fenwei	氛围
gaige kaifang	改革开放
gangtie shi zenyang liancheng de	钢铁是怎样练成的
Gao Xixi	高希希
gongnong jiaoyu	工农教育
gongren julebu	工人俱乐部
gongren wenhuagong	工人文化宫
gongshe	公社

guangming ribao	光明日报
guanxishi	盥洗室
gudong	鼓动
guoji daxiyuan	国际大戏院
guojie	过节
guonan shiqi jiaoyu fang'an	国难时期教育方案
guotai dianyingyuan	国泰电影院
heping	和平
hong deng ji	红灯记
hongse niangzijun	红色娘子军
hongyan	红岩
huabei lianda	华北联大
huaihai	淮海
huandeng	幻灯
huandengji	幻灯机
huandengpian	幻灯片
Huang Jiamo	黄嘉谟
Huang Shiren	黄世仁
huaqiao nongchang	华侨农场
huodong yingxi bu	活动影戏部
Huo Jianqi	霍建起
ka'erdeng	卡尔登
kan renao	看热闹
kangmei yuanchao	抗美援朝
kuaiban	快板
Jia Ding	甲丁
jiaoyu	教育
jianlou	简陋
Jiang Qing	江青
Jiang Wen	姜文
jiaoyu yu minzhong	教育与民众
jiedao	街道
jieshuo	解说
jingyingdeng	镜影灯
jinling daxue	金陵大学

jintian wo xiuxi	今天我休息
jiqing ranshao de suiyue	激情燃烧的岁月
jiyu	机遇
jizhen yingyuan	集镇影院
jizhi	机制
laodong renmin wenhuagong	劳动人民文化宫
lao san pian	老三篇
laojiao	劳教
Lei Feng	雷锋
Li Qiang	李樯
Li Shuangshuang	李双双
Li Xiangyang	李向阳
Liang Shangbo	梁山伯
liehuo zhong yongsheng	烈火中永生
liening zai 1918	列宁在1918
liening zai shiyue	列宁在十月
linjia puzi	林家铺子
Liu Jin	刘劲
Liu Xiang	刘向
liudong dianying fangyingdui	流动电影放映队
Lu Xun	鲁迅
Lü Zichen	吕自臣
lun chijiuzhan	论持久战
lutian dianying	露天电影
Ma Changchun	马长春
Ma Weidu	马未都
maihua guniang	卖花姑娘
meishu	美术
mi	米
minzhong jiaoyu	民众教育
mu	亩
Nan Guonong	南国农
nandao fengyun	南岛风云
nanjing daxiyuan	南京大戏院
nanzheng beizhan	南征北战

nashan, naren, nagou	那山、那人、那狗
neihang	内行
ni shuo bu shuo	你说不说
Nie Er	聂耳
ningsi buqu	宁死不屈
Pan Dongzi	潘冬子
paopian	跑片
Peng Zhen	彭真
pingfeng	屏风
pingmin jiaoyu	平民教育
pingmu	屏幕
pingtan	评弹
pingyuan youjidui	平原游击队
pu bu mie de huoyan	扑不灭的火焰
puji	普及
qianyi mohua	潜移默化
qifen	气氛
qingchun zhi ge	青春之歌
qingwa gongzhu	青蛙公主
qiqie chengqun	妻妾成群
qiye	企业
qunzhong luxian	群众路线
Ren Ming	任鸣
renmin dianyingyuan	人民电影院
renmin meishu chubanshe	人民美术出版社
renmin ribao	人民日报
ruanxing dianying	软性电影
sanfan yundong	三反运动
shanshan de hongxing	闪闪的红星
shanghai qingnian hui	上海青年会
shangwu yinshu guan	商务印书馆
shaolin si	少林寺
shehuizhuyi jiaoyu yundong	社会主义教育运动
shehuizhuyi xinren	社会主义新人
Shen Enfu	沈恩孚

shengchan dadui	生产大队
shengli	胜利
shenguai	神怪
shenru shenghuo	深入生活
shuo yuan	说苑
shuoming shu	说明书
sihao	四好
Songshan	嵩山
Su Tong	苏童
suiyi	随意
Sun Mingjing	孙明经
Sun Xisheng	孙熹圣
taiyang zhaochang shengqi	太阳照常升起
Tao Zhu	陶铸
tiedao youjidui	铁道游击队
tigao	提高
tongxin huifang	童心回放
tu	土
tuolaji shou	拖拉机手
waihang	外行
wang	旺
Wang Shuo	王朔
Wang Xiaoshuai	王小帅
Wang Zhong	王中
Wang Zhong'an	王仲安
wei gongnongbing fuwu	为工农兵服务
weida de qidian	伟大的起点
weile liushiyi ge jieji xiongdi	为了六十一个阶级兄弟
weilüe	魏略
wenhua gongzuozhe	文化工作者
wenhui bao	文汇报
wenyi	文艺
wo de fuqin muqin	我的父亲母亲
Wu Manyou	吴满有
wuqi ganxiao	五七干校

wutai jiemei	舞台姐妹
wuxia	武侠
Xi'er	喜儿
xihan	稀罕
Xiwang	喜旺
Xizi	喜子
xiatian de gushi	夏天的故事
Xiang Hong	项红
Xiang Xiuli	向秀丽
Xiao Shuzi	萧树滋
Xiaobing Zhang Ga	小兵张嘎
xin shiqi	新时期
xingfen	兴奋
xingfu de shenghuo	幸福的生活
xingua	新寡
xinhua	新华
xinxian	新鲜
Xu Xuehui	徐学慧
Xu Zhuodai (Xu Fulin)	徐卓呆 (徐傅霖)
xuanchuan	宣传
xuanchuan gongju	宣传工具
xuni	虚拟
Yan Yangchu	晏阳初
Yan'an dianying tuan	延安电影团
Yang Bailao	杨白劳
yangbanxi	样板戏
yangge	秧歌
yangguang canlan de rizi	阳光灿烂的日子
Yi Xiangdong	衣向东
yinghou taolun	映后讨论
yingjian chahua	映间插话
yingqian xuanchuan	映前宣传
yingxing dianying	硬性电影
yinmu	银幕
yong bu xiaoshi de dianbo	永不消逝的电波

Yongcheng xianzhi	永成县志
Yu Dong	郁冬
Yu Huan	鱼豢
yule pian	娱乐片
yuanxianzhi	院线制
Zhai Junjie	翟俊杰
zhanzuo	占座
Zhang Wentian	张闻天
Zhang Yimou	张艺谋
Zhang Yuan	张元
Zhao Shuli	赵树理
Zhao Yiman	赵一曼
Zhao Zhankui	赵占魁
zhazi dong	渣滓洞
Zheng Zhenhuan	郑振环
zhenya fangeming	镇压反革命
zhiqing	知青
zhiqu huashan	智取华山
Zhong Dianfei	钟惦棐
zhongguo meishujia xiehui	中国美术家协会
zhonghua quanguo zong gonghui	中华全国总工会
zhongxin gongzuo	中心工作
zhongying gongsi	中影公司
Zhou Yang	周扬
Zhu Yingtai	祝英台
zhuanqu	专区

Notes

INTRODUCTION

1. Sontag, "Decay of Cinema."

2. Li Aidong, ed., *Dianying*, 4: 114. All translations of Chinese texts are mine unless otherwise noted.

3. In most cases, Chinese names are rendered in this book in the Chinese custom with last name first followed by the first name. Authors of English sources who are of Chinese origin are cited according to the ways their names appeared in the original publications.

4. Sontag, "Decay of Cinema."

5. For reforms of the Chinese film industry from the late 1970s to the early 2000s, see Tang Rong, "Sanshinian zhongguo dianying tizhi gaige licheng huigu (shang)" and "Sanshinian zhongguo dianying tizhi gaige licheng huigu (xia)"; Xie Fei, "Zhongguo dianying zhuanxing 30 nian"; Rosen, "Film and Society in China"; Yi Lu, "The Malling of the Movies."

6. Gaudreault and Marion, *End of Cinema?*

7. Assmann, "Collective Memory and Cultural Identity."

8. Larkin, *Signal and Noise*, 78–79.

9. See Aveyard and Moran, eds., *Watching Films*; Biltereyst, Maltby, and Meers, eds., *Cinema, Audiences and Modernity*; Christie, ed., *Audiences*; Maltby, Stokes, and Allen, eds., *Going to the Movies*; Maltby, Biltereyst, and Meers. eds., *Explorations in New Cinema History*; Reinhard and Olson, eds., *Making Sense of Cinema*. As an exception, two articles on Chinese rural film exhibition can be found in Gennari, Hipkins, and O'Rawe, eds., *Rural Cinema Exhibition and Audiences*: Goode, "UNESCO, Mobile Cinema, and Rural Audiences"; Johnson, "Reconsidering Post-Revolutionary Cultural Change."

10. Casetti, *Lumière Galaxy*, 5.

11. Pickowicz, "From Yao Wenyuan to Cui Zi'en," 47.

12. Rushton and Bettinson, *What Is Film Theory?*, 1.

13. Ferencz-Flatz and Hanich. "Editors' Introduction," 3.

14. See Sobchack, *Address of the Eye* and *Carnal Thoughts*; Barker, *Tactile Eye*; Hanich, *Cinematic Emotion*; Wilson, *Spectatorship, Embodiment and Physicality*.

15. Wilson, *Spectatorship, Embodiment and Physicality*, 4–5.

16. Paul, *When Movies Were Theater*, 2.

17. Other examples of scholarly works that address the identity of cinema in the digital age include Belton, "If Film Is Dead"; Casetti, *Lumière Galaxy*; Van de Vijver, "Cinema Is Dead"; Prince, *Digital Cinema*.

18. A great example of this approach to cinema can be found in David Derwei Wang, ed., *New Literary History of Modern China*, in which Wang considers literature, films, songs, costumes, and other cultural forms all under the traditional Chinese concept of *wen*, which originally meant ornamentation, pattern, sign, or inscription (5–6, 21–22).

19. Yingjin Zhang, "Ethnicity, Nationality, Translocality," 243.

20. Yingjin Zhang, *Screening China*, 119.

21. Pickowicz, "From Yao Wenyuan to Cui Zi'en," 47.

22. Yeh, "Pitfalls of Cross-Cultural Analysis," 439.

23. Ibid., 439.

24. Zhang, *Screening China*, 143.

25. Casetti, *Theories of Cinema*, 2.

26. Fan, *Cinema Approaching Reality*, 8.

27. Larkin, *Signal and Noise*, 79–86.

28. Manovich, *Language of the New Media*, 62–115.

29. de Souza e Silva and Firth, *Mobile Interfaces in Public Spaces*, 5.

30. Galloway, *Interface Effect*.

31. Hookway, *Interface*.

32. Xiao Liu, *Information Fantasies*, 25–26.

33. Jeong. *Cinematic Interfaces*, 11.

34. Fiske, *Introduction to Communication Studies*, 2; Bao, *Fiery Cinema*, 9.

35. Mittler, *Continuous Revolution*, 375.

36. Srinivas, *House Full*, 12.

37. Recent monographs on Chinese socialist culture include Clark, *The Chinese Cultural Revolution*; Hung, *Mao's New World*; Mittler, *Continuous Revolution*; Van Fleit Hang, *Literature the People Love*; Zhuoyi Wang, *Revolutionary Cycles*; DeMare, *Mao's Cultural Army*; Volland, *Socialist Cosmopolitanism*; Laikwan Pang, *Art of Cloning*; Denise Ho, *Curating Revolution*; Wilcox, *Revolutionary Bodies*; Chan, *Chinese Revolutionary Cinema*; Xiaoning Lu, *Moulding the Socialist Subject*.

38. Mittler, *Continuous Revolution*, 11.

39. Hung, *Mao's New World*.

40. Peters, *Marvelous Clouds*, 17.

41. Ibid., 18.

42. Ibid., 37.

43. Hung, *Mao's New World*, 5.

44. The mechanism and efficacy of subject formation is the focus of Laikwan Pang, *Art of Cloning* and Xiaoning Lu, *Moulding the Socialist Subject*. For a similar approach in the North Korean context, see Mironenko, "North Koreans at the Movies."

45. After a hiatus during the Cultural Revolution, *Film Projection* resumed distribution in 1975. *Film Projection* became *Film Popularization* in 1981, which was then merged with another journal to become *Film Projection and Popularization* (*Dianying fangying puji*) in 1988. After more editorial changes, this journal became *China Film Market* (*Zhongguo dianying shichang*) in 1993.

46. Tina Mai Chen, "Propagating the Propaganda Film," 155.

47. Ibid., 177–84.

48. I have not been able to identify the particular documentary he referenced.

49. Interview with Mr. Cheng on March 17, 2014.

50. I have offered preliminary analysis of these phenomena in my dissertation "Socialism Off-Screen: Moviegoing in Socialist China, 1949–1976" (Stanford, 2016).

51. Ten of the interviews were conducted by Lu Yunnan in the Xinjiang Uyghur Autonomous Region.

52. Li Aidong, ed., *Dianying*, 1–4.

53. Huyssen, *Twilight Memories*, 3.

54. There is a vast literature on memory research from the disciplines of cognitive psychology, developmental psychology, and neuroscience. For memory reconsolidation, see Alberini, "Role of Reconsolidation"; Alberini and LeDoux, "Memory Reconsolidation"; and Ecker, "Memory Reconsolidation Understood and Misunderstood." For the influence of language on memory, see Loftus and Palmer, "Reconstruction of Automobile Destruction"; for the impact of collective memory on individual memory, see Gagnepain et al., "Collective Memory Shapes the Organization of Individual Memories."

55. Thomson, "Memory and Remembering," 84–85.

56. Interview with Mr. Chen and Mrs. Feng on April 19, 2014.

57. Interview with Mr. Zhou on April 8, 2014.

58. Stacey, *Star Gazing*, 64.

59. Kuhn, "What to Do with Cinema Memory."

60. Dirlik, "Postsocialism?"

61. Berry, *Postsocialist Cinema*, 1.

62. Yingjin Zhang, "Directors, Aesthetics, Genres."

63. McGrath, *Postsocialist Modernity*, 2–4.

64. Xudong Zhang, *Postsocialism and Cultural Politics*, 9–10.

65. Ban Wang, *Illuminations from the Past*, 219.

66. For the phenomenon of "Mao-Craze," see Barmé, *Shades of Mao*.

67. For an overview of the nostalgia industry, see Li Zeng, "Road to the Past." For the nostalgia of *zhiqing* in particular, see Guobin Yang, "China's Zhiqing Generation."

68. Lu, "History, Memory, Nostalgia."

69. Chu, "Displacing Red Childhood."

70. Lingchei Letty Chen, *Great Leap Backward*, 4.

71. Denton, *Exhibiting the Past*, 214–42; Chunfeng Lin, "Red Tourism."

72. Li and Zhang, "Introduction," 18–19.

73. Veg, "Introduction," 1–2, 9–10.

74. Liu Jian, "Huaijiu, xiandaixing," 246–47.

75. For the role of the dominant narrator, see Cuc et al., "On the Formation of Collective Memories"; Coman et al., "Collective Memory from a Psychological Perspective," 132–34.

CHAPTER 1. SPACE

1. Yingjin Zhang, *Chinese National Cinema*, 190.

2. Cheng Jihua, *Zhongguo dianying*, 4.

3. Cheng Jihua, *Zhongguo dianying*, 8–11; Zhen Zhang, *Amorous History*, chapters 2 and 3.

4. Chen Yiyu, "Zhongguo zaoqi dianying guanzhong shi," 75–79.

5. A short opera film called *Dingjun Mountain* (*Dingjun shan*), supposedly made by the Fengtai Photo Studio in Beijing in 1905, was long considered the first-ever Chinese film. But Chinese scholar Huang Dequan argues that this alleged film was never made (see Huang, "Xiqu dianying dingjun shan"). Commenting on this debate, Emilie Yueh-yu Yeh calls for more primary research to reexamine prevalent claims about Chinese film history that have long been taken for granted (Yeh, "Translating Yingxi," 33).

6. Pickowicz, "Melodramatic Imagination," 300–301; Clark, *Chinese Cinema*, 10.

7. Zhen Zhang, *Amorous History*, 123. For a survey of Republican-era Shanghai movie theaters, see Huang Dequan, *Minguo shanghai yingyuan*.

8. "Yuandong weiyi da jianzhu."

9. Huang Dequan, *Mingguo shanghai yingyuan*, 165.

10. T.H.C, "Tantan guotai dianyingyuan," 544.

11. Quoted in Fu, *Between Shanghai and Hong Kong*, 36.

12. Ibid., 36.

13. Yao Fangzao, "Xinhua daxiyuan," 29.

14. Wu Di (Qi Zhi), *Mao Zedong shidai de renmin dianying*, 19.

15. Mao, *Selected Works*, 69.

16. Ban Wang, *Sublime Figure of History*, 209.

17. Mittler, *Continuous Revolution*, 24.

18. Van Fleit Hang, *Literature the People Love*, 8.

19. Mao, *Selected Works*, 235.

20. Holm, *Art and Ideology in Revolutionary China*, 96.

21. Meisner, *Mao's China and After*, 42–44.

22. Mao, *Selected Works*, 93.

23. Wang Hui, "Qu zhengzhihua de zhengzhi," 51.

24. Mao, *Selected Works*, 235.

25. Ibid., 82 (emphasis mine).

26. Ibid., 86.

27. Liu Hailong, "Hanyu zhong xuanchuan gainian," 104.

28. According to Chunfeng Lin, the preaching practice of Confucius was considered an epitome of *xuanchuan* by Chinese scholars (Lin, "Red Tourism," 330–31).

29. Bao, *Fiery Cinema*, 300.

30. Kenez, *The Birth of the Propaganda State*, 5–7.

31. Zhang Wentian, "Dang de xuanchuan gudong gangling," 150–61.

32. Kenez, 109–10.

33. These examples are taken from *People's Daily* (August 5, 1949; March 31, 1950; April 20, April 22, May 9, May 21, May 23, 1950).

34. "Shenme shi shenru shenghuo."

35. Li Xing, "Guanzhong xuyao."

36. Zhong Dianfei, "Dianying de luogu."

37. Zhong Dianfei, "Lun dianying zhidao sixiang zhong de jige wenti." According to Wu Di, this article, written in 1956, was originally intended for publication in *People's Daily*, but it was not published at the time due to negative reactions from cultural administrators (Wu, *Zhongguo dianying yanjiu ziliao*, 20).

38. Dazhong dianying bianji bu, "Jianjue hanwei," 145.

39. Cai Chusheng, "Mantan 'sihao.'"

40. "Lin Biao tongzhi."

41. Zhong Yingbin, "'Huizhan' fangying hao," 15.

42. Lefebvre, *The Production of Space*, 33, 38.

43. de Certeau, *The Practice of Everyday Life.*

44. Yingjin Zhang, *Chinese National Cinema*, 191; Chen Bo, *Zhongguo dianying biannian jishi*, 1.

45. Paul, "K-Mart Audience," 80.

46. "Shanghai shi dianyingyuan"; Zhang Shuoguo, *"Shiqi nian" shanghai dianying*, 51. The conversion rate between the old RMB and the new RMB adopted in 1955 was of 10,000 old RMB = 1 new RMB.

47. "Qing yingyuan laoban men kaolü," 2.

48. Zhang Shuoguo, *"Shiqi nian" shanghai dianying*, 51–53.

49. Liu Siyu, "Dianyingyuan yu guojia," 53.

50. "Shanghai shi dianyingyuan ge lei piaojia mingxibiao."

51. According to a 1935 issue of the magazine *Qingqing Film* (*Qingqing dianying*), tickets to the Grand Theater had three tiers: 0.6 *yuan*, 1 *yuan*, and 1.5 *yuan* ("Shanghai dianyingyuan," 1). For workers' wages, see Li Jiaqi et al., *Shanghai gongyun zhi*, 147.

52. Wu Yigong, *Shanghi dianiyng zhi*, 620.

53. Yao Fangzao, "Xinhua daxiyuan."

54. Cohen, "Forgotten Audiences in the Passion Pits."

55. Athique and Hill, *Multiplex in India*, 134–35.

56. Jin Xian, "Jingjin (1)."

57. Li Cun, "Guoji daxiyuan fuwu zhoudao."

58. "Xin zhongguo diyi suo."

59. Jin Xian, "Jingjin (1)" and "Jingjin (2)."

60. Yao, "Xinhua daxiyuan." A similar statement can be found in a 1951 work report of the Shanghai Movie Theaters Guild. The report states that

after several months of reform, movie theaters in Shanghai have "gradually transformed theaters that used to only serve a handful of leisurely class to lecture halls for the great masses" ("Shanghai shi dianyingyuan shangye tongye gonghui," 1).

61. Xi Wen and Ji Jin'an, *Shanghai qunzhong wenhua zhi*, 64–67.

62. Chen Shao, "Laodong renmin wenhua gong."

63. "Shanghai gongren."

64. "Jinyibu xiezhu gonghui juleibu."

65. Hung, "Political Park."

66. "Beijing shi gequ gongren julebu," 2.

67. Ke, "Xin zhongguo gongren."

68. Lihsin Yang, "A Visit to the Shanghai Workers' Club," 53 (emphasis mine).

69. Bray, *Social Space and Governance*, 94.

70. Walder, *Communist Neo-Traditionalism*, 16.

71. Lu Duanfang, *Remaking Chinese Urban Form*, 52–58.

72. Interview with Mrs. Dai on April 3, 2014. Film theaters also arranged late-night showings to accommodate workers. A 1960 article in the journal *Film Exhibition* reported that a theater in Guangzhou showed films at 11:30 p.m., 1:30 a.m., and 3:30 a.m. in an effort to serve production and fulfill the principle of "serving workers, peasants, and soldiers." (Gao Naiyan, "Weile gongren").

73. Interview with Mr. Wang on September 17, 2013.

74. Jin Lisheng, "Juexin dapo."

75. Chen Bo, *Zhongguo dianying biannian jishi*, 4.

76. Tina Mai Chen, "Propagating the Propaganda Film" and "Textual Communities"; Liu Guangyu, "1949–1976 nian," "Xin zhongguo chengli yilai"; Yanping Guo, "Film Propaganda as Medium of Perception"; Xiaoning Lu, *Moulding the Socialist Subject*, 142–64.

77. Set up in the 1950s, communes may be seen as the rural equivalence of work units. They managed agricultural production and distribution in villages (Ogden, "Communes"). Communes were further divided into production brigades, which were made up of production teams. A village corresponded to either a team or a brigade depending on size. The system remained in place until the 1980s. As an initiative developed during the Great Leap Forward (1958–1961), organizing projection teams at the commune level was aimed at increasing the frequency of film screenings for rural viewers. But in many places this initiative was never actualized. In his investigation of the history of rural film exhibition in Jiangjin County, Sichuan province, Liu Guangyu ("1949–1976 nian," 62) notes that in an attempt to realize decentralization, Jiangjin county asked each administrative district to recommend three people for projectionist training. The program was terminated after a few months, possibly due to a lack of funds. What eventually allowed film projection teams to be housed within communes and production brigades was the introduction of 8.75 mm projectors in the early '70s.

78. Chen Bo, *Zhongguo dianying biannian jishi*, 7, 48.

79. Zhongguo dianying faxing fangying gongsi, *Zhongguo dianying faxing fangying*, 8.

80. Tina Mai Chen, "Propagating the Propaganda Film" and "Textual Communities."

81. Sun Xuewen and Liu Shulin, "Xuanchuan hongqi piao"

82. "Yinmu guashang Daba shan"; Chen Yingba, "Dianying songdao wu-zhishan"; Xu Ruzhong, "Zhishi weile ba dianying songshang haidao."

83. "Guanyu jianguo yilai."

84. Deng Xiaoping, *Deng Xiaoping wenxuan*, 354–74.

85. Rong Liangqian, "Cong shiji chufa," 7.

86. You Ming, "Guanyu kaifa nongcun dianying shichang," 2–3.

87. "Shanghai shi dianying fangyingdui qingkuang," 11.

88. "Shanghai shi wenhua ju guanyu dianyingyuan xuanchuan."

89. "Shanghai shi yingyuan, juchang."

90. You Ming, "Guanyu kaifa nongcun dianying shichang," 2; Tang Ruxin, "Zhuanhuan jingying fangshi," 3.

91. Gao Baolin, "Zhuanye dianyingyuan," 6.

CHAPTER 2. LABOR

1. "Yinmu guashang Daba shan."

2. "Classical cinema" has been widely used in film studies to refer to film styles and modes of production, distribution, and reception typified by Holly-wood during the studio era (1910s–1960s). See Bordwell, Staiger, and Thompson, *The Classical Hollywood Cinema*; Hansen, "The Mass Production of Senses" and "Fallen Women."

3. Li Meng and Cheng Weimin, "Laishui sanjiemei dianying fangyingdui."

4. Kenez, *Birth of the Propaganda State*, 58–62. Heftberger, "Soviet Agit-Trains."

5. DeMare, *Mao's Cultural Army*, 146.

6. Hongwei Thorn Chen, "Cinemas, Highways."

7. "Dianying fangyingdui buyao pa."

8. "Special districts" became "districts" (*diqu*) after 1970.

9. Liu Guangyu, *Xin zhongguo chengli yilai*, 48–57.

10. "Yinmu gua shang daba shan."

11. Baudry, "Ideological Effects," 40.

12. Zhongguo dianying faxing fangying gongsi, *Zhongguo dianying faxing fangying*.

13. Ibid., 65, 91.

14. Ibid., 110–76.

15. Mrs. Zhou from Beijing recalled vividly how the audience was left waiting impatiently in the middle of a film because the theater did not have the rest of the film yet. They all cheered when the theater worker came back with the remaining film reels (interview on September 11, 2013).

16. According to Paul Clark, the film *The Lin Family Shop* (*Linjia puzi*, 1959), adapted from Mao Dun's novel of the same name, was not released in 16 mm prints until thirteen months after its initial 35 mm run (Clark, "Closely Watched Viewers," 82). See the same article by Clark for more on the differential treatment of 35 mm and 16 mm copies. The fact that rural audiences were

not prioritized in film distribution is one reason why Zhang Shuoguo suggests that the principle of "serving workers, peasants, and soldiers" was not really implemented in practice (*"Shiqinian" shanghai dianying*, 1–22).

17. Liu Dishan, "'Shiqinian' shiqi yizhipian chuanbo," 105.

18. Bao, *Fiery Cinema*, 9.

19. Jeong, *Cinematic Interfaces*, 8.

20. Merleau-Ponty, *Basic Writings*, 87–94.

21. Mauss, *Techniques, Technology, and Civilization*, 77–95.

22. Gallagher and Zahavi, *Phenomenological Mind*, 157.

23. "Dapo yandong bu huodong de chengui," 24.

24. "Yingyao songchu ershi li," 24.

25. "Huoyue zai qunshan zhong."

26. I was able to find one such booklet published by the Fujian Provincial Cultural Bureau in 1962 on the secondhand book website Kongfuzi. The articles in the booklet discuss both technical knowledge and administrative tips on how to promote the practice of *aiji hupian* on an institutional level.

27. Tang Peize, "Guojingxian shang."

28. Meng Ling, "Tapo bingshan wei mumin," 8–9.

29. Li Ruidong, "Fangyingyuan zhi ge," 22.

30. Li Shu, "Xin chengli de hubei nüzi fangyingdui," 18.

31. Xiaoning Lu, *Moulding the Socialist Subject*, 153.

32. Tina Mai Chen, "The Human-Machine Continuum."

33. Siegert, *Cultural Techniques*, 2.

34. Krajewski, "The Power of Small Gestures," 94.

35. Barnard, "The 'Machine Operator.'"

36. Ibid., 70.

37. For the role of the projectionist in life sciences around 1900, see Cartwright, "The Hands of the Projectionist." Recent scholarship on the projectionist has emerged out of the Projection Project, a British research project that ran from 2014 to 2018 by scholars from the University of Warwick (Charlotte Brunsdon, Jon Burrows, Claire Jesson, Michael Pigott, and Richard Wallace). Their work can be seen on https://projectionproject.warwick.ac.uk/ (accessed July 24, 2020) and in a special issue on projection of *Journal of British Cinema and Television* (15, no. 1, 2018). See also Brunsdon, "This Is Not a Cinema."

38. Baudry, "Ideological Effects."

39. Li Shukai, "Wo shi yige," 23.

40. Rancière, *The Politics of Aesthetics*.

41. Yi Xiangdong, *Aiqing xijie*, 8.

42. Li, "Wo shi yige," 23.

43. Tina Main Chen, "Textual Communities," 65.

44. Barnard, "The 'Machine Operator.'"

45. Hongwei Thorn Chen, "Cinemas, Highways," 28–29.

46. Quoted in Liu Guangyu, *Xin zhongguo chengli yilai*, 69.

47. For socialist visual representations of laborers, see Tina Mai Chen, "Proletarian White and Working Bodies"; Laikwan Pang, "Visual Representation of the Barefoot Doctor"; Wang Zheng, *Finding Women in the State*, 78–111.

48. Miin-ling Yu, "Labor Is Glorious," 235.

49. Ibid., 238.
50. Ibid.; Yinghong Chen, *Creating the "New Man,"* 76–100.
51. "Yinmu guashang daba shan."
52. "Dianying fangyingdui buyao pa jin shanqu."
53. Meisner, *Mao's China and After*, 42.
54. Funari and Mees, "Socialist Emulation in China."
55. Sheridan, "The Emulation of Heroes," 52–54.
56. Pingdu dianying fangyingdui, "Rang shehuizhuyi sixiang chuanbian xin nongcun," 6.
57. Kashi zhuanqu, "Mao Zedong sixiang," 13.
58. Chen, *Creating the "New Man,"* 76.
59. Gimple, "Civilizing Bodies."
60. Dutton, "Disciplinary Projects and Carceral Spread."
61. Baudry, "Ideological Effects."
62. Althusser, *Lenin and Philosophy*, 109.
63. Wollen, "Godard and Counter Cinema."

CHAPTER 3. MULTIMEDIA

1. Qu Youliang, "Dang de zhongxin gongzuo."
2. Sugawara, "Toward the Opposite Side of 'Vulgarity.'"
3. Matthew Johnson, "Science Education Film," 35–36.
4. Bao, *Fiery Cinema*, 278.
5. Ibid., 297.
6. Matthew Johnson, "Science Education Film."
7. Bao, *Fiery Cinema*, 299.
8. A Lunna, "Zhongguo dianhua jiaoyu," 66.
9. The following survey of *dianjiao* in Republican China is based on A Lunna, "Dianhua jiaoyu de yunyu" and "dianhua jiaoyu shiye."
10. The first color film made in China is conventionally believed to be a Peking opera film from 1948 called *A Wedding in the Dream (Sheng si hen*, dir. Fei Mu). However, A Lunna suggests that a science education film produced by Jinling University in 1936 called *Solar Eclipse in Republican Year 25 (Minguo ershiwu nian zhi rishi)* was the first Chinese film shot in color ("Dianhua jiaoyu de yunyu," 118). Though beyond the scope of this book, how audiovisual education motivated the development of cinematic technologies and how Chinese film history can be revised to better integrate education cinema are both subjects that call for more scholarly attention.
11. One source of continuity is personnel. For example, Xiao Shuzi (1914–2002), who was sent to the United States to study audiovisual education by the GMD Ministry of Education in the late '40s, taught a session on slide projection for the program organized by the Ministry of Culture in Nanjing in 1950, which trained more than fifteen hundred film projectionists (A Lunna, "Zhongguo dianhua jiaoyu," 63).
12. For a history of different Chinese terms for the magic lantern, see Sun Qing, "Modeng jingying."
13. Wu Dinghong, *Huandeng gongzuo shouce*, 71–103.

14. Ding Li, "Huandeng."

15. Wang Mingxun, "Xiwang ba huandeng pian shenru nongcun."

16. See Christie, "Through a Glass Brightly"; Fawcett, "Visual Facts"; Lacoste et al., *History of Projected Photography*; Lamarre, "Magic Lantern"; Musser, "Towards a History of Screen Practice"; Nelson, "Windows to the American Past"; Rossell, "Double Think"; Stange, "Jacob Riis and Urban Visual Culture"; Vogl-Bienek and Crangle, eds., *Screen Culture and the Social Question*.

17. van Dooren, "Our Magic Lantern Heritage," 185.

18. Eisenhauer, "Next Slide Please."

19. For education technology in the United States, see Cuban, *Teachers and Machines*; Petrina, "Getting a Purchase"; Terzian, "History of Technology." According to Terzian, most historical research on technology in education tends to focus on North America, in particular the United States (Terzin, "History of Technology"). For the use of cinema in American classrooms, see Acland, "Curtains, Carts, and Mobile Screen"; Orgeron, et al., *Learning with the Lights Off*.

20. Wue, "China in the World;" Sugawara, "Toward the Opposite Side of 'Vulgarity'"; Laura Jo-Han Wen, "Magic Lantern Shows."

21. Sun Qing, "Modeng jingying."

22. Tang Hongfeng, "Xuni yingxiang."

23. Yu Zixia, Qiao Jinxia, Yu Wendu, "Chuanjiaoshi." British missionary John Hepburn Dudgeon (Dezhen, 1837–1901) published "On the Magic Lantern" (*Jingyingdeng shuo*) in 1873, one of the earliest Chinese articles introducing the magic lantern, in which he advocated using lantern for the purpose of *xuanchuan* and lecturing.

24. Loiperdinger, "Social Impact," 17.

25. Li Qiongzhi, "Huandeng jiaoyu."

26. Jin Liangbi, "Xiangcun minzhong jiaoyu."

27. Schmalzer, *Red Revolution*, 34–38.

28. "Jinli zuohao."

29. "Shanghai shi dianyingyuan shangye tongye gonghui."

30. Wu Wei, "Liyong huandeng pian."

31. Kong Ru, "Tongyi yinfa."

32. Guangdong sheng wenhuaju, "Nongcun dianying fangyingdui," 29–30.

33. A Lunna, "Zhongguo dianhua," 63.

34. He Baoyu, "Huandeng," 31. Dong Cunrui (1929–1948) was a PLA soldier well known in China for blowing himself up in an attempt to bomb a Guomindang bunker during the Chinese Civil War. Liang Shanbo and Zhu Yingtai are characters in a classic folk love story, known in the West as "The Butterfly Lovers."

35. Meng Chao, "Duoduo chuangzuo," 20.

36. He Baoyu, "Huandeng"; Meng, "Duoduo chuangzuo."

37. Meng Chao, "Duoduo chuangzuo," 20–21.

38. He Baoyu, "huandeng," 31.

39. Liu Guangyu, *Xin zhongguo chengli yilai*, 195.

40. Ibid., 186–96.

41. Ibid., 193.

42. For a history of the Chinese television industry, see Keane, *The Chinese Television Industry*.

43. Bao, *Fiery Cinema*, 297.

44. Liu, *Xin zhongguo chengli yilai*, 189.

45. Yongcheng xian difang shizhi bianzuan weiyuanhui, "Huandeng."

46. Liu, *Xin zhongguo chengli yilai*, 192.

47. Chen Bo, *Zhongguo dianying biannian*, 58–59.

48. Yongcheng xian difang shizhi bianzuan weiyuanhui, "Huandeng."

49. Ibid.

50. He Licheng, "Yao zuzhi huandengji shengchan."

51. Musser, "Toward a History of Screen Practices."

52. Okubo, "Magic Lantern Show."

53. For the role played by *benshi* in early Japanese cinema, see Akihiro and Thomas, "The Alluring Voice"; Fujiki, "*Benshi* as Stars"; Gerow, *Visions of Japanese Modernity*, 133–73; Standish, "Mediators of Modernity."

54. Li Keng, "Wo dui jieshuo de yidian tihui," 22.

55. Qian Zhengzhuan, "Zenyang zai yingqian xuanchuan," 10.

56. Ibid., 10. The original Chinese verses are: 各位观众不要吵, 听我把影片内容表一表: 从前有个抗日英雄叫蒋三, 胆量枪法数他高。原先是个八路军, 后来又把游击队员来领导。鬼子汉奸见他都害怕, 人民群众称他是英豪。

57. Holm, *Art and Ideology*, chapter 1.

58. For analyses of this classic tale, see Li Haiyan, "Huashuo baimaonü"; Meng Yue, "Baimaonü yanbian de qishi"; Jixian He, "White-Haired Girl."

59. Peterson, "Peasant Education," 221.

60. Liu Guangyu, *Xin zhongguo chengli yilai*, 185–86.

61. Zhao Liyan, "Jiading xian," 10.

62. Lacasse, "Film Lecturer"; Hansen, *Babel and Babylon*, 96.

63. Gunning, *D. W. Griffith*, 92–93.

64. Hansen, *Babel and Babylon*, 96–99.

65. Zhen Zhang, *Amorous History*, 157.

66. Chen Yiyu, "Zhongguo zaoqi dianying guanzhong shi," 40.

67. Guan Wenqi, "Women yiding yao," 32.

68. "Shanghai shi dianyingyuan shangye tongye gonghui."

69. Guangdong sheng wenhuaju, "Nongcun dianying fangyingdui," 30.

70. Ibid., 30–31.

71. Shi Yongsen, "Weile rang nongmin kandong dianying," 15.

72. "Dianying fangying gongzuo shang."

73. Qian Zhengzhuan, "Zenyang zai yingqian xuanchuan," 11.

74. Quoted in Xu Xiaxiang, "Nongcun fangyingdui," 50. Translation is mine.

75. Shi Yongsen, "Weile rang nongmin kandong dianying," 17.

76. Hebei changli xian diyi fangyingdui, "Didao zhan yingjian jieshuo," 19–20.

CHAPTER 4. ATMOSPHERE

1. King, *Coen Brothers*, 185.

2. In the United States, the nickelodeon theater, also known as storefront theater, flourished from around 1905 to 1915. Usually of a small, rectangular shape, the nickelodeon is considered the first dedicated indoor showplace for

cinema. The first movie palaces emerged around 1913–1914. These were luxurious, single-auditorium theaters that could accommodate thousands of visitors. Studies of these exhibition sites are numerous. See, for example, Hark, ed., *Exhibition*; Paul, *When Movies Were Theater*.

3. Bamford, "Sun Pictures."

4. Mentzelopoulos, "Athenian Summer Cinemas"; "Take in a Movie under the Stars."

5. See Li Daoxin, "Lutian dianying." Li, however, conflates the categories of open-air cinema and mobile projection. For example, he cites a *People's Daily* article from 1950 to discuss the itinerant film exhibition network in the Soviet Union, but it is unclear to what extent Soviet itinerant screenings were outdoor screenings. According to Vance Kepley Jr., Soviet village screenings in the 1920s were held in various locations, including schools, libraries, huts, and open village squares in warm weather, whereas urban audiences relied on commercial movie theaters and cinema clubs (Kepley, "Cinefication"). My current research suggests open-air screenings were not as widespread in the Soviet Union as in China.

6. Rice, "British Empire's Forgotten Propaganda Tool"; Larkin, *Signal and Noise*, 73–122.

7. See Chen Yiyu, "Zhongguo zaoqi dianying guanzhong shi," 23–27.

8. Zhen Zhang, *Amorous History*, 61–62.

9. Huang Dequan, *Minguo shanghai yingyuan gaiguan*.

10. Liu Sijia, "Qiantan minguo lutian dianying," 43.

11. For an introduction of Program 2131, see Tina Mai Chen, "Mobile Film Projection."

12. For Chinese scholarship on open-air cinema, see Li Daoxin, "Lutian dianying"; Zhang Qizhong, "'Lutian dianying'"; Liu Jian, "huaijiu, xiandaixing"; Liu Sijia, "Qiantan minguo lutian dianying."

13. Hanich, *Audience Effect*, 3.

14. Ibid., 27.

15. Allen, "Relocating American Film History," 51.

16. Baudry, "Ideological Effects," 44–45.

17. Flitterman-Lewis, "Psychoanalysis, Film, and Television," 168–69.

18. For a summary of early movie show places in the United States, see Herzog, "The Movie Palace." For early screenings venues in China, see Zhen Zhang, *An Amorous History*; Pang, "Walking into and out of the Spectacle"; Yeh, "Translating Yingxi."

19. Gunning and Gaudreault, "Le cinéma des premiers temps"; Gunning "The Cinema of Attractions." For a history of the term "cinema of attractions," see Strauven, "Introduction to an Attractive Concept."

20. For the drive-in theater, see Cohen, "Forgotten Audiences"; for how film screenings became part of museum programing, see Wasson, *Museum Movies*; for the employment of "useful cinema" in educational and industrial contexts, See Acland, "Curtains, Carts and Mobile Screen"; Acland and Wasson, eds., *Useful Cinema*; for contemporary community film exhibition, see Ross, "Interstitial Film Viewing"; for domestic film viewing, see Klinger, *Beyond the Multiplex*.

21. Since the 1960s, the multiplex gradually gained prominence as the most dominant site of film exhibition globally. See Acland, *Screen Traffic*; Egerton, "The Multiplex"; Hubbard, "Fear and Loathing" and "A Good Night Out."

22. For an ethnographic study of moviegoing in Indian cinema halls, see Srinivas, *House Full.*

23. Acland, "Curtains, Carts, Mobile Screen," 148.

24. Casetti, "Cinema Lost and Found."

25. Roquet, *Ambient Media,* 3.

26. The earliest usage of this meaning can be found in volume 18 of Liu Xiang's *Garden of Stories (Shuo yuan).*

27. See Peters, *Marvelous Clouds.*

28. Casetti, "Screening."

29. Bao, *Fiery Cinema.*

30. Although popcorn became a staple of the American movie theater concession stand in the 1930s as a result of the Great Depression (Smith, *Popped Culture*), the phrase "popcorn movie" appears to be much more recent.

31. *Ambience* and *atmosphere* are synonyms in English. *Ambience*, for Roquet, puts more emphasis on subjective elements in mediation and thus foregrounds agency in personal uses of media. *Atmosphere*, on the other hand, can be understood as having a more public dimension, describing a shared, collective milieu. See Roquet, *Ambient Media,* 3.

32. Ibid., 10–11.

33. See the restaurant's website at http://foreigncinema.com/films/.

34. For a description of the project and interview with the director, see "SLEEPCINEMAHOTEL."

35. According to Yi Lu, the current multiplexes in China constitute heterotopias in the sense that they simultaneously offer utopia moments and discipline audiences' behaviors. The multiplex is thus like a "utopian Panopticon." See Lu, "Malling of the Movies," 216–21.

36. Ross, "Interstitial Film Viewing," 452.

37. Larkin, *Signal and Noise,* 152.

38. The AIRSCREEN Company, "History of Open-air Cinema," PRLOG, June 4, 2012, https://www.prlog.org/11891213-the-history-of-open-air-cinema .html. The company's Instagram account reinforces this message by featuring many spectacular photos of their inflatable screens in front of historical landmarks. See https://www.instagram.com/airscreen/.

39. Interview by Lu Yunnan on February 15, 2014.

40. Interview with Mrs. Nie on September 13, 2013.

41. Interview on September 30, 2013.

42. Interview on September 11, 2013.

43. See Lu Shukun's story in chapter 5.

44. Ma Weidu, "Lutian dianying."

45. Su Tong, *Lutian dianying,* 28.

46. Peters, *Marvelous Clouds,* 10.

47. Casetti, "Filmic Experience," 60.

48. Mentzelopoulos, "Athenian Summer Cinemas."

49. Li Daoxin, "Lutian dianying," 100–101.

50. Warden and Chen, "When Hot and Noisy Is Good."

51. Pan, "*Renao.*"

52. See Ackerman and Walker, "Consumption of *Renao.*"

53. Interview on September 19, 2013.

54. See, for example, Hua, "*Renao*, Deities' Efficacy"; Virgil Kit Yiu Ho, "Why Don't We Take Drama as Facts"; David Johnson, *Spectacle and Sacrifice*; and Ward, "Not Merely Players."

55. Ward, "Not Merely Players," 29.

56. Similarly, Zhiya Hua observes that *renao* at temple festivals in Hebei Province is seen as an exterior indicator of the efficacy of deities (see Hua, "Renao, Deities' Efficacy").

57. CCP's policy on religion was inconsistent over time. See Xiaoxun Wang, "Dilemma of Implementation."

58. Virgil Kit Yiu Ho, "Why Don't We Take Drama as Facts," 184.

59. Deng Yiwen, "Xin shiqi xiangcun."

60. Li Aidong, ed., *Dianying*, 1: 17.

61. Interviews by Lu Yunnan on February 16, February 13, and February 13, 2014.

62. Staiger, *Perverse Spectators*, 21–22.

63. Berry, *Postsocialist Cinema*, chapter 2.

64. For preferences of rural film viewers, see Zhou Jianming, "Nongcun yingpian gongying de maodun." Drama workers also reported that peasants liked *renao* and music in shows and did not like dialogues (DeMare, *Mao's Cultural Army*, 162).

65. For strategies employed in such emotion work, see Perry, "Moving the Masses."

66. Hanich, *Audience Effect*, 113.

67. Tina Mai Chen, "Propagating the Propaganda Film," 162.

68. Sun Shungen, "Zhao Yiman jiaoyu le wo," 24.

69. Interview with Mr. Zhou (b. 1936) on April 8, 2014.

70. Interview with Mr. Qin (b. 1937) on May 9, 2014.

71. Such instances are mentioned in Guan Wenqi, "Women yiding yao bangzhu nongmin" and a 1953 document from the Shanghai Municipal Archive ("Shanghai shi wenhua ju guanyu dianying fangyingdui qingkuang de baogao").

72. Interview with Mr.Chen (b. 1936) on May 9, 2014.

73. See Shen Enfu, "Yingxi yu jiaoyu."

74. Liu Jian, "Huaijiu, xiandaixing," 250. For more on popular film genres and the introduction of Western film theory in the 1980s, see Xiao Liu, *Information Fantasies*, 195–254.

75. Yu Zhen, "Bandeng shang guanying."

76. Liu Jian, "Huaijiu, xiandaixing," 246.

77. Dai Jinhua, "Imagined Nostalgia."

78. Lu, "Malling of the Movies," 206.

79. "China Reports."

80. See news articles such as "Hollywood Says"; "China to Be the World's Largest Film Market by 2020."

81. "China Reports."

82. Casetti, *Lumière Galaxy*, 3 (emphasis mine).
83. Statista, "Number of Movie Tickets Sold in China"; Statista, "Number of Movies Tickets Sold."
84. Chen Bo, *Zhongguo dianying biannian jishi*, 272–79.
85. Shu Weina, "Liuguang suiyue."
86. Boym, *Future of Nostalgia*, xviii.

CHAPTER 5. DISCOMFORT

1. Li Aidong, ed., *Dianying*, 1:212.
2. "Handling the Visitor," 66.
3. Stacey, *Star Gazing*, 184.
4. https://www.amctheatres.com/recliner-seating, accessed August 26, 2020.
5. Zhen Zhang, *Amorous History*, 124–25.
6. T.H.C, "Tantan guotai dianyingyuan."
7. Poshek Fu, *Between Shanghai and Hong Kong*, 36.
8. "Sheng guang zuo," 2.
9. Huang Jiamo, "Yingxing yingpian."
10. Sun Zhe, "Shenyang tiexi gongren qu."
11. Zhu Qi, "Wulumuqi shi."
12. Gerth, "Compromising with Consumerism," 211.
13. Dazhong dianying bianji bu, "Kan hao yingpian juefei langfei," 66.
14. "Shanghai shi wenhua ju guanyu dianying fangyingdui qingkuang de baogao."
15. Zheng Yiliu, "Wo cengjing fengkuang," 11.
16. Luo Ziliang, "Hao dianying guwu xia," 18. I thank Perry Link for help with the translation of the film's title.
17. "Duo yin zai nongmin zhong," 3.
18. Li Aidong, ed., *Dianying*, 1:109.
19. Interview with Mr. Zou on September 30, 2013.
20. Su Tong, *Lutian dianying*, 29.
21. Li Aidong, ed., *Dianying* 2:134.
22. Jie Li, "Cinematic Guerrillas," 224.
23. Li Aidong, ed., *Dianying* 1, 187.
24. Yi Xiangdong, *Aiqing xijie*, 29.
25. Mr. Chen recalls an incident he heard about as a teenager that involved a stampede at an open-air screening. The screening was allegedly sabotaged by "bad elements," and many people died during the stampede. (Interview by Lu Yunnan on February 13, 2014).
26. Interview by Lu Yunnan on February 13, 2014.
27. Duanfang Lu, *Remaking Chinese Urban Form*, 8–9.
28. Interview on September 13, 2013.
29. Interview on September 24, 2013.
30. Interview on April 19, 2014.
31. Interview with Mrs. Zhou by Lu Yunnan on February 15, 2014.
32. Chen Mo, *Huaji fangying*, 34–35.
33. Li Aidong, ed., *Dianying*, 1:109.

34. Studlar, "Masochism."
35. Neroni, *Subject of Torture*, 23–48.
36. Plantinga, *Moving Views*, 12.
37. Williams, *Marxism and Literature*, 131.
38. Mazlish, *The Revolutionary Ascetic*; Meisner, *Marxism, Maoism, Utopianism*.
39. Meisner, *Marxism, Maoism, Utopianism*, 119–20.
40. Mittler, *Continuous Revolution*, 203.
41. According to Miin-Ling Yu, two million copies of the novel were sold between October 1949 and December 1952 (Yu, "A Soviet Hero," 336). In addition, two Soviet film adaptations of the novel were released in China, one in 1951 and the other in 1957. The two adaptations were *Heroes Are Made* (*Kak zakalyalas stal/Gangtie shi zenyang liancheng de*, 1942) and *Pavel Korchagin* (*Bao'er kechajin*, 1957). For discussions of the changing reception of *How the Steel Was Tempered* in China, see Donghui He, "Coming of Age."
42. Ostrovsky, *How the Steel Was Tempered*, 271.
43. Meisner, *Marxism, Maoism, Utopianism*, 129
44. Ibid., 120–21.
45. According to Pang Xianzhi et al., eds., *Mao Zedong nianpu*, 27–28, the original lines that Mao wrote in his diary in 1916 were "与天奋斗, 其乐无穷; 与地奋斗, 其乐无穷; 与人奋斗, 其乐无穷." The most circulated version of this quote substitutes 奋斗 with 斗. This small difference has led to different interpretations of Mao's thought on the relationship with nature. Judith Shapiro, for example, quotes a Chinese scholar who evokes the "*yu tian dou*" version to criticize Mao's harmful policies on nature (*Mao's War against Nature*, 9). Her misquotation is in turn criticized by Dongping Han ("China's Urbanization Drive," 206).
46. Quoted in Meisner, *Marxism, Maoism, Utopianism*, 129.
47. Ban Wang, *Sublime Figure of History*, 143.
48. Nussbaum, *Upheavals of Thought*.
49. Interview on April 15, 2014.
50. Li, ed., *Dianying*, 2:112.
51. Berry, "Lust, Caution," 82–83.
52. Wang Zheng, "Call me *Qingnian*," 15–16.
53. Ibid., 17.
54. Li, ed., *Dianying*, 1:228–29.
55. Portelli, "Peculiarities of Oral History," 99–100.
56. Rae Yang, *Spider Eaters*, 108–20.
57. Scarry, *The Body in Pain*, 27.
58. Ibid., 34.
59. Wu Xiangyu, "Lun hongyan de shenti geming yishi," 136.
60. Luo Guangbin and Yang Yiyan, *Hongyan*, 504.
61. Rae Yang, *Spider Eaters*, 110.
62. Xiaobing Tang, *Chinese Modern*, 1.
63. Ibid., 4.
64. Sobchack, *Carnal Thoughts*, 60.

65. Sobchack, *Address of the Eye*, 179.
66. Ibid.
67. Marks, *Skin of the Film*.
68. Barker, *Tactile Eye*.
69. Ibid., 2.
70. Wilson, *Spectatorship, Embodiment and Physicality*, 3.
71. Hanich, *Cinematic Emotion*, 57–62.
72. Ferencz-Flatz and Hanich. "Editors' Introduction," 3.

CHAPTER 6. SCREEN

1. Bruno, *Surface*, 56.
2. Ibid, 3.
3. Li Aidong, ed., *Dianying*, 4:113.
4. Ross, "Interstitial Film Viewing," 450.
5. Li Aidong, ed., *Dianying*, 4:11–12.
6. Ibid., 4:113–14.
7. Ibid., 4:12.
8. Ibid., 4:108.
9. Ibid., 1:17.
10. Ibid., 1:202.
11. Kuhn, "What to Do with Cinema Memory?" 93.
12. Andrea Kelley, "Bedsheet Cinema."
13. In fact, Chinese film practitioners had long recognized that films could be shown from both sides of a translucent screen. In *Methods of Film Projection* (*Dianying fangying fa*), a booklet published in 1938 under the name Xu Fulin, writer and filmmaker Xu Zhuodai (1881–1958) also known as "China's Chaplin," explicitly discusses the advantages and disadvantages of using white sheets for double-sided projection (Xu Fulin, *Dianying fanying fa*, 50–55).
14. Li Aidong, ed., *Dianying*, 1:91–92.
15. Keathley, *Cinephilia and History*, 7.
16. Li Aidong, ed., *Dianying*, 1:9.
17. Ibid., 1: 17–18.
18. For similar incidents, see Tina Mai Chen, "Textual Communities," 66; Yanping Guo, "Film Propaganda as Medium of Perception," 78.
19. Li Aidong, ed., *Dianying*, 1:76
20. It should be noted that in my research, stories of rural audiences mistaking films as reality mostly come from oral accounts of film projectionists collected by other scholars and myself. In contemporaneous reports or government documents, I have only come across one of such reports from a 1955 issue of *Mass Cinema*, which is referenced in Jie Li, "Cinematic Guerrillas." According to this report, when peasants on an island first saw *The White-Haired Girl*, several older women got up to make way for Huang Shiren when he yelled "Get out of the way" ("Dianyingdui"). I have not seen sources from the early 1950s describing rural audiences' "first contact" with cinema in these terms. In a 1951

article that I will cite below, rural audiences are described as watching the film *The White-Haired Girl* in complete silence and immersion.

21. Li Aidong, ed., *Dianying*, 1:180–81.
22. Ibid., 1:181.
23. McGrath, "Cultural Revolution Model Opera Films," 343.
24. Lu Fu, "Shanghai jiaoqu nongmin," 20.
25. McGrath, "Cultural Revolution Model Opera Films," 343.
26. Gunning, "Aesthetic of Astonishment," 115.
27. Ibid.
28. Loiperdinger, "Lumière's *Arrival of the Train*," 96.
29. Hansen, *Babel and Babylon*, 25–28; Elsaesser, "Discipline through Diegesis."
30. Strauven, "Early Cinema's Touch(able) Screens."
31. Gunning, "Aesthetic of Astonishment," 118.
32. Hung Wu, "The Painted Screen," 45.
33. deGravelles, "You Be Othello," 159.
34. West-Knight, "The List."
35. Interview with Mr. Tang on August 24, 2013.
36. "Budui kan baimaonü."
37. DeMare, *Mao's Cultural Army*, 1–2.
38. Strauven, "Observers' Dilemma."
39. Hansen, "Room-for-Play."
40. Bak, "Ludic Archive," 2.
41. Strauven, "Observers' Dilemma."
42. Beeler, "DVD Screen Culture for Children."
43. Strauven, "Observer's Dilemma," 158.
44. Ibid., 158.
45. Huhtamo, "Elements of Screenology," 32.
46. Ibid., 33.
47. Strauven, "Early Cinema's Touch(able) Screens."
48. Chateau and Moure, "Introduction," 13–14.
49. Ibid., 17.
50. The term *buwo* appears in "Danguiyuan guan yingxi zhilue"; *buman* in "Guan yingxi ji"; *bumu* in "Tianhua chayuan guan waiyang xifa."
51. "Using white sheet as a barrier" (*yi baibu zuozhang*) is mentioned in "Guan meiguo yingxi ji."
52. Hongwei Thorn Chen, "Screens," 27.
53. Li Aidong, ed., *Dianying*, 4:139.
54. Bateson, "Theory of Play and Fantasy."
55. Seligman et al., *Ritual and Its Consequences*, 20–23.
56. Ibid., 74–75.
57. Huizinga, *Homo Ludens*, 8–11.
58. Staiger, *Perverse Spectators*, 45–46.
59. For a brief discussion of hand shadows in Europe, see Huhtamo, "Elements of Screenology," 39–40. For Chinese shadow theater, see Fan-Pen Li Chen, *Chinese Shadow Theatre*.
60. Gunning, "Aesthetic of Astonishment," 117.

POSTSCRIPT

1. Li Daoxin, "Dianying shiming de qianye."
2. Wilkinson, "*Gemini Man.*"
3. "Pioneering 120fps HFR cinema."
4. "Huaxia Film debuts CINITY Cinema."
5. Li Daoxin, "Dianying shiming de qianye."
6. Casetti, *Lumière Galaxy*, 208–11.
7. Guerrasio, "'*Gemini Man*' Was Made."
8. Wilkinson, "*Gemini Man.*"
9. Evangelista, "No Movie Theater in the U.S."
10. Phipps, "Ang Lee."
11. Zhou Liming, "Shuangzi shashou."
12. Daqite (Grinch), "Shuangzi shashou jishu zhixia."
13. Xiu Long, "Li An weishenme sike 120 zhen."
14. Casetti, *Lumière Galaxy*, 5.
15. ripple, "Gaozhen wei yingxiang dailai le shenme."
16. Brunsdon, "'This Is Not a Cinema,'" 546.
17. Gunning, "Moving Away from the Index," 36.
18. Belton, "If Film Is Dead," 470.
19. Ibid., 470.
20. Casetti, *Lumière Galaxy*, 209.
21. Wittgenstein, *Philosophical Investigations*, 317–18.
22. Quoted in Phipps, "Ang Lee."

Bibliography

ENGLISH-LANGUAGE SOURCES

Ackerman, David, and Kristen Walker. "Consumption of *Renao* at a Taiwan Night Market." *International Journal of Culture, Tourism and Hospitality Research* 6, no. 3 (2012): 209–22.

Acland, Charles R. "Curtain, Carts, and Mobile Screen." *Screen* 50, no. 1 (2009): 148–66.

———. *Screen Traffic: Movies, Multiplexes, and Global Culture*. Durham, NC: Duke University Press, 2003.

Acland, Charles R., and Haidee Wasson. *Useful Cinema*. Durham, NC: Duke University Press, 2011.

Akihiro, Kitada, and Stefanie Thomas. "The Alluring Voice/the Allure of Film (Theaters): The Formation of the Voice in the Japanese Cinema of the Prewar Period." *Japan Forum* 30, no. 3 (2018): 352–76.

Alberini, Cristina M. "The Role of Reconsolidation and the Dynamic Process of Long-Term Memory Formation and Storage." *Frontiers in Behavioral Neuroscience*, March 7, 2011.

Alberini, Cristina M., and Joseph E. LeDoux. "Memory Reconsolidation." *Current Biology* 23, no. 17 (2013): 746–50.

Allen, Robert C. "Relocating American Film History: The 'Problem' of the Empirical." *Cultural Studies* 20 (2006): 48–88.

Althusser, Louis. *Lenin and Philosophy and Other Essays*. New York: Monthly Review Press, 1972.

Assmann, Jan. "Collective Memory and Cultural Identity." Translated by John Czaplicka. *New German Critique* 65 (1995): 125–33.

Athique, Adrian, and Douglas Hill. *The Multiplex in India: A Cultural Economy of Urban Leisure*. London: Routledge, 2010.

Aveyard, Karina, and Albert Moran, eds., *Watching Films: New Perspectives on Movie-Going, Exhibition and Reception.* Bristol, UK: Intellect Books Ltd, 2013.

Bak, Meredith. "The Ludic Archive: The Work of Playing with Optical Toys." *The Moving Image* 16, no. 1 (2016): 1–16.

Bamford, Matthew. "Sun Pictures Celebrates 100 Years in the Kimberley." ABC News, December 2, 2016. https://www.abc.net.au/news/2016-12-02/outback-cinema-turns-100/8088844.

Bao, Weihong. *Fiery Cinema: The Emergence of an Affective Medium in China, 1915–1945.* Minneapolis: University of Minnesota Press, 2015.

Barker, Jennifer. *The Tactile Eye: Touch and the Cinematic Experience.* Berkeley: University of California Press, 2009.

Barmé, Geremie. *Shades of Mao: The Posthumous Cult of the Great Leader.* London: Taylor & Francis, 2016.

Barnard, Timothy. "The 'Machine Operator': Deus Ex Machina of the Storefront Cinema." *Framework* 43, no. 1 (2002): 40–75.

Bateson, Gregory. "A Theory of Play and Fantasy." In *Ritual, Play, and Performance: Readings in the Social Sciences/Theatre*, edited by Richard Schechner and Mady Shuman, 67–73. New York: Seabury Press, 1976.

Baudry, Jean-Louis, "Ideological Effects of the Basic Cinematographic Apparatus." Translated by Alan Williams. *Film Quarterly* 28, no. 2 (1974–1975): 39–47.

Beeler, Karin. "DVD Screen Culture for Children: Theories of Play and Young Viewers." *Screening the Past* 32 (2011). Accessed September 4, 2020. http://www.screeningthepast.com/2011/11/dvd-screen-culture-for-children-theories-of-play-and-young-viewers/.

Belton, John. "If Film Is Dead, What Is Cinema?" *Screen* 55, no. 4 (2013): 460–70.

Berry, Chris. "*Lust, Caution*: Torture, Sex, and Passion in Chinese Cinema." In *Screening Torture: Media Representations of State Terror and Political Domination*, edited by Michael Flynn and Fabiola F. Salek, 71–92. New York: Columbia University Press, 2012.

———. *Postsocialist Cinema in Post-Mao China: The Cultural Revolution after the Cultural Revolution.* New York: Routledge, 2004.

Biltereyst, Daniel, Richard Maltby, and Philippe Meers, eds. *Cinema, Audiences and Modernity: New Perspectives on European Cinema History.* London: Routledge, 2012.

Bordwell, David, Janet Staiger, and Kristin Thompson. *The Classical Hollywood Cinema: Film Style and Mode of Production to 1960.* London: Routledge, 1988.

Boym, Svetlana. *The Future of Nostalgia.* New York: Basic Books, 2001.

Bray, David. *Social Space and Governance in Urban China: The Danwei System from Origins to Reform.* Stanford, CA: Stanford University Press, 2005.

Bruno, Giuliana. *Surface: Matters of Aesthetics, Materiality, and Media.* Chicago: University of Chicago Press, 2014.

Brunsdon, Charlotte. "'This Is Not a Cinema': The Projectionist's Tale." *Screen* 60, no. 4 (2019): 527–47.

Cartwright, Lisa. "The Hands of the Projectionists." *Science in Context* 24, no. 3 (2011): 443–64.

Casetti, Francesco. "Cinema Lost and Found: Trajectories of Relocation." *Screening the Past* 32 (2011). Accessed September 4, 2020. http://www .screeningthepast.com/2011/11/cinema-lost-and-found-trajectories-of -relocation/#lightbox%5B1828%5D/o/.

———. "Filmic Experience." *Screen* 50, no. 1 (2009): 56–66.

———. *The Lumière Galaxy: Seven Keywords for the Cinema to Come.* New York: Columbia University Press, 2015.

———. "Screening: A Counter-Genealogy of the Silver Screen." Paper presented at the Society of Cinema and Media Studies Annual Conference, Fairmount Chicago, March 24, 2017.

———. *Theories of Cinema, 1945–1995.* Austin: University of Texas Press, 1999.

Chan, Jessica Ka Yee. *Chinese Revolutionary Cinema: Propaganda, Aesthetics and Internationalism, 1949–1966.* London: I.B. Tauris, 2019.

Chateau, Dominique, and José Moure. "Introduction: A Concept in Progress." In *Screens: From Materiality to Spectatorship—A Historical and Theoretical Reassessment,* edited by Dominique Chateau and José Moure, 13–22. Amsterdam University Press, 2016.

Chen, Fan-Pen Li. *Chinese Shadow Theatre: History, Popular Religion, and Women Warriors.* Montreal: McGill-Queen's University Press, 2007.

Chen, Hongwei Thorn. "Cinemas, Highways, and the Making of Provincial Space: Mobile Screenings in Jiangsu, China, 1933–1937." *Wide Screen* 7, no. 1 (2018): 1–34. http://widescreenjournal.org/index.php/journal/article /view/116.

———. "Screens." *Journal of Chinese Cinemas* 10, no. 1 (2016): 26–30.

Chen, Lingchei Letty. *The Great Leap Backward: Forgetting and Representing the Mao Years.* Amherst, NY: Cambria Press, 2020.

Chen, Tina Mai. "The Human-Machine Continuum in Maoism: The Intersection of Soviet Socialist Realism, Japanese Theoretical Physics, and Chinese Revolutionary Theory." *Cultural Critique* 80 (2012): 151–82.

———. "Mobile Film Projection in Socialist and Post-Socialist China." *China Policy Institute Blog,* May 8, 2015. https://blogs.nottingham.ac.uk /chinapolicyinstitute/2015/05/08/enduring-themes-of-propaganda-mobile -film-projection-in-socialist-and-post-socialist-china/.

———. "The Proletarian White and Working Bodies in Mao's China." *Positions: East Asia Cultures Critique* 11, no. 2 (2003): 361–93.

———. "Propagating the Propaganda Film: The Meaning of Film in Chinese Communist Party Writings, 1949–1965. *Modern Chinese Literature and Culture* 15, no. 2 (2003): 154–93.

———. "Textual Communities and Localized Practices of Film in Maoist China." In *Film, History, and Cultural Citizenship: Sites of Production,* edited by Tina Mai Chen and David S. Churchill, 61–80. New York: Routledge, 2007.

Chen, Yinghong. *Creating the "New Man": From Enlightenment Ideals to Socialist Realities.* Honolulu: University of Hawai'i Press, 2009.

"China Reports the World's Largest Number of Film Screens." *Xinhua Net*, July 26, 2019. http://www.xinhuanet.com/english/2019-07/26/c_138259990 .htm.

"China to Be the World's Largest Film Market by 2020." *China Daily*, updated August 30, 2017. http://www.chinadaily.com.cn/business/2017-08/30/content _31328301.htm.

Christie, Ian, ed. *Audiences: The Key Debates*. Amsterdam: Amsterdam University Press, 2012.

———. "Through a Glass Brightly: The Magic Lantern in History." *British Academy Review* 5 (2001): 21–23.

Chu, Kiu-wai. "Displacing Red Childhood: Representation of Childhood during Mao's Era in Little Red Flowers." In *Lost and Othered Children in Contemporary Cinema*, edited by Debbie Olsen and Andrew Scahill, 175–98. Lanham, MD: Lexington Books, 2012.

Clark, Paul. *Chinese Cinema: Culture and Politics Since 1949*. Cambridge: Cambridge University Press, 1987.

———. *The Chinese Cultural Revolution: A History*. Cambridge: Cambridge University Press, 2008.

———. "Closely Watched Viewers: A Taxonomy of Chinese film Audiences from 1949 to the Cultural Revolution Seen from Hunan." *Journal of Chinese Cinemas* 5 no. 1 (2011): 73–89.

Cohen, Mary Morley. "Forgotten Audiences in the Passion Pits: Drive-in Theatres and Changing Spectator Practices in Post-War America," *Film History* 6, no. 4 (1994): 470–86.

Coman, Alin, Adam D. Brown, Jonathan Koppel, and William Hirst. "Collective Memory from a Psychological Perspective." *International Journal of Politics, Culture, and Society* 22, no. 2 (2009): 125–41.

Cuban, Larry. *Teachers and Machines: The Classroom Use of Technology*. New York: Teachers College Press, 1986.

Cuc, Alexandru, Yasuhiro Ozuru, David Manier, and William Hirst. "On the Formation of Collective Memories: The Role of a Dominant Narrator." *Memory & Cognition* 34, no. 4 (2006): 752–62.

Dai, Jinhua. "Imagined Nostalgia." Translated by Judy T. H. Chen. In *Postmodernism and China*, edited by Arif Dirlik and Xudong Zhang, 205–21. Durham, NC: Duke University Press, 2000.

de Certeau, Michel. *The Practice of Everyday Life*. Translated by Steven Rendall. Berkeley: University of California Press, 1988.

deGravelles, Karin H. "You Be Othello: Interrogating Identification in the Classroom." *Pedagogy* 11, no. 1 (2011): 153–75.

DeMare, Brian. *Mao's Cultural Army: Drama Troupes in China's Rural Revolution*. Cambridge: Cambridge University Press, 2015.

Denton, Kirk. *Exhibiting the Past: Historical Memory and the Politics of Museum in Postsocialist China*. Honolulu: University of Hawai'i Press, 2014.

de Souza e Silva, Adrianna, and Jordan Firth. *Mobile Interfaces in Public Spaces: Locational Privacy, Control, and Urban Sociability*. New York: Routledge, 2012.

Dirlik, Arif. "Postsocialism? Reflections on Socialism with Chinese Character-istics." In *Marxism and the Chinese Experience: Issues in Contemporary Chinese Socialism*, edited by Arif Dirlik and Maurice Meisner, 361–84. Armonk, NY: M. E. Sharpe, 1989.

Dutton, Michael. "Disciplinary Projects and Carceral Spread: Foucauldian The-ory and Chinese Practice." *Economy and Society* 21, no. 3 (1992): 276–94.

Ecker, Bruce. "Memory Reconsolidation Understood and Misunderstood." *International Journal of Neuropsychotherapy* 3, no. 1 (2015): 2–46.

Egerton, Gary. "The Multiplex: The Modern American Motion Picture The-ater as Message." In *Exhibition: The Film Reader*, edited by Ina Rae Hark, 155–59. London: Routledge, 2002.

Eisenhauer, Jennifer F. "Next Slide Please: The Magical, Scientific, and Corpo-rate Discourses of Visual Projection Technologies." *Studies in Art Education* 47, no. 3 (2006): 198–214.

Elsaesser, Thomas. "Discipline through Diegesis: The Rube Film between 'Attraction' and 'Narrative Integration.'" In *The Cinema of Attractions Reloaded*, edited by Wanda Stauven, 205–23. Amsterdam: Amsterdam Uni-versity Press, 2006.

Evangelista, Chris. "No Movie Theater in the U.S. Will Be Screening 'Gemini Man' as Director Ang Lee Intended." *Slash Film*, October 9, 2019. https://www.slashfilm.com/gemini-man-high-frame-rate/.

Fan, Victor. *Cinema Approaching Reality: Locating Chinese Film Theory*. Min-neapolis: University of Minnesota Press, 2015.

Fawcett, Trevor. "Visual Facts and the Nineteenth-Century Art Lecture." *Art History* 5, no. 4 (1983): 443–60.

Ferencz-Flatz, Christian, and Julian Hanich. "Editors' Introduction: What Is Film Phenomenology?" *Studia Phaenomenologica* 16 (2016): 11–61.

Fiske, John. *Introduction to Communication Studies*, 2nd edition. London; New York: Routledge, 1990.

Flitterman-Lewis, Sandy. "Psychoanalysis, Film, and Television." In *Channels of Discourse: Television and Contemporary Criticism*, edited by Robert C. Allen, 172–210. Chapel Hill: University of North Carolina Press, 1987.

Fu, Poshek. *Between Shanghai and Hong Kong: The Politics of Chinese Cin-emas*. Stanford, CA: Stanford University Press, 2003.

Fujiki, Hideaki, "*Benshi* as Stars: The Irony of the Popularity and Respectabil-ity of Voice Performance in Japanese Cinema." *Cinema Journal* 45, no. 2 (2006): 68–84.

Funari, Rachel, and Bernard Mees. "Socialist Emulation in China: Worker Heroes Yesterday and Today." *Labor History* 54, no. 3 (2013): 240–55.

Gagnepain, Pierre, Thomas Vallée, Serge Heiden, et al. "Collective Memory Shapes the Organization of Individual Memories in the Medial Prefrontal Cortex." *Nature Human Behavior* 4 (2020): 189–200.

Gallagher, Shaun, and Dan Zahavi. *The Phenomenological Mind: An Intro-duction to Philosophy of Mind and Cognitive Science*. London: Routledge, 2008.

Galloway, Alexander. *The Interface Effect*. Malden, MA: Polity Press 2012.

Gaudreault, André, and Philippe Marion. *The End of Cinema? A Medium in Crisis in the Digital Age*. Translated by Timothy Barnard. New York: Columbia University Press, 2015.

Gerow, Aaron. *Visions of Japanese Modernity: Articulations of Cinema, Nation, and Spectatorship, 1895–1925*. Berkeley, CA: University of California Press, 2010.

Gerth, Karl. "Compromising with Consumerism in Socialist China: Transnational Flows and Internal Tensions in 'Socialist Advertising.'" *Past & Present* 218, no. 8 (2013): 203–32.

Gimple, Denise. "Civilizing Bodies: Somatic Engineering in China." In *Sports across Asia: Politics, Cultures, and Identities*, edited by Katrin Bromber, Birgit Krawietz, and Joseph Maguire, 32–58. New York: Routledge, 2013.

Goode, Ian. "UNESCO, Mobile Cinema, and Rural Audiences: Exhibition Histories and Instrumental Ideologies of the 1940s." In *Rural Cinema Exhibition and Audiences in a Global Context*, edited by Daniela Treveri Gennari, Danielle Hipkins, and Catherine O'Rawe, 219–35. New York: Palgrave Macmillan, 2018.

Guerrasio, Jason. "'*Gemini Man*' Was Made in Such a Technically Advanced Way that Zero Movie Theaters in the US Can Show It as Intended." *Business Insider*, October 11, 2019. https://www.businessinsider.com/gemini-man-so-advanced-no-theater-can-show-as-intended-2019-10.

Gunning, Tom. "An Aesthetic of Astonishment: Early Film and the (In)Credulous Spectator." In *Viewing Positions: Ways of Seeing*, edited by Linda Williams, 114–33. New Brunswick, NJ: Rutgers University Press, 1995.

———. "The Cinema of Attractions: Early Film, Its Spectator and the Avant-Garde." In *Early Cinema: Space Frame Narrative*, edited by Thomas Elsaesser, 56–62. London: British Film Institute, 1990.

———. *D. W. Griffith and the Origins of American Narrative Film: The Early Years at Biograph*. Urbana: University of Illinois Press, 1991.

———. "Moving Away from the Index: Cinema and the Impression of Reality." *Differences: A Journal of Feminist Cultural Studies* 18, no. 1 (2007): 29–52.

Gunning, Tom, and André Gaudreault, "Le cinéma des premiers temps: Un défi à l'histoire du cinema." In *Histoire du cinema: Nouvelles approaches*, edited by Jacques Aumont, André Gaudreault, and Michel Marie, 49–63. Paris: Sorbonne, 1989.

Guo, Yanping. "Film Propaganda as Medium of Perception: Early Rural Screening in Maoist China (1949–1965)." PhD dissertation, The Chinese University of Hong Kong, 2017.

Han, Dongping. "China's Urbanization Drive and Its Consequences: The Jimo Case." *Philosophy Study* 6, no. 4 (2016): 204–18.

"Handling the Visitor (1909)." In *Moviegoing in America: A Sourcebook in the History of Film Exhibition*, edited by Gregory A. Waller, 66–67. Malden, MA: Blackwell Publishers, 2002.

Hanich, Julian. *The Audience Effect: On the Collective Cinema Experience*. Edinburgh: University of Edinburgh Press, 2018.

———. *Cinematic Emotion in Horror Films and Thrillers: The Aesthetic Paradox of Pleasurable Fear*. Hoboken, NJ: Taylor & Francis, 2010.

Hansen, Miriam. *Babel and Babylon: Spectatorship in American Silent Film.* Cambridge, MA: Harvard University Press, 1991.

———. "Fallen Women, Rising Stars, New Horizons: Shanghai Silent Film as Vernacular Modernism." *Film Quarterly* 54, no. 1 (2000): 10–22.

———. "The Mass Production of the Senses: Classical Cinema as Vernacular Modernism." *Modernism/Modernity* 6, no. 2 (1999): 59–77.

———. "Room-for-Play: Benjamin's Gamble with Cinema." *October* 109 (2004): 3–45.

Hark, Ian Rae, ed. *Exhibition: The Film Reader.* London: Routledge, 2002.

He, Donghui. "Coming of Age in the Brave New World: The Changing Reception of *How the Steel Was Tempered* in the People's Republic of China." In *China Learns from the Soviet Union, 1949 to the Present,* edited by Thomas P. Bernstein and Hua-yu Li, 393–420. Lanham, MD: Lexington Books, 2010.

He, Jixian. "*The White-Haired Girl*: Limitations and Potential of the New Interpretation." Translated by Ping Zhu and Chenshu Zhou. In *Debating the Socialist Legacy and Capitalist Globalization in China,* edited by Ban Wang & Xueping Zhong, 219–38. New York: Palgrave Macmillan, 2014.

Heftberger, Adelheid. "Soviet Agit-Trains from the Vertov Collection of the Austrian Film Museum." *INCITE Journal of Experimental Media.* Accessed September 2, 2020. http://www.incite-online.net/heftberger4.html.

Herzog, Charlotte. "The Movie Palace and the Theatrical Sources of Its Architecture Style." In *Exhibition: The Film Reader,* edited by Ina Rae Hark, 51–65. London: Routledge, 2002.

Ho, Denise. *Curating Revolution: Politics on Display in Mao's China.* Cambridge: Cambridge University Press, 2017.

Ho, Virgil Kit Yiu. "'Why Don't We Take Drama as Facts?' Observations on Cantonese Opera in a Rural Setting." *Journal of the Royal Asiatic Society Hong Kong Branch* 53 (2013): 183–214.

"Hollywood Says China Will Soon Be World's Top Film market, as Ticket Sales Overtake US-Canada in 2018." *South China Morning Post,* April 5, 2018. https://www.scmp.com/culture/film-tv/article/2140381/china-will-soon-be -worlds-top-film-market-having-overtaken-us-canada.

Holm, David. *Art and Ideology in Revolutionary China.* Oxford: Clarendon Press, 1990.

Hookway, Branden. *Interface.* Cambridge MA: MIT Press, 2014.

Hua, Zhiya. "*Renao* (Heat-noise), Deities' Efficacy, and Temple Festivals in Central and Southern Hebei Province." *Journal of Cambridge Studies* 8, nos. 3–4 (2013): 1–18.

"Huaxia Film debuts CINITY Cinema with Ang Lee's *Gemini Man* Advanced-Format Trailer." *Box Office Pro,* August 29, 2019. https://www.boxofficepro .com/huaxia-film-debuts-cinity-cinema-with-ang-lees-gemini-man-advanced -format-trailer/.

Hubbard, Phil. "Fear and Loathing at the Multiplex: Everyday Anxiety in the Post-industrial City." *Capital and Class* 27, no. 2 (2003): 51–75.

———. "A Good Night Out? Multiplex Cinema as Sites of Embodied Leisure." *Leisure Studies* 22 (2003): 255–72.

Huhtamo, Erkki. "Elements of Screenology: Toward an Archaeology of the Screen." *Iconics: International Studies of the Modern Image* 7 (2004): 31–82.

Huizinga, John. *Homo Ludens: A Study of the Play-Element in Culture*. Boston: Beacon, 1950.

Hung, Chang-tai. *Mao's New World: Political Culture in the Early People's Republic*. Ithaca, NY: Cornell University Press, 2011.

———. "A Political Park: The Working People's Cultural Palace in Beijing." *Journal of Contemporary History* 48, no. 3 (2013): 556–77.

Huyssen, Andreas. *Twilight Memories: Marking Time in a Culture of Amnesia*. New York: Routledge, 1995.

Jeong, Seung-hoon. *Cinematic Interfaces: Film Theory after New Media*. London: Routledge, 2013.

Johnson, David. *Spectacle and Sacrifice: The Ritual Foundations of Village Life*. Cambridge, MA: Harvard University Asia Center: Distributed by Harvard University Press, 2009.

Johnson, Matthew D. "Reconsidering Post-Revolutionary Cultural Change: Rural Film Projection Teams in Shaanxi Province, 1949–1956." In *Rural Cinema Exhibition and Audiences in a Global Context*, edited by Daniela Treveri Gennari, Danielle Hipkins, and Catherine O'Rawe, 237–60. New York: Palgrave Macmillan, 2018.

———. "The Science Education Film: Cinematizing Technocracy and Internationalizing Development." *Journal of Chinese Cinemas* 5, no. 1 (2011): 31–53.

Keane, Michael. *The Chinese Television Industry*. London: Palgrave, 2015.

Keathley, Christian. *Cinephilia and History; or, The Wind in the Trees*. Bloomington: Indiana University Press, 2006.

Kelley, Andrea J. "Bedsheet Cinema: The Materiality of the Segregating Screen." *Film History* 31, no. 3 (2019): 1–26.

Kenez, Peter. *The Birth of the Propaganda State: Soviet Methods of Mass Mobilization, 1917–1929*. London: Cambridge University Press, 1985.

Kepley, Vance, Jr. "'Cinefication': Soviet Film Exhibition in the 1920s." *Film History* 6, no. 2 (1994): 262–77.

King, Lynnea Chapman. *The Coen Brothers Encyclopedia*. Lanham, MD: Rowman and Littlefield, 2014.

Klinger, Barbara. *Beyond the Multiplex: Cinema, New Technologies, and the Home*. Berkeley: University of California Press, 2006.

Krajewski, Marcus. "The Power of Small Gestures: On the Cultural Technique of Service." *Theory, Culture & Society* 30, no. 6 (2013): 94–109.

Kuhn, Annette. "What to Do with Cinema Memory?" In *Explorations in New Cinema History: Approaches and Case Studies*, edited by Richard Maltby, Daniel Biltereyst, and Philippe Meers, 85–98. Malden, MA: Wiley-Blackwell, 2011.

Lacasse, Germain. "The Film Lecturer." In *A Companion to Early Cinema*, edited by Nicolas Dulac, André Gaudreault, and Santiago Hidalgo, 487–97. Malden, MA: Wiley-Blackwell, 2012.

Lacoste, Anne, et al. *Slides: The History of Projected Photography.* Lausanne: Éditions Noir sur Blanc, 2017.

Lamarre, Thomas. "Magic Lantern, Dark Precursor of Animation." *Animation: An Interdisciplinary Journal* 6, no. 2 (2011): 127–48.

Larkin, Brian. *Signal and Noise: Media, Infrastructure, and Urban Culture in Nigeria.* Durham, NC: Duke University Press, 2008.

Lefebvre, Henri. *The Production of Space.* Translated by Donald Nicolson-Smith. Oxford: Blackwell, 1991.

Li, Jie. "Cinematic Guerrillas in Mao's China." *Screen* 61, no. 2 (2020): 207–29.

Li, Jie and Enhua Zhang. "Introduction." In *Red Legacies in China: Cultural Afterlives of the Communist Revolution*, edited by Jie Li and Enhua Zhang, 1–22. Cambridge, MA: Harvard University Asia Center, 2016.

Lin, Chunfeng. "Red Tourism: Rethinking Propaganda as a Social Space." *Communication and Critical Cultural Studies* 12, no. 3 (2015): 328–46.

Liu, Xiao. *Information Fantasies: Precarious Mediation in Postsocialist China.* Minneapolis: University of Minnesota Press, 2019.

Loftus, Elizabeth, and John C Palmer. "Reconstruction of Automobile Destruction: An Example of the Interaction between Language and Memory." *Journal of Verbal Learning and Verbal Behavior* 13, no. 5 (1974): 585–89.

Loiperdinger, Martin. "Lumière's *Arrival of the Train*: Cinema's Founding Myth." Translated by Bernd Elzer. *The Moving Image* 4, no. 1 (2004): 89–118.

———. "The Social Impact of Screen Culture: 1880–1914." In *Screen Culture and the Social Question, 1880–1914*, edited by Ludwig Vogl-Bienek and Richard Crangle, 9–20. Bloomington: Indiana University Press, 2013.

Lu, Duanfang. *Remaking Chinese Urban Form: Modernity, Scarcity, and Space, 1949–2005.* London: Routledge, 2006.

Lu, Sheldon. "History, Memory, Nostalgia: Rewriting Socialism in Chinese Cinema and Television Drama." *Asian Cinema* 16, no. 2 (2005): 2–22.

Lu, Xiaoning. *Moulding the Socialist Subject: Cinema and Chinese Modernity (1949–1966).* Brill, 2020.

Lu, Yi. "The Malling of the Movies: Film Exhibition Reforms, Multiplexes, and Film Consumption in the New Millennium in Urban China." *Journal of Chinese Cinemas* 10, no. 3 (2016): 205–27.

Manovich, Lev. *The Language of the New Media.* Cambridge MA: MIT Press, 2002.

Mao, Zedong. *Selected Works of Mao Tse-Tung, vol. 3.* Beijing: Foreign Languages Press, 1967.

Marks, Laura. *The Skin of the Film: Intercultural Cinema, Embodiment, and the Senses.* Durham, NC: Duke University Press, 2000.

Maltby, Richard, Daniel Biltereyst, and Philippe Meers. eds., *Explorations in New Cinema History: Approaches and Case Studies.* Malden, MA: Wiley-Blackwell, 2011.

Maltby, Richard, Melvyn Stokes, and Robert C. Allen, eds., *Going to the Movies: Hollywood and the Social Experience of Cinema.* Exeter: University of Exeter Press, 2007.

Mauss, Marcel. *Techniques, Technology and Civilization*, edited by Nathan Schlanger. New York: Durkheim Press/Berghahn Books, 2006.

Mazlish, Bruce. *The Revolutionary Ascetic: Evolution of a Political Type*. New York: Basic Books, 1976.

McGrath, Jason. "Cultural Revolution Model Opera Films and the Realist Tradition in Chinese Cinema." *The Opera Quarterly* 26, nos. 2–3 (2010): 343–76.

———. *Postsocialist Modernity: Chinese Cinema, Literature, and Criticism in the Market Age*. Stanford, CA: Stanford University Press, 2008.

Meisner, Maurice. *Mao's China and After*. New York: Free Press, 1986.

———. *Marxism, Maoism, Utopianism: Eight Essays*. Madison: University of Wisconsin Press, 1982.

Mentzelopoulos, Haris. "The Athenian Summer Cinemas." *Visit Greece*. Accessed January 2, 2020. http://www.visitgreece.gr/en/leisure/going_out/the _athenian_summer_cinemas.

Merleau-Ponty, Maurice. *Maurice Merleau-Ponty: Basic Writings*. Edited by Thomas Baldwin. London: Routledge, 2004.

Mironenko, Dima. "North Koreans at the Movies: Cinema of Fits and Starts and the Rise of Chameleon Spectatorship." *Journal of Japanese and Korean Cinema* 8, no. 1 (2016): 25–44.

Mittler, Barbara. *A Continuous Revolution: Making Sense of Cultural Revolution Culture*. Cambridge, MA: Harvard University Asia Center, 2012.

Musser, Charles. "Toward a History of Screen Practices." *Quarterly Review of Film Studies* 9, no. 1 (1984): 59–69.

Nelson, Robert. "Windows to the American Past: Lantern Slides as Historic Evidence." *Visual Resources* 5, no. 1 (1988): 1–15.

Neroni, Hilary. *The Subject of Torture: Psychoanalysis and Biopolitics in Television and Film*. New York: Columbia University Press, 2015.

Nussbaum, Martha. *Upheavals of Thought: The Intelligence of Emotions*. Cambridge: Cambridge University Press, 2001.

Ogden, Chris. "Communes." In *A Dictionary of Politics and International Relations in China*. Oxford: Oxford University Press, 2019. https://www-oxford reference-com.proxy.library.nyu.edu/view/10.1093/acref/9780191848124 .001.0001/acref-9780191848124-e-39.

Okubo, Ryo. "The Magic Lantern Show and Its Spectators during Late Nineteenth Century Japan: Control of Perception in Lantern Shows for Education and News Report of Sino-Japanese War." *Iconics* 11 (2014): 7–26.

Orgeron, Devin, Marsha Orgeron, and Dan Streible, eds. *Learning with the Lights Off: Educational Film in the United States*. New York: Oxford University Press, 2012.

Ostrovsky, Nikolay. *How the Steel Was Tempered: A Novel in Two Parts*. Translated by R. Prokofieva. Moscow: Progressive Publishers, 1976.

Pan, Ing-hai. "*Renao*: A Socio-psychological Phenomenon of Chinese," *Indigenous Psychological Research* 1 (1993): 330–37.

Pang, Laikwan. *The Art of Cloning: Creative Production during China's Cultural Revolution*. London: Verso, 2017.

————. "The Visual Representation of the Barefoot Doctor: Between Medical Policy and Political Struggle." *Positions: Asia Critique* 22, no. 4 (2014): 837–75.

————. "Walking into and out of the Spectacle: China's Earliest Film Scene." *Screen* 47, no. 1 (2006): 66–80.

Paul, William. "The K-Mart Audience at the Mall Movies." In *Exhibition: The Film Reader*, edited by Ina Rae Hark, 77–88. London: Routledge, 2002.

————. *When Movies Were Theater: Architecture, Exhibition, and the Evolution of American Film*. New York: Columbia University Press, 2016.

Perry, Elizabeth J. "Moving the Masses: Emotion Work in the Chinese Revolution." *Mobilization: An International Journal* 7, no. 2 (2002): 111–28.

Peters, John Durham. *The Marvelous Clouds: Toward an Elemental Philosophy of Media*. Chicago: University of Chicago Press, 2015.

Peterson, Glen. "Peasant Education and the Reconstruction of Village Society." In *Education, Culture, and Identity in Twentieth-Century China*, edited by Glen Peterson, Ruth Hayhoe, and Yongling Lu, 217–37. Ann Arbor: The University of Michigan Press, 2001.

Petrina, Stephen. "Getting a Purchase on 'The School of Tomorrow' and Its Constituent Commodities: Histories and Historiographies of Technologies." *History of Education Quarterly* 42, no. 1 (2002): 75–111.

Phipps, Keith. "Ang Lee and the Uncertain Future of High-Frame-Rate Filmmaking." *The Ringer*, October 15, 2019. https://www.theringer.com/movies/2019/10/15/20915467/ang-lee-gemini-man-will-smith-high-frame-rate-billy-lynns-long-halftime-walk.

Pickowicz, Paul G. "From Yao Wenyuan to Cui Zi'en: Film, History, Memory." *Journal of Chinese Cinemas* 1, no. 1 (2007): 41–53.

————. "Melodramatic Representations and the May Fourth Tradition of Chinese Cinema." In *From May Fourth to June Fourth: Fiction and Film in Twentieth-Century China*, edited by Ellen Widmer and David Wang, 295–326. Cambridge, MA: Harvard University Press, 1993.

"Pioneering 120fps HFR cinema with Paramount Pictures' *Gemini Man*, from Legendary Filmmaker Ang Lee." *DCinema Today*, October 3, 2019. https://www.dcinematoday.com/dc/pr?newsID=5575.

Plantinga, Carl. *Moving Viewers: American Film and the Spectator's Experience*. Berkeley: University of California Press, 2009.

Portelli, Alessandro. "The Peculiarities of Oral History." *History Workshop* 12 (1981): 96–107.

Prince, Stephen. *Digital Cinema*. New Brunswick, NJ: Rutgers University Press, 2019.

Rancière, Jacques. *The Politics of Aesthetics: The Distribution of the Sensible*. Translated by Gabriel Rockhill. London: Continuum, 2004.

Reinhard, Carrielynn D., and Christopher J. Olson, eds. *Making Sense of Cinema: Empirical Studies into Film Spectators and Spectatorship*. New York: Bloomsbury Academic, 2016.

Rice, Tom. "British Empire's Forgotten Propaganda Tool for 'Primitive People': Mobile Cinema." *The Conversations*, August 24, 2016. https://theconversation

.com/british-empires-forgotten-propaganda-tool-for-primitive-peoples-mobile
-cinema-64275.

Roquet, Paul. *Ambient Media: Japanese Atmospheres of Self.* Minneapolis: University of Minnesota Press, 2016.

Rosen, Stanley. "Film and Society in China: Logic of the Market." In *A Companion to Chinese Cinema*, edited by Yingjin Zhang, 197–217. Malden, MA: Blackwell Publishing: 2012.

Ross, Miriam. "Interstitial Film Viewing: Community Exhibition in the Twenty-First Century." *Continuum: Journal of Media & Cultural Studies* 27, no. 3 (2013): 446–57.

Rossell, Deac. "Double Think: The Cinema and Magic Lantern Culture." In *Celebrating 1895: The Centenary of Cinema*, edited by John Fullerton, 27–36. London: John Libbey, 1998.

Rushton, Richard and Gary Bettinson. *What Is Film Theory?* Maidenhead, UK: McGraw-Hill Education, 2010.

Scarry, Elaine. *The Body in Pain: The Making and Unmaking of the World.* New York: Oxford University Press, 1985.

Schmalzer, Sigrid. *Red Revolution, Green Revolution: Scientific Farming in Socialist China.* Chicago: University of Chicago Press, 2016.

Seligman, Adam B., Robert P. Weller, Michael Puett, and Bennett Simon. *Ritual and Its Consequences: An Essay on the Limits of Sincerity.* London: Oxford University Press, 2008.

Shapiro, Judith. *Mao's War against Nature: Politics and the Environment in Revolutionary China.* Cambridge: Cambridge University Press, 2001.

Sheridan, Mary. "The Emulation of Heroes." *China Quarterly* 33 (1968): 47–72.

Siegert, Bernhard. *Cultural Techniques: Grids, Filters, Doors, and Other Articulations of the Real.* Translated by Geoffrey Winthrop-Young. New York: Fordham University Press, 2015.

"SLEEPCINEMAHOTEL: Where They Want You to Fall Asleep." Produced by Sophie van Brugen and Kaona Pongpipat. BBC, February 2, 2018. Video. https://www.bbc.com/news/av/entertainment-arts-42905498/sleepcinema hotel-where-they-want-you-to-fall-asleep.

Smith, Andrew F. *Popped Culture: A Social History of Popcorn in America.* Columbia: University of South Carolina Press, 1999.

Sobchack, Vivian. *The Address of the Eye: A Phenomenology of Film Experience.* Princeton, NJ: Princeton University Press, 1992.

———. *Carnal Thoughts: Embodiment and Moving Image Culture.* Berkeley: University of California Press, 2004.

Sontag, Susan. "The Decay of Cinema." *New York Times*, February 25, 1996.

Srinivas, Lakshmi. *House Full: Indian Cinema and the Active Audience.* Chicago: The University of Chicago Press, 2016.

Stacey, Jackie. *Star Gazing: Hollywood Cinema and Female Spectatorship.* London: Routledge, 1993.

Staiger, Janet. *Perverse Spectators: The Practices of Film Reception.* New York: New York University Press, 2000.

Standish, Isolde. "Mediators of Modernity: 'Photo-interpreters' in Japanese Silent Cinema." *Oral Tradition* 20, no. 1 (2005): 93–110.

Stange, Maren. "Jacob Riis and Urban Visual Culture: The Lantern Slide Exhibition as Entertainment and Ideology." *Journal of Urban History* 15, no. 3 (1989): 274–303.

Statista. "Number of Movie Tickets Sold in China from 2010 to 2020." Chart. January 15, 2021. *Statista*. Accessed February 16, 2021. https://www.statista.com/statistics/260333/number-of-movie-tickets-sold-in-china/.

———. "Number of Movie Tickets Sold in the U.S. and Canada from 1980 to 2020 (in Millions)." Chart. January 22, 2021. Accessed February 16, 2020. https://www.statista.com/statistics/187073/tickets-sold-at-the-north-american -box-office-since-1980/

Strauven, Wanda. "Early Cinema's Touch(able) Screens: From Uncle Josh to Ali Barbouyou." *NECSUS*, November 22, 2012. https://necsus-ejms.org/early -cinemas-touchable-screens-from-uncle-josh-to-ali-barbouyou/.

———. "Introduction to an Attractive Concept." In *The Cinema of Attractions Reloaded*, edited by Wanda Strauven, 11–27. Amsterdam University Press, 2006.

———. "The Observer's Dilemma: To Touch or Not to Touch' in *Media Archaeology: Approaches, Applications, and Implications*, edited by E. Huhtamo and J. Parikka, 148–63. Berkeley: University of California Press, 2011.

Studlar, Gaylyn. "Masochism and the Perverse Pleasures of the Cinema." *Quarterly Review of Film Studies* 9, no. 4 (1984): 267–82.

Sugawara, Yoshino. "Toward the Opposite Side of 'Vulgarity': The Birth of Cinema as a 'Healthful Entertainment' and the Shanghai YMCA." In *Early Film Culture in Hong Kong, Taiwan, and Republican China: Kaleidoscopic Histories*, edited by Emilie Yueh-yu Yeh, 179–201. Ann Arbor, MI: University of Michigan Press, 2018.

"Take in a Movie under the Stars in Greece," *The Telegraph*, May 20, 2015. https://www.telegraph.co.uk/travel/destinations/europe/greece/captivating -holidays/outdoor-cinemas-in-athens/.

Tang, Xiaobing. *Chinese Modern: The Heroic and the Quotidian*. Durham, NC: Duke University Press, 2000.

Terzian, Sevan. "The History of Technology and Education." *The Oxford Handbook of the History of Education*, edited by John L. Rury and Eileen H. Tamura, 554–65. New York: Oxford University Press, 2019.

Thomson, Allistair. "Memory and Remembering in Oral History." In *The Oxford Handbook of Oral History*, edited by Donald A. Ritchie, 77–95. Oxford: Oxford University Press, 2011.

Van de Vijver, Lies. "The Cinema Is Dead, Long Live the Cinema: Understanding the Social Experience of Cinema-Going Today." *Participations* 14, no. 1 (2017): 129–44.

Van Dooren, Ine. "Our Magic Lantern Heritage: Archiving a Past Medium That Nearly Never Was." In *Screen Culture and the Social Question, 1880–1914*, edited by Ludwig Vogl-Bienek and Richard Crangle, 183–90. Bloomington: Indiana University Press, 2013.

Van Fleit Hang, Krista. *Literature the People Love: Reading Chinese Texts from the Early Maoist Period (1949–1966)*. New York: Palgrave Macmillan, 2013.

Vogl-Bienek, Ludwig, and Richard Crangle. *Screen Culture and the Social Question, 1880–1914.* Bloomington: Indiana University Press, 2013.

Volland, Nicolai. *Socialist Cosmopolitanism: The Chinese Literary Universe, 1945–1965.* New York: Columbia University Press, 2017.

Walder, Andrew. *Communist Neo-Traditionalism: Work and Authority in Chinese Industry.* Berkeley: University of California Press, 1986.

Wang, Ban. *Illuminations from the Past: Trauma, Memory, and History in Modern China.* Stanford, CA: Stanford University Press, 2004.

———. *The Sublime Figure of History: Aesthetics and Politics in Twentieth-Century China.* Stanford: Stanford University Press, 1997.

Wang, David Der-wei. *A New Literary History of Modern China.* Cambridge, MA: Harvard University Press, 2018.

Wang, Xiaoxuan. "The Dilemma of Implementation: The State and Religion in the People's Republic of China, 1949–1990." In *Maoism at the Grassroots: Everyday Life in China's Era of High Socialism,* edited by Jeremy Brown and Matthew D. Johnson, 258–78. Cambridge, MA: Harvard University Press, 2015.

Wang, Zheng. "Call me *Qingnian,* but Not *Funü:* A Maoist Youth in Retrospect." *Feminist Studies* 27, no. 1 (2001): 9–34.

———. *Finding Women in the State: A Socialist Feminist Revolution in the People's Republic of China, 1949–1964.* Oakland: University of California Press, 2017.

Wang, Zhuoyi. *Revolutionary Cycles in Chinese Cinema, 1951–1979.* New York: Palgrave Macmillan, 2014.

Ward, Barbara E. "Not Merely Players: Drama, Art, and Ritual in Traditional China." *Man, NS* 14, no. 1 (1979): 18–39.

Warden, Clyde A., and Judy F. Chen. "When Hot and Noisy Is Good: Chinese Values of *Renao* and Consumption Metaphors." *Asia Pacific Journal of Marketing and Logistics* 21, no. 2 (2009): 216–31.

Wassen, Haidee. *Museum Movies: The Museum of Modern Art and the Birth of Art Cinema.* Berkeley, CA: University of California Press, 2005.

Wen, Laura Jo-Han. "Magic Lantern Shows and Screen Modernity in Colonial Taiwan." In *Early Film Culture in Hong Kong, Taiwan, and Republican China: Kaleidoscopic Histories,* edited by Emilie Yueh-yu Yeh, 19–50. Ann Arbor: University of Michigan Press, 2018.

West-Knight, Imogen. "The List: Four of the Strangest Theatrical Interruptions." *Financial Times,* July 11, 2015. https://www.ft.com/content/ed235438-2646 -11e5-9c4e-a775d2b173ca.

Wilcox, Emily. *Revolutionary Bodies: Chinese Dance and the Socialist Legacy.* Oakland: University of California Press, 2019.

Wilkinson, Alisa. "Gemini Man, Starring Will Smith, Spells Catastrophe for the Future of Movies." *Vox,* October 9, 2019. https://www.vox.com/culture /2019/10/9/20905020/gemini-man-review-will-smith.

Williams, Raymond. *Marxism and Literature.* London: Oxford University Press, 1977.

Wilson, Laura. *Spectatorship, Embodiment and Physicality in the Contemporary Mutilation Film.* New York: Palgrave Macmillan, 2015.

Wittgenstein, Ludwig. *Philosophical Investigations*, 3rd edition. Translated by G. E. M Anscombe. Oxford, UK: Basil Blackwell, 1967.

Wollen, Peter. "Godard and Counter Cinema: Vent d'Est," *Afterimage* 4 (Autumn 1972): 6–17.

Wu, Hung. "The Painted Screen." *Critical Inquiry* 23 (1996): 23–79.

Wue, Roberta. "China in the World: On Photography, Montages, and the Magic Lantern." *History of Photography* 41, no. 2 (2017): 171–87.

Veg, Sebastian. "Introduction: Trauma, Nostalgia, Public Debate." In *Popular Memories of the Mao Era: From Critical Debate to Reassessing History*, edited by Sebastian Veg, 1–18. Hong Kong: Hong Kong University Press, 2019.

Yang, Guobin. "China's Zhiqing Generation: Nostalgia, Identity, and Cultural Resistance in the 1990s." *Modern China* 29, no. 3 (2003): 267–96.

Yang, Lihsin. "A Visit to the Shanghai Workers' Club." *China Monthly Review*, April 1, 1953: 52–55.

Yang, Rae. *Spider Eaters: A Memoir*. Berkeley: University of California Press, 2013.

Yeh, Emilie Yueh-yu. "Pitfalls of Cross-Cultural Analysis: Chinese *Wenyi* Film and Melodrama." *Asian Journal of Communication* 19, no. 4 (2009): 438–52.

———. "Translating Yingxi: Chinese Film Genealogy and Early Cinema in Hong Kong." In *Early Film Culture in Hong Kong, Taiwan, and Republican China: Kaleidoscopic Histories*, edited by Emilie Yueh-yu Yeh, 51–70. Ann Arbor: University of Michigan Press, 2018.

Yu, Miin-ling. "Labor Is Glorious: Model Laborers in the People's Republic of China." In *China Learns from the Soviet Union 1949–Present*, edited by Thomas P. Bernstein and Hua-yu Li, 231–58. Lanham, MD: Lexington, 2010.

———. "A Soviet Hero, Pavel Korchagin, Comes to China." *Russian History* 29, nos. 2–4 (2002): 329–55.

Zeng, Li. "The Road to the Past: Socialist Nostalgia in Postsocialist China." *Visual Anthropology* 22 (2009): 108–22.

Zhang, Xudong. *Postsocialism and Cultural Politics: China in the Last Decade of the Twentieth Century*. Durham, NC: Duke University Press, 2008.

Zhang, Yingjin. *Chinese National Cinema*. New York: Routledge, 2004.

———. "Directors, Aesthetics, Genres: Chinese Postsocialist Cinema, 1979–2010." In *A Companion to Chinese Cinema*, edited by Yingjin Zhang, 57–74. Hoboken, NJ: John Wiley & Sons, 2012.

———. "Ethnicity, Nationality, Translocality: A Critical Reflection on the Questions of Theory in Chinese Film Studies." In *Contemporary Chinese Art and Film: Theory Applied and Resisted*, edited by Jason C. Kuo, 243–60. Washington, DC: New Academia Publishing, 2013.

———. *Screening China: Critical Interventions, Cinematic Reconfigurations, and the Transnational Imaginary in Contemporary Chinese Cinema*. Ann Arbor, MI: Center for Chinese Studies, 2002.

Zhang, Zhen. *An Amorous History of the Silver Screen: Shanghai Cinema, 1896–1937*. Chicago: University of Chicago Press, 2005.

CHINESE-LANGUAGE SOURCES

Abbreviations

DYFY   *Dianying fangying* [Film Projection]

DYPJ   *Dianying puji* [Film popularization]

DZDY   *Dazhong dianying* [Mass cinema]

GMRB   *Guangming ribao* [Guangming Daily]

RMRB   *Renmin ribao* [People's Daily]

SMA   Shanghai Municipal Archive

A Lunna. "Dianhua jiaoyu shiye de chuchuang" [The beginning of the audiovisual education enterprise]. *Dianhua jiaoyu yanjiu* [E-Education Research] 5 (2011): 110–20

———. "Dianhua jiaoyu de yunyu yu dansheng" [The incubation and birth of audiovisual education]. *Dianhua jiaoyu yanjiu* 12 (2010): 111–20.

———. "Zhongguo dianhua jiaoyu (jiaoyu jishu) nianbiao 2" [Chronology of audiovisual education in China]. *Dianhua jiaoyu yanjiu* 12 (2006): 63–70.

"Beijing shi gequ gongren julebu gongzuo zanxing tiaoli" [Temporary regulations for district-level workers' clubs in Beijing], 1958. Beijing Municipal Archive 101-001-00690.

"Budui kan baimaonü weihe guiding zidan buzhun shangtang" [Why the military forbids loaded guns at performances of *The White-Haired Girl*]. *Dongfang wang*, April 30, 2014. http://history.eastday.com/h/20140430/u1a8061969.html.

Cai Chusheng. "Mantan 'sihao': zai yici zuotanhui shang de fayan" [Thoughts on the 'Four Goods': Speech delivered at a conference]. *DZDY* 8 (1961): 5–6.

Chen Bo. *Zhongguo dianying biannian jishi: faxing fangying juan* [Chronicles of Chinese cinema: Volume on distribution and exhibition]. Beijing: Zhongyang wenxian chuban she, 2005.

Chen Mo. *Huaji fangying: Shanxi nüzi fangying ren* [Projection in the flower season: Female projectionists from Shaanxi]. Beijing: Zhongguo dianying chubanshe, 2014.

Chen Shao. "Laodong renmin wenhuagong xunli" [A tour of the Working People's Cultural Palace]. *GMRB*, April 30, 1950.

Chen Yingba. "Dianying songdao wuzhishan" [Delivering cinema to Wuzhi Mountain]. *DYFY* 4 (1957): 23.

Chen Yiyu. "Zhongguo zaoqi dianying guanzhong shi (1896–1949)" [A history of early Chinese film audience, 1896–1949]. PhD Dissertation, Chinese National Academy of Arts, 2013.

Cheng Jihua. *Zhongguo dianying fazhan shi* [A history of the development of Chinese cinema]. Beijing: Zhongguo dianying, 1980.

"Danguiyuan guan yingxi zhilue" [Watching shadowplay in Dangui Garden]. *Shen Bao* [Shanghai News], October 17, 1887.

"Dapo yandong bu huodong de chengui" [Breaking the old rule of no screening in the winter]. *Dianying fangying ziliao* [Film Projection Resources] 3 (1956): 24.

Daqite (Grinch). "Shuangzi shashou jishu zhixia, shi ta laolaoshishi zuo dianying de yongxin" [Beneath the technology of *Gemini Man* is his dedication to making films with heart]. *Douban*, September 27, 2019. https://movie.douban.com/review/10531960/.

Dazhong dianying bianji bu [Editorial office of *Mass Cinema*]. "Jianjue hanwei shehuizhuyi de dianying shiye" [Determined to safeguard the socialist film enterprise]. In *Zhongguo dianying yanjiu ziliao: 1949–1976, zhongjuan* [A sourcebook for Chinese cinema studies: 1949–1976, vol. 2], edited by Wu Di, 144–49. Beijing: Wenhua yishu chubanshe, 2006.

———. "Kan hao yingpian jue fei langfei [Watching good films is by no means wasteful]. *DZDY* 1–2 (1952): 66.

Deng, Xiaoping. *Deng Xiaoping wenxuan, di er juan* [Selected works of Deng Xiaoping, vol. 2]. Beijing: Renmin chubanshe, 1994.

Deng, Yiwen. "Xin shiqi xiangcun lutian dianying minsu" [Folk culture of open-air cinema in the new era]. *Dianying pingjie* [Movie Review] 11 (2007): 37.

"Dianying fangyingdui buyao pa jin shanqu" [Film projection teams should not be afraid of entering mountainous areas]. *RMRB*, September 2, 1953.

"Dianying fangying gongzuo shang de yige zhongda chuangzao" [A major innovation in the work of film exhibition]. *RMRB*, December 16, 1964.

"Dianyingdui lai le" [The film projection team is here]. *DZDY* 1 (1955): 36–37.

Ding Li. "Huandeng" [Slide projection]. *DZDY* 4 (1950): 29

"Duo yin zai nongmin zhong fanxiang qianglie" [Peasants greeted *The Fight for Power* with enthusiasm]. *DYFY* 9 (1964): 3.

Gao Baolin. "Zhuanye dianyingyuan de gaizao shi chengshi dianying shiye fazhan de zhongyao tujing" [The renovation of purpose-built movie theaters is an important way to develop the urban film enterprise]. *DYPJ* 8 (1987): 5–6.

Gao Naiyan. "Weile gongren, ban buyetian dianyingyuan" [Running a 24-hour movie theater for workers]. *DYFY* 5 (1960): 16–17.

"Guan meiguo yingxi ji" [Watching American shadowplay]. *Youxi bao* [The Amusement Paper] 74, September 5, 1897.

Guan Wenqi. "Women yiding yao bangzhu nongmin kan dong dianying" [We must help peasants understand films]. *DZDY* 6 (1953): 32–33.

"Guan yingxi ji" [Watching shadowplay]. *Shen Bao*, August 29, 1889.

Guangdong sheng wenhua ju. "Nongcun dianying fangyingdui xuanchuan gongzuo zanxing xize" [Tentative guidelines for the propaganda work of rural film projection teams]. *Dianying Fangying Ziliao* 3 (1956): 26–33.

"Guanyu jianguo yilai dang de ruogan lishi wenti de jueyi" [Decisions on several historical problems of the party since the founding of the nation]. *Zhonghua renmin gongheguo zhongyang renmin zhengfu* [the State Council of the People's Republic of China], June 23, 2008. http://www.gov.cn/test/2008-06/23/content_1024934.htm.

He Baoyu. "Huandeng, qunzhong xi'ai de yishu huaduo" [Slide projection: An artistic gem loved by the people]. *Meishu* [Fine Arts] 3 (1958): 31–32.

He Licheng. "Yao zuzhi huandengji shengchan" [The production of slide projectors should be organized]. *DYPJ* 9 (1983): 22.

Hebei changli xian diyi fangyingdui [Number One Film Projection Team of Changli County, Hebei Province]. "Didao zhan yingjian jieshuo" [Lecturing script for *Tunnel Warfare*]. DYFY 3 (1966): 19–20.

Huang Dequan. *Minguo shanghai yingyuan gaiguan* [Overview of movie theaters in Republican Shanghai]. Beijing: Zhongguo dianying chubanshe, 2014.

———. "Xiqu dianying dingjun shan zhi youlai yu yanbian" [The origin and development of the opera film *Dingjun Mountain*] *Dangdai dianying* [Contemporary Cinema] 2 (2008): 104–11.

Huang Jiamo, "Yingxing yingpian yu ruanxing yinggpian" [Hard film and soft film]. *Xiandai dianying* [Modern Cinema] 1, no. 6 (1933): 3.

"Huoyue zai qunshan zhong de dianying fangyingdui" [A film projection team active in the mountains]. RMRB, June 13, 1963.

"Jinli zuohao dianying fangying de xuanchuan jieshi gongzuo" [Trying our best in the propaganda and lecturing work in film exhibition]. DZDY 5 (1952): 32.

"Jinyibu xiezhu gonghui juleibu jinxing gongzuo" [Providing more assistance to the work of workers' clubs]. GMRB, January 27, 1955.

Jin Liangbi. "Xiangcun minzhong jiaoyu shiji wenti taolun: huandeng shijiao fangfa de jieshao" [A discussion of practical issues in rural mass education: Introducing methods in slide education]. *Nongmin jiaoyu* [Peasant Education] 2, no. 8 (1932): 22–24.

Jin Lisheng. "Juexin dapo meiyue fangying ershiliu chang de zhibiao" [Determined to break the record of twenty-six screenings per month]. *Dianying fangying ziliao* 6 (1956): 8.

Jin Xian. "Jingjin, dongbei gedi yingyuan canguan ji (1)" [Touring movie theaters in Beijing, Tianjin, and the Northeast, part 1]. DZDY 24 (1951): 20–21.

———. "Jingjin, dongbei gedi yingyuan canguan ji (2)" [Touring movie theaters in Beijing, Tianjin, and the Northeast, part 2]. DZDY 25 (1951): 22.

Kashi zhuanqu dianying faxing fangying gongsi [Kashi special district film distribution and exhibition company]. "Mao Zedong sixiang geile tamen qianjin de liliang" [Mao Zedong Thought gives them the power to charge forward]. DYFY 1–2 (1966): 13.

Ke Ke. "Xin zhongguo gongren de wenhua shenghuo" [Workers' cultural life in the new China]. GMRB, August 12, 1951.

Kong Ru. "Tongyi yinfa yingpian shuomingshu yu fangying qian jia gushi jianjie luyin" [I agree that we should print plot sheets and play audio introductions before screenings]. DZDY 5 (1952): 33.

Li Aidong, ed. *Dianying: Women gongtong de ji yi, 1–4* [Cinema: Our shared memory, vols. 1–4]. Beijing: zhongguo dianying chubanshe, 2007.

Li Cun. "Guoji daxiyuan fuwu zhoudao" [Thoughtful service at the International Theater]. DZDY 8 (1951): 16.

Li Daoxin. "Dianying shiming de qianye, Li An de gudu yu kongju" [The night before cinema loses its sight: The loneliness and fear of Ang Lee]. *Beiqing yiping* [Beiqing art review], October 26, 2019. https://mp.weixin.qq.com/s/VH2KdTFexMoQTlVnDSc28A.

———. "Lutian dianying de zhengzhi jingjixue" [The political economy of open-air cinema]. *Dangdai dianying* 3 (2006): 97–101.

Li Haiyan. "Huashuo Baimaonü: Minzu xushi zhong de jieji yu xingbie zheng-zhi" [*The white-haired girl*: class and gender politics in a national narrative]. *Ershiyi shiji* [Twenty-first Century] 52 (1999): 110–18.

Li Jiaqi, et al. *Shanghai gongyun zhi* [Shanghai gazetteer of labor movements]. Shanghai: shanghai shehui kexueyuan chubanshe, 1997.

Li Keng. "Wo dui jieshuo de yidian tihui" [Some thoughts on lecturing]. *DYFY* 1 (1957): 22–25.

Li Meng and Cheng Weimin. "Laishui sanjiemei dianying fangyingdui jinian-guan jiepai" [Memorial museum for the Laishui Three Sisters Film Projection Team opened]. *Sohu*, August 28, 2016. https://m.sohu.com/n/466395781 /?wscrid=95360_6.

Li Qiongzhi. "Huandeng jiaoyu" [Slide education]. *Jiaoyu yu minzhong* [Education and the Masses] 1, no. 6 (1930): 1–12.

Li Ruidong, "Fangyingyuan zhi ge (shi pei hua)" [The projectionist's song (illustrated poem)]. *DYFY* 1–2 (1966): 22.

Li Shu. "Xin chengli de hubei nüzi fangying dui" [A newly formed all-female projection team from Hubei]. *DZDY* 1(1953): 18.

Li Shukai. "Wo shi yige xin zhongguo de nü fangyingyuan" [I am a female film projectionist of the new China]. *DZDY* 26 (1951): 23.

Li Xing. "Guanzhong xuyao kan shenmeyang de yingpian" [What kinds of films do audiences want to watch?]. *Wenhui bao* [Wenhui Daily], December 17, 1956.

"Lin Biao tongzhi weituo Jiang Qing tongzhi zhaokai de budui wenyi gongzuo zuotanhui jiyao" [Summary of the forum on literature and art for the armed forces organized by Jiang Qing as commissioned by comrade Lin Biao]. *RMRB*, May 29, 1967.

Liu Dishan. "'Shiqinian' shiqi yizhipian chuanbo de chengxiang zhi bie" [Urban-rural differences in the circulation of dubbed foreign films during the Seventeen Years]. *Wenyi yanjiu* [Studies of Literature and Arts] 2 (2013): 98–106.

Liu Guangyu. "1949–1976 nian: Jiangjin nongcun dianying fangyingdui de lishi yange ji yunzuo jizhi" [The history and operation of Jiangjin showing team from 1949 to 1976]. *Dangdai dianying* 10 (2008): 61–65.

———. *Xin zhongguo chengli yilai nongcun dianying fangying yanjiu* [A study of rural film exhibition since the founding of the new China]. Beijing: Wen-hua yishu chubanshe, 2015.

Liu Hailong. "Hanyu zhong xuanchuan gainian de qiyuan yu yiyi bianqian" [The origin and changing meaning of *xuanchuan* in Chinese]. *Guoji xinwen jie* [International News] 11 (2011): 103–7.

Liu Jian. "Huaijiu, xiandaixing, yu linglei gonggong kongjian: 20 shiji 80 nian-dai lutian dianying wenhua yanjiu" [Nostalgia, modernity, and alternative public sphere: A study of open-air cinema culture in the 1980s]. *Wenhua yu shixue* [Literature and the Arts] 2 (2016): 244–63.

Liu Sijia. "Qiantan minguo lutian dianying de fazhan yu yanbian" [A brief discussion of the evolution of open-air cinema during the Republican era] *Dianying wenxue* [Film Literature] 5 (2019): 42–45.

Liu Siyu. "Dianyingyuan yu guojia zhengzhi dongyuan" [Movie theaters and state political mobilization]. *Dangdai dianying* 11 (2013): 52–57.

Lu Fu. "Shanghai jiaoqu nongmin zai huore de tugai yundong zhong kan ying-pian baimaonü" [Peasants in the suburbs of Shanghai watch *The White-Haired Girl* in the heat of land reform] *DZDY* 26 (1951): 20–21.

Luo Guangbin and Yang Yiyan. *Hongyan* [Red crag]. Beijing: Zhongguo qing-nian chubanshe, 1961.

Luo Ziliang. "Hao dianying guwu xia de nantong guanzhong" [Nantong audi-ences under the encouragement of good films]. *DYFY* 7 (1959): 18–19.

Ma Weidu, "Lutian dianying" [Open-air cinema]. *Weibo*, September 29, 2017. https://www.weibo.com/ttarticle/p/show?id=2309404157243070238403& infeed=1.

Meng Chao. "Duoduo chuangzuo huandengpian" [Create more slides]. *Meishu* 1 (1956): 20–21.

Meng Ling. "Tapo bingshan wei mumin" [Traverse the icy mountain for the herders]. *DYFY* 12 (1964): 8–9.

Meng Yue. "Baimaonü yanbian de qishi: Jianlun yan'an wenyi de lishi duozhix-ing" [Revelations of the evolution of *The White-Haired Girl*: On the het-erogeneity of Yan'an literature and arts]. In *Zai jiedu: dazhong wenyi yu yishixingtai* [Re-interpretation: mass literature and arts and ideology], edited by Tang Xiaobing, 48–69. Beijing: Beijing daxue chubanshe, 2007.

Pang Xianzhi et al., eds. *Mao zedong nianpu, 1893–1949, shangjuan* [A chroni-cal of Mao Zedong, 1893–1949, part 1]. Beijing: zhongyang wenxian chu-banshe, 1993.

Pingdu dianying fangying dui [Pingdu Film Projection Team]. "Rang shehu-izhuyi sixiang chuanbian xin nongcun: tan nongcun puji fangying de jige guanjian wenti" [Let socialist thought spread across the new countryside: Discussing a few key problems in the popularization of rural film exhibi-tion]. *DYFY* 8 (1964): 6.

Qian Zhengzhuan. "Zenyang zai yingqian xuanchuan, zai yingjian chahua [How to propagate before screenings and insert comments during screen-ings]. *DYFY* 10 (1958): 10–11.

"Qing yingyuan laobanmen kaolü guanzhong yijian" [Theater owners, please consider the requests of audiences]. *DZDY* 10 (1950): 2.

Qu Youliang. "Dang de zhongxin gongzuo shi shenme women jiu xuanch-uan shenme" [We propagate whatever the Party's central task is]. *DYFY* 2 (1960): 15–16.

ripple. "Gaozhen wei yingxiang dailai le shenme" [What has HFR brought to the image?]. *Douban*, October 23, 2019. https://movie.douban.com/review /10593204/.

Rong Liangqian. "Cong shiji chufa zuohao dianying fangyingwang de tiaozheng gongzuo" [Adjust the film distribution and exhibition network according to reality]. *DYPJ* 9 (1981): 6–8.

"Shanghai dianyingyuan" [Movie theaters in Shanghai]. *Qingqing dianying* [Qingqing Film] 2, no. 4 (1935): 1.

"Shanghai gongren de wenhua shenghuo riyi fengfu duocai" [The cultural life of Shanghai workers is becoming increasingly diverse]. *GMRB*, Septem-ber 23, 1954.

"Shanghai shi dianying fangyingdui qingkuang" [The status of Shanghai film projection teams], 1953. SMA B172-4-259.

"Shanghai shi dianyingyuan ge lei piaojia mingxibiao" [Admission prices at movie theaters in Shanghai], 1959. SMA B172-5-124-63.

"Shanghai shi dianyingyuan shangye tongye gonghui 1951 nian gongzuo zongjie baogao" [1951 annual report of the Shanghai movie theater guild], 1952. SMA C48-2-313.

"Shanghai shi dianyingyuan yewu zhuangkuang diaochabiao" [Survey of the business status of Shanghai movie theaters], 1950. SMA B172-4-48.

"Shanghai shi wenhuaju guanyu dianyingyuan xuanchuan he zuzhi guanzhong gongzuo zongjie chugao" [Draft report by the Shanghai Municipal Cultural Bureau on the work of propaganda and audience organization of movie theaters], 1954. SMA B172-1-145-34.

"Shanghai shi yingyuan, juchang, shuchang, youlechang, fangyingdui gongzuo huiyi: Li juzhang baogao" [Presentation by Chief Li at the conference on the work of movie theaters, theaters, storytelling parlors, entertainment halls, and projection teams], 1959. SMA B172-5-1.

Shen Enfu. "Yingxi yu jiaoyu" [Shadowplay and Education]. Dianying zazhi [Film Magazine] 1 (1924): 1–2.

"Sheng guang zuo: xiyuan de jiegou" [Sound, light, seats: The structure of a theater]. Dahua daxiyuan kaimu jinian kan [Special issue on the opening of the Roxy theater] (1940): 2.

"Shenme shi shenru shenghuo: cong Zhao Shuli de xiaoshuo tanqi" [What is delving into life: The fiction of Zhao Shuli]. Zhongguo shehui kexue wang [Chinese Social Sciences Net], May 21, 2016. http://lit.cssn.cn/wx/wx_zjzl/201611/t20161114_3275536.shtml?COLLCC=1198396219&.

Shi Yongsen. "Weile rang nongmin kandong dianying: Hai'an xian disi fangyingdui zhuanxie Li Shuangshuang chahua gao jingyan jieshao" [In order for peasants to understand films: Introducing the experience of Number Four Projection Team of Hai'an County in writing the commentary for Li Shuangshuang]. DYFY 3 (1963): 15–18.

Shu Weina. "Liuguang suiyue li de dianying qingjie" [Love for cinema in the flow of time]. Mala tan 271 (2014). Accessed September 3, 2020. https://cq.qq.com/zt2014/mlt271/.

Su Tong. Lutian dianying: Su Tong sanwen [Open-air cinema: Essays by Su Tong]. Hangzhou: Zhejiang wenyi chubanshe, 2014.

Sun Qing. "Modeng jingying: 18–20 shiji zhongguo zaoqi huandeng de fangying, zhizuo, yu chuanbo" [Mirror images through magic lanterns: The presentation, production and circulation of the early magic lantern in 18th–20th Century China]. Jindai shi yanjiu [Modern Chinese History Studies] 4 (2018): 65–83.

Sun Shungen. "Zhao Yiman jiaoyu le wo" [Zhao Yiman educated me]. DZDY 5 (1950): 24.

Sun Xuewen and Liu Shulin. "Xuanchuan hongqi piao: qingling xiang fangying dui de xuanchuan gongzuo" [The red flag of propaganda waves: Work experience of the Qingling Township projection team]. DYFY 5 (1959): 7–9.

Sun Zhe. "Shenyang tiexi gongrenqu xinjian yizuo dianyingyuan" [A new movie theater was built in the Tiexi workers district in Shenyang]. *GMRB*, November 1, 1954.

Tang Hongfeng. "Xuni yingxiang: zhongguo zaoqi dianying meijie kaogu" [Virtual images: Media archeology of early Chinese cinema]. *Dianying yishu* [Film Art] 3 (2018): 3–10.

Tang Peize. "Guojingxian shang de yizhi fangyingdui" [A film projection team on the national border]. *RMRB*, August 23, 1956.

Tang Rong. "Sanshi nian zhongguo dianying tizhi gaige licheng huigu (shang)" [Reform of the Chinese film system in the last thirty years (1)]. *Zhongguo dianying bao* [China film news], October 9, 2008.

———. "Sanshi nian zhongguo dianying tizhi gaige licheng huigu (xia)" [Reform of the Chinese film system in the last thirty years (2)]. *Zhongguo dianying* bao, October 16, 2008.

Tang Ruxin. "Zhuanhuan jingying fangshi shi nongcun dianying shichang fazhan de biyouzhilu" [Changing the business model is the necessary road in the development of rural film market]. *DYPJ* 12 (1992): 3–4.

T.H.C. "Tantan guotai dianyingyuan" [Let's talk about Cathay theater]. *Funü shenghuo* [Women's Life] 1, no. 21 (1932): 544.

"Tianhua chayuan guan waiyang xifa gui shu suojian" [Recording what I saw after returning from a trip to Tianhua teahouse to watch foreign tricks]. *Youxi bao* 54, August 16, 1897.

Wang Hui. "Qu zhengzhihua de zhengzhi: baquan de duochong goucheng yu liushi niandai de xiaoshi" [Depoliticized politics: multiple components of hegemony and the eclipse of the 1960s] *Kaifang shidai* [Open Times] 2 (2007): 5–41.

Wang Mingxun, "Xiwang ba huandeng pian shenru nongcun" [I hope to see more slides in the countryside]. *DZDY* 23 (1951): 31.

Wu Di (Qi Zhi). *Mao Zedong shidai de renmin dianying, 1949–1966 nian* [People's cinema in the era of Mao Zedong, 1949–1966]. Taipei: Xiuwei zixun keji gufen youxian gongsi, 2010.

———. *Zhongguo dianying yanjiu ziliao: 1949–1976 (zhongjuan)* [A sourcebook for Chinese cinema studies: 1949–1976, vol. 2]. Beijing: Wenhua yishu chubanshe, 2006.

Wu Dinghong. *Huandeng gongzuo shouce* [Handbook for slide projection]. Beijing: Wenhua xueshe, 1953.

Wu Wei. "Liyong huandengpian jiejue le yin shuomingshu de kunnan" [Using slides to solve the difficulty of printing plot sheets]. *DZDY* 5 (1952): 33.

Wu Xiangyu. "Lun hongyan de shenti geming yishi" [The bodily revolution of *Red Crag*]. *Zhongguo kuangye daxue xuebao* [Journal of Chinese University of Mining and Technology] 2 (2007): 132–36.

Wu Yigong. *Shanghai dianying zhi* [Shanghai film gazetteer]. Shanghai: Shanghai kexueyuan chubanshe, 1999.

Xi Wen and Ji Jin'an, eds. *Shanghai qunzhong wenhua zhi* [Shanghai gazetteer of mass culture]. Shanghai: Shanghai wenhua chubanshe, 1999.

Xie Fei. "Zhongguo dianying zhuanxing 30 nian" [The transition of Chinese cinema in the last thirty years]. *Liaowang zhoukan* [Outlook Weekly] 1 (2009): 60–63.

"Xin zhongguo diyi suo ertong dianyingyuan" [The first children's cinema in the new China]. *GMRB*, May 19, 1954.

Xiu Long. "Li An weishenme sike 120 zhen" [Why is Ang Lee so obsessed with 120fps]. *Dianying zazhi* [Movie]. October 22, 2019. https://mp.weixin.qq.com/s/1x3be6dxCDL_Bq_u_vrKtw.

Xu Fulin. *Dianying fangying fa* [Methods of Film Projection]. Changsha: Shangwu yinshuguan, 1938.

Xu Ruzhong, "Zhishi weile ba dianying songshang haidao" [The only goal is to deliver film to islands]. *DYFY* 3 (1957): 27–31.

Xu Xiaxiang. "Nongcun dianying fangyingdui yu nongmin de 'zaizao'" [Rural film projection teams and the 'remaking' of peasants]. *21 Shiji shuangyuekan* [Twenty-First Century Bi-monthly] 122 (2010): 47–55.

Yao Fangzao. "Xinhua daxiyuan fangwen ji" [A trip to the Xinhua Theater]. *DZDY* 4 (1951): 29.

Yi Xiangdong. *Aiqing xijie* [West love street]. Guilin: Guangxi shifan daxue chubanshe, 2008.

"Yinmu gua shang Daba shan—Shaanxi Pingli xian dianying fangying dui disandui de yingxiong gushi" [Raising the screen on Daba Mountain: The heroic deeds of the Number Three Film Projection Team of Pingli County, Shaanxi Province]. *RMRB*, June 13, 1960.

"Yingyao song chu ershi li" [Determined to take the films out for 20 *li*]. *Dianying fangying ziliao* 3 (1956): 24.

Yongcheng xian difang shizhi bianzuan weiyuanhui [Yongcheng commission on the compilation of local gazetteers]. "Huandeng" [Slide projection]. In *Yongcheng Xianzhi* [Yongcheng gazatteer]. Beijing: Xinhua chubanshe, 1991. Accessed September 4, 2020. http://www.hnsqw.com.cn/sqssjk/sqxqz/ycxz/.

You Ming. "Guanyu kaifa nongcun dianying shichang de jidian sikao" [Thoughts on the development of rural film market]. *DYPJ* 8 (1987): 2–4.

Yu Zhen. "Bandeng shang guanying de shaonian jiyi" [Youthful memory of watching movies from the campstool]. *Meiri toutiao* [Kk news], August 26, 2016. https://kknews.cc/history/8zb33q.html.

Yu Zixia, Qiao Jinxia, and Yu Wendu. "Chuanjiaoshi yu jindai zhongguo dianhua jiaoyu de xingqi" [Missionaries and the rise of modern Chinese audiovisual education]. *Huazhong shifan daxue xuebao* [Journal of Huazhong Normal University] 54, no. 1 (2015): 168–76.

"Yuandong weiyi da jianzhu: da guangming yingxiyuan" [The only grand architecture in the Far East: Grand Theater]. *Shen Bao*, June 13, 1933.

Zhang Qizhong. "'Lutian dianying' yu nongcun de wenhua qimeng: Shiqinian nongcun dianying fangyingwang de lishi fenxi" [Open-air cinema and the cultural enlightenment of the countryside: A historical analysis of the rural film exhibition network of the Seventeen Years]. *Yishu pinglun* [Arts Criticism] 8 (2010): 49–54.

Zhang Shuoguo. "*Shiqi nian*" shanghai dianying wenhua yanjiu [Studies of Shanghai film culture during the "seventeen years"]. Beijing: Shehui kexue wenxian chubanshe, 2014.

Zhang Wentian. "Dang de xuanchuan gudong gangling" [Party guidelines for propaganda and agitation]. In *Zhang Wentian wenji, di san juan* [Collected works of Zhang Wentian, vol. 3], 150–61. Beijing: Zhonggong dangshi chubanshe, 1994.

Zhao Liyan. "Jiading xian peihe liangshi wenti xuanchuan fangfa duo" [Jiading County uses different ways to propagate about grain problems]. *DYFY* 12 (1957): 10–11.

Zheng Yiliu. "Wo cengjing fengkuang de miguo Beidi Gelanbao, xianzai zhengtuo le meidi yingpian de mozhang" [I used to be crazy about Betty Grable; now I have escaped the evil hand of American imperialist films]. *DYFY* 4 (1950): 11.

Zhong Dianfei. "Dianying de luogu" [The gongs and drums of film]. *Wenhui bao*, December 21, 1956.

———. "Lun dianying zhidao sixiang zhong de jige wenti" [A few problems in the guiding principles of film administration]. In *Zhongguo dianying yanjiu ziliao, di er ce*, edited by Wu Di, 20–29. Beijing: Wenhua yishu chubanshe, 2006.

Zhong Yingbin. "'Huizhan' fangying hao" [Exhibition "battles" are good]. *Dianying xuanchuan faxing fangying gongzuo qingkuang jianbao* [Newsletter on film propaganda, distribution, and exhibition] 1 (1972): 15–19.

Zhongguo dianying faxing fangying gongsi [China Film Corporation]. *Zhongguo dianying faxing fangying tongji ziliao huibian (1958–1960), di yi ce* [Sourcebook for Chinese film distribution and exhibition 1958–1960, Vol. 1]. Beijing: Zhongguo dianying faxing fangying gongsi, 1961.

Zhou Jianming. "Nongcun yingpian gongying de maodun" [Contradictions in the supply of films in the countryside]. *DYFY* 5 (1957): 6–7.

Zhou Liming. "Shuangzi shashou, Li An zai dianying geming zhong de guzhuyizhi" [*Gemini Man*: Ang Lee's gamble in the cinematic revolution]. *Tengxun wang*, October 24, 2019. https://new.qq.com/rain/a/20191024A0KWZ5.

Zhu Qi. "Wulumuqi shi renmin dianyingyuan wangong" [Construction of Urumqi's People's Theater is complete]. *GMRB*, February 22, 1955.

Index

Founded in 1893,
UNIVERSITY OF CALIFORNIA PRESS
publishes bold, progressive books and journals
on topics in the arts, humanities, social sciences,
and natural sciences—with a focus on social
justice issues—that inspire thought and action
among readers worldwide.

The UC PRESS FOUNDATION
raises funds to uphold the press's vital role
as an independent, nonprofit publisher, and
receives philanthropic support from a wide
range of individuals and institutions—and from
committed readers like you. To learn more, visit
ucpress.edu/supportus.

www.ingramcontent.com/pod-product-compliance
Lightning Source LLC
Chambersburg PA
CBHW030347270326
41926CB00009B/997